Towards a Comprehensive Theory of Human Learning

Lifelong Learning and the Learning Society, Volume I

In recent years the idea of lifelong learning and the learning society has become central to both society and to everyone involved in education throughout the world but, as yet, no truly exhaustive study has been made of these phenomena. This ground-breaking distillation of Peter Jarvis' thoughts on lifelong learning will comprehensively correct that omission.

This book, the first in a forthcoming series, concentrates on the processes of human learning and considers the fact that research into learning itself has hitherto been unsystematic and, for a while, mainly psychological. In the first section of this book the author argues that learning is existential, and so its study must be complex and interdisciplinary. A number of the existing theories of learning are then critically examined, in order to see how they can be reconciled with a more complex model. Applying his expert analytical approach to this wide-ranging topic Professor Jarvis looks in detail at

- Learning in the social context
- The transformation of experience
- The outcomes of learning
- Learning and action
- Cognitive theories
- Emotions and learning
- Experiential learning.

Although it is acknowledged from the outset that a totally comprehensive theory of learning is not possible, the ultimate goal of this book (and its forthcoming companion volumes) is nothing less than an endeavour to construct an integrated but critical theory of lifelong learning and the learning society. It will be essential reading for students in education, HRD and teaching and learning generally, in addition to academics and informed practitioners.

Peter Jarvis is an internationally renowned expert in the field of adult learning and continuing education. He is Professor of Continuing Education at the University of Surrey, UK, and honorary Adjunct Professor in Adult Education at the University of Georgia, USA.

Towards a Comprehensive Theory of Human Learning

Lifelong Learning and the Learning Society, Volume I

Peter Jarvis

Routledge
Taylor & Francis Group

LONDON AND NEW YORK

First published 2006
by Routledge
2 Park Square, Milton Park, Abingdon, Oxon OX14 4RN

Simultaneously published in the USA and Canada
by Routledge
270 Madison Ave, New York, NY 10016

Routledge is an imprint of the Taylor & Francis Group

Typeset in Goudy by RefineCatch Ltd, Bungay, Suffolk
Printed and bound in Great Britain by
The Cromwell Press, Trowbridge, Wiltshire

British Library Cataloguing in Publication Data
A catalogue record for this book is available from the British Library

Library of Congress Cataloging in Publication Data
Jarvis, Peter, 1937–
    Towards a comprehensive theory of human learning / Peter Jarvis.
        p.   cm.
    Includes bibliographical references and index.
    1. Learning. 2. Learning, Psychology of. 3. Social learning.
    4. Experiential learning. 5. Continuing education. I. Title.
    LB1060.J38 2006
    370.15′23–dc22
                                            2005016863

ISBN10: 0–415–35540–0 (hbk)
ISBN10: 0–415–35541–9 (pbk)

ISBN13: 978–0–415–33540–7 (hbk)
ISBN13: 978–0–415–33541–4 (pbk)

Contents

Figures and tables

Figures

Tables

The author

Peter Jarvis is Professor of Continuing Education at the University of Surrey and adjunct Professor of Adult Education at the University of Georgia in the United States. In addition, he has been awarded a University Professorship *cum laudis* at the University of Pécs in Hungary. He holds the following degrees: B.D. (University of London); B.A. (Econ) (University of Sheffield); M.Soc.Sc. (University of Birmingham); Ph.D. (University of Aston); D.Litt. (University of Surrey). He has also been awarded an honorary doctorate by the University of Helsinki. He is a Fellow of the Royal Society of Arts. Among the honours that he has received are: the Cyril O. Houle World Award for Literature in Adult Education, the American Association of Adult and Continuing Education; a fellowship of the Japan Society for the Promotion of Science (University of Tokyo) to research into the education of adults; induction in the International Hall of Fame of Adult and Continuing Education in the USA; and the Comenius Award of the International ESVA Foundation. He was the Hon. President of the British Association of International and Comparative Education in 1999–2000 and he is an honorary life member of a number of associations of adult education in different parts of the world. Over the past twenty years he has been visiting professor in a number of universities in the United States, Canada and Europe and guest professor in a number of others. He is a frequent speaker at conferences around the world.

Peter Jarvis has authored many books: *Adult Education in a Small Centre: A Case Study*, University of Surrey, Dept. of Educational Studies (1982); *Professional Education*, Croom Helm (1983); *Adult and Continuing Education: Theory and Practice*, Croom Helm (1983) – now in its third edition as *Adult Education and Lifelong Learning: Theory and Practice*, RoutledgeFalmer (2004); *The Sociology of Adult and Continuing Education*, Croom Helm (1985); *Sociological Perspectives on Lifelong Education and Lifelong Learning*, University of Georgia, Dept. of Adult Education (1986); *Adult Learning in the Social Context*, Croom Helm (1987); *International Dictionary of Adult and Continuing Education*, Routledge (1990); *Paradoxes of Learning*, Jossey Bass (1992); *Adult Education and the State*, Routledge (1993); *Ethics and the Education of Adults* in *Later Modern Society*, NIACE (1997); *The Practitioner Researcher*, Jossey-Bass (1999); *Learning in Later Life*, Kogan Page (2001); *Universities and Corporate Universities: The Lifelong Learning Industry and Global Society*, Kogan Page (2001).

He has co-authored the following: *The Teacher Practitioner in Nursing, Midwifery and Health Visiting*, Croom Helm (1985) – published as second edition *The Teacher Practitioner and Mentor in Nursing, Midwifery, Health Visiting and the Social Services*, Thorne (1997); *The Human Resource Development Handbook*, Kogan Page (1998); *The Theory and Practice of Learning*, Kogan Page (1998) – second edition (2003).

He has also edited *Twentieth Century Thinkers in Adult Education*, Croom Helm (1987) – second edition *Twentieth Century Thinkers in Adult and Continuing Education*, Kogan Page (2001); *Britain: Policy and Practice in Continuing Education*, Jossey Bass (1988); *Perspectives in Adult Education and Training in Europe*, NIACE (1992); *The Age of Learning*, Kogan Page (2000); *Theory and Practice of Teaching in a Learning Society*, Kogan Page (2001); *Adult and Continuing Education: major themes since the Enlightenment* (5 vols) with Colin Griffin, Routledge (2003); *From Adult Education to Lifelong Learning*, RoutledgeFalmer (forthcoming).

He has also co-edited: *Training Adult Educators in Western Europe*, Routledge (1991); *Adult Education: Evolution and Achievements in a Developing Field of Study*, Jossey Bass (1991); *Adult Education and Theological Interpretations*, Krieger (1993); *Developments in the Education of Adults in Europe*, Peter Lang (1994); *International Perspectives on Lifelong Learning*, Kogan Page (1998); *Human Learning: a holistic approach*, Routledge (forthcoming); *Living, Learning and Working*, Palgrave (forthcoming).

His books and papers have been translated into about twenty languages.

He is also founding editor of *The International Journal of Lifelong Education*, Chair of the Board of Editors of *Comparative Education* and he serves on a number of other editorial boards in Europe, Asia and the USA.

Preface and acknowledgements

Contemporary science has made a singular contribution to our knowledge of man [*sic*] by showing that he is biologically unfinished. One might say that he never does become an adult, that his existence is an unending process of completion and learning. It is essentially that incompleteness that sets him apart from other living beings, the fact that he must draw from his surroundings the techniques for living which nature and instinct fail to give him. He is obliged to learn unceasingly in order to survive and evolve.

(Faure Report, 1972: 157)

Every individual must be in a position to keep learning throughout his life. The idea of lifelong education is the keystone to the learning society.

(Faure Report, 1972: 181)

The Faure Report captures something of the concerns of this book: it is about being, becoming and learning throughout life. It is an attempt to understand human learning and these quotations reflect these emphases.

This volume, the first of three, seeks to understand human learning in all its complexity; it offers a theory of learning in the first seven chapters which has emerged from my own research over the past twenty years. Basically it seeks to move our thinking from a narrow restricted psychological investigation into a complex interdisciplinary study of the human processes of being-in-the-world and learning to be a self in society. Learning is the driving force that combines with our bodily drives to make us what we are – we are learned beings.

The fact that learning is the single most significant element moulding our being suggests that all the different theories of learning should be able to be understood within a single comprehensive framework, and so the second part of the book examines a number of the theories of learning in order to see how they fit into the model suggested in the first part. In a sense, they also test the validity of the initial discussion. While all the theories can be fitted within this framework, the final conclusion to this study is that we do not know enough about human learning to be able to produce a single comphensive theory. In fact, we might never know enough to be able to do this because, if we did, we would fully understand the mysteries of human functioning and even of life itself. However, that all human beings do keep on learning throughout their lives leads to another conclusion – one highlighted in the Faure Report but argued more forcibly by others (Simpson 1995) – that lifelong learning is an indication that humanity remains an unfinished project.

I have been working on this subject for two decades now and have published many books and papers about it. In a sense, this book gathers together much of my understanding. Over that period and around the world, I have conducted my learning workshops more times than I have counted and I have given more lectures and classes on the topic that I care to remember, and yet those who have undertaken the workshop and students who have listened to the lectures have been unstinting in giving me feedback about how they understand learning. In addition, many colleages who have heard my lectures and read papers have also been generous in their criticism of my work. Naturally, they have all enriched my thinking and I am enormously grateful to them.

Dr Alison le Cornu has commented on the first chapter of this book – she has over many years been a student, friend and critic of my work as she engaged with it first in her own research. I am tremendously grateful to her not only for reading the chapter but also for the times she has challenged my thinking as I have read her work. Many other colleagues have helped me but I want to mention one in particular, Dr Pauline Jeffree, who has encouraged me to work both by her friendship and her example.

Naturally, what I have written is my responsibility and nobody else's. I have written it in the profound hope that it might help others who want to know a little more about teaching and learning: this includes students and teachers, course designers and educational managers, and also policy makers. All that I can hope is that in some ways it may prove useful to those who do me the honour of reading my work.

This is the first volume in the trilogy *Lifelong Learning and the Learning Society* and as this focuses on the person and comes from a psychological and philosophical framework, the second volume, *Learning and Society*, will start from a sociological perspective and takes me back to my early writings on sociology of adult and continuing education. The third volume is provisionally entitled either *Realising the Learning Society?* or *Beyond the Learning Society*, although this might change a little over the next year and a half. I am, however, immensely grateful to Philip Mudd of Routledge who encouraged me to write the trilogy and trusted me to complete it. I am only a third of the way along the route, but I hope that I am beginning to repay that trust.

Around the time I started this work I had a little health scare and writing this has been extremely beneficial to me. However, one person above all has supported and encouraged me, has always been there when I needed her, and without whom this book would never have seen the light of day, and that is my wife Maureen. It is to her that I dedicate this trilogy in love and gratitude.

Peter Jarvis
Thatcham
May, 2005

Part I

Human learning

Chapter 1

A philosophical perspective on human learning

Learning is like food, ingest it and it will enrich the human being: unlike food, it is difficult to have too much. It is possible to eat the wrong things and it is likewise possible to learn the wrong things; Dewey (1938), for instance, used the term 'miseducation' to describe this. Nevertheless, the processes of learning are a fundamental stimulus for life itself and without it the human body could never transcend its biological state, nor could the individual function effectively in the wider society. It is essential to our humanity and, in fact, it is an existential process. This does not mean that studies of learning need only to be philosophical, but it does demand that we recognise the philosophical underpinnings of all theories of learning, in whatever academic discipline they are based. Moreover, since learning is a human phenomenon, it might be asked whether all the theories of learning are only aspects of the same human process. Consequently, it is necessary here to understand some of the basic philosophical arguments, especially the tenets of existentialism, that are important to our thinking about learning and the first part of this book will briefly explore these.

At the same time, this work is the culmination of over twenty years of thinking about and researching human learning. In that time I have published many books and papers about these human processes, a number of which have elaborated ideas that were previously published, and while it is unnecessary to review all of these here, it is important to demonstrate how my understanding has grown and developed and even to point out where I think I have made mistakes in the past, and so the second part of this chapter will offer a very brief overview of these develotments. My brief critique of my own work will in part be based on the philosophical ideas that I discuss in this book. This discussion is important since I am going to examine other theories of learning in the second part of this volume and demonstrate how all of these are attempts to understand the same human process which we call human learning, and which is located within the wider context of human society. Overall, this book is a quest to understand human learning a little better.

I will, therefore, then present my own current definition and models of learning and discuss them briefly and show that learning is a very complex human and lifelong process. This means that we should not seek to regard children's learning, for example, as necessarily different from adult learning – even though there may be different processes and it occurs in different social contexts. But this does not mean that animal learning can be equated with human learning, although the two can be compared and contrasted. This also points us to the fact that the study of learning is interdisciplinary although there might, indeed should, be different emphases in specific studies.

Underlying this study is a fundamental belief that human learning is a complex set of human processes that are in some ways extremely difficult to understand. I have used the term 'human learning' here because some scholars, notably some of those from an organisational learning background, want to use the term to refer to change and development in organisations and even to society. We will look at 'learning organisations' in the second volume of this study. However, I will argue that this is a false understanding of learning, or at the very least a de-personalised concept of a human process, although there are considerable similarities between aspects of human learning and organisational change, since both have outcome, function, development and process. There is, however, is one fundamental difference: learning is about experience, usually conscious experience. Organisations may have a life of their own but they do not have experiences and so, for instance, their learning cannot begin from seeing a green apple fall to the ground! It takes a member of the organisation to have that experience and then to implement whatever learning that has occurred into the organisation's procedures and structures in order to change them, thereby changing other people, their social context and their actions. To use learning to describe organisational processes is to try to de-humanise something that lies at the heart of humanity itself, of personhood, and while it may reflect the tenor of this age, using the term in this way deprives learning of something fundamental to itself.

Heidegger makes the significant point that the human being must be understood as person and that 'Persona means the actor's mask through which his dramatic tale is sounded. Since man is the percipient who perceives what is, we can think of him as persona, the mask, of Being' (1968: 62). Learning, then, is a essential element of Being. Learning, it is maintained here, lies at the heart of our humanity – it is a driving force in human existence – so that our theories of learning must embrace an holistic and existentialist perspective.

Additionally, it is surmised here that researchers from different academic disciplines have unintentionally done the study of learning something of a disservice when they have failed to achnowledge that their single-discipline approach is but one of a number of different ways of understanding it.

Some relevant tenets of existentialism

This is not a study of existentialism (see Macquarrie 1973; Cooper 1990; *inter alia*) since this would entail an examination of many of the leading philosophers of the twentieth century, which is not only beyond the scope of this work, it is beyond my ability. However, Cooper (1990: 2–3) makes the point that there are two main bases of existentialist thought: 'existence' refers to the kind of existence enjoyed by human beings and it also refers to a form of existence which distinguishes it from all others. This leads us to recognise that existence always precedes essence. In a sense, existence is the process of realising what we might become – being is always becoming: human becoming is achieved both through our learning and our physical maturing, so that we will need to explore the mind–body relationship in the next chapter. However, it is also important in passing to note that we cannot escape from the concepts of space and time in our thinking about learning – both past time and future time – for we learn by reflecting upon the past and also from planning for future activities, and we also do so within a social context. We shall return to these on a number of occasions.

Existence is, therefore, assumed and never needs to be proven. This means that the Cartesian dictum 'I think, therefore I am' is unnecessary – but this does not automatically exclude some form of dualist argments about the relationship between the mind and the body. I am! But what does existence actually mean? I know I am, and I do not need to prove it to myself. Because I am, I think. Macquarrie (1973: 125) writes:

> But what does it mean to say, 'I am'? 'I am' is the same as 'I exist'; but 'I exist', in turn, is equivalent to 'I-am-in-the-world', or again 'I-am-with-others'. So the premise of the argument is not anything so abstract as 'I think' or even 'I am' if it is understood in some isolated sense. The premise is the immediately rich and complex reality, 'I-am-with-others-in the world'.

But Bergson (1998 [1911]: 7) makes another vitally important point:

> for a conscious being to exist is to change, to change is to mature, to mature is to go on creating oneself endlessly.

Existence, then, is never unchanging and always social; we live and move and have our being in a social context. We will argue throughout this volume that learning is the driving force of human change through which the human essence emerges and is nurtured. But also 'I-am-in-the-world' and 'I-am-with-others' are different phenomena: in the former we are in the wider world, but the latter can refer to our life-world (see Luckmann 1983; Habermas 1987; Williamson 1998). Habermas (1987: 118) made an important distinction between the social system and life-world and he proposed that we need to conceptualise society as being both simultaneously. But we know that we are in the world because we act, as MacMurray argued, 'We know existence by participating in existence' (1979 [1961]: 17), or as Husserl said, 'I live *in* my Acts' (cited in Schutz 1967: 51). I am, therefore I act, but also I act, therefore I am. But action is rarely meaningless, so that underlying action lies intention and meaning but, paradoxically, we have to learn meaning. Being, and therefore becoming, lie at the heart of our thinking about learning, but – and we need to emphasise this from the outset – thinking per se is but one element in it. Thinking is a function of our existence and not the proof of it. Because we are, we both think and act and by so doing we learn and, therefore, continue to become. Learning is the process of being in the world. At the heart of all learning is not merely what is learned, but what the learner is becoming (learning) as a result of doing and thinking – and feeling. Indeed, the mind really is not like a computer just performing functions, as it does experience the outcomes of sensations and we shall discuss this further below and in the following chapters. While it is conceptually mistaken to liken the mind to a computer, the computer may have some similarities to our brain. But as human beings we are much more than these computational functions. We do have experiences, feel and have emotions. And we do learn from and through our feelings. At the heart of this process, therefore, is the learner as a whole person and, therefore, the learner's self. But self is formed through existing and interacting with people. We actually learn to become a person and this occurs within our own life-world; it is a social process (see Mead in Strauss 1964; Schutz 1967). Indeed, the demands of our life-world also determine to a great extent the opportunities that we have to learn.

Learning, then, is a much more profound phenomenon than just teaching dogs to salivate or rats to explore the mystery of a maze in search of food; it is fundamental to our humanity and to our society. It is about the way that human beings are in the world and the world in them – it occurs at the intersection of humanity and society – it is more than experiential, more than physiological, psychological and so on. Understanding it more fully is a momentous integrated multi-disciplinary project. Illeris (2002: 43) also captures something of the significance of human learning when he writes:

> The human ability to learn developed together with other characteristics of our species in the struggle for survival of the various species, and this can be understood as one of several tools for the continued struggle.

Our action is always in the world, always engagement with the world (both the physical and the human social world) that we experience and these experiences become data for our own thinking, so that the idea of experiential learning points us in the direction of philosophy, amongst other things, and it is what we 'do' with our experience that lies at the heart of our understanding of learning. Our experience occurs at the intersection of the inner self and the outer world and so learning always occurs at this point of interaction, usually when the two are in some tension, even dissonance, which I have always called 'disjuncture'. In fact, the desire to overcome this sense of dissonance and to return to a state of harmony might be seen as a fundamental motivating force in learning, and the disjunctural state may be said to be one in which a need has to be satisfied.

Cooper (1990: 79–94) highlights four perennial problems that are resolved through existentialist thought: subjects versus objects; mind versus body; reason versus passion; fact versus value. In the first instance, we do not stand over against the world, as a subject to an object, but we are in the world and it is 'impregnated with human purposes and concerns' (Cooper 1990: 80), but we are also partly the outcome of our interaction with the world. This is a dialectical relationship in which we also need an awareness to be able to respond to what we perceive to be the needs of the world. Second, the mind is embedded within the neurological mechanism of the brain and cannot either be separated from it nor confused with it; indeed, we cannot separate a self from its body nor a living body from its self. We are both physical and mental entities. Hence, when I do something it is not a mindless activity, but neither is it two activities – thinking and doing – but it is one human phenomenon since I am my body (Marcel 1976: 12, cited by Cooper 1990: 83) as well as my mind. Nevertheless, we will argue that my meanings and the bodily sensations that contribute to them are not synonymous, so that there is some form of dualism that we have to consider; something to which we will return below and more so in the next chapter when we explore it in greater depth, and later in the book when we discuss theory and practice, amongst other things. At the same time, a claim is being made here that all statements about mental states cannot be reduced to statements about physiological conditions without loss of meaning. Third, when we think something, we have emotions about it but, by contrast, when we desire something we are likely to think about it, even rationally plan how it can be obtained and so on. We are rarely such 'cold fishes' that our thinking is not in some way infused with our emotions about what we are thinking, but 'emotion has to be subjected to reflection' (Macquarrie 1973: 155) in existentialist thought, Indeed, even when we are committed to the rationalist answers to our own questions, we invest some emotion in the state of being committed to our answer. This is a very important point when we consider the processes of human learning. There is a sense in which emotion is a simultaneous combination of physical experiences and thought, but ultimately it is not merely physical. Finally, we exist in the world, a world which is impregnated with human purposes and concerns, and in some other ways we mirror our world, so that facts can only have value when they have meaning and objects only have meaning when we are aware and conscious of them. The resolution of these dualisms is crucial to our understanding human learning.

It is partially upon these premises that I have criticised my own work, and in the following section I want to review and criticise something of the process whereby my own ideas of learning have been changed and have developed.

Learning about human learning

During the mid-1980s I became profoundly dissatisfied with the many different approaches to learning, many of which were psychological and based on work with animals or children and, as an adult educator, I felt that these neglected major elements in our humanity. Additionally, I was unable to accept the traditional view of theory being learned in the classroom and then applied in practice, since the latter tended to suggest that people act without learning, which I could not accept. Fortunately, I had opportunity to develop a research project into human learning, which was later published as *Adult Learning in the Social Context* (Croom Helm, 1987).[1]

My research initially consisted of getting individuals who were participating in adult education workshops to write down a learning incident from their own lives, then to compare and contrast their learning incidents with another participant in the workshop, and then the pairs were combined into larger groups of four in order to discuss their findings about their own learning. Then each group of four was given a copy of Kolb's learning cycle (Figure 1.1) and they were told that they did not necessarily have to accept the model but that they should reconstruct it to fit their four learning stories.

Each group redrew the cycle to fit their four experiences and then reported back to the whole group. I collected the models and retained them. I was fortunate enough to be able to repeat this workshop nine times between September 1985 and April 1986 in both the United Kingdom and the United

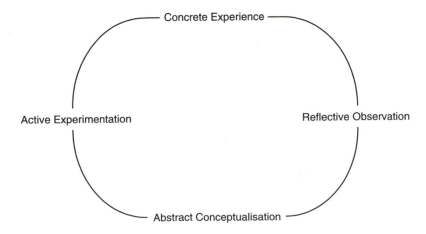

Figure 1.1 Kolb's learning cycle.

States. From these workshops and the different models that were presented I was able to construct a much more sophisticated learning cycle (Figure 1.2 – from Jarvis 1987: 26). In total about two hundred participants contributed to the construction of the model from their own reflection on their own learning and it demonstrates a great deal more of the complexity of learning than does Kolb's model. This model has been tested out in subsequent workshops over many years and gradually it has been adapted as more points have emerged from different participants. Initially, however, we will refer to the original model, reproduced in Figure 1.2.

There are a number of strengths in this research approach that need to be emphasised here, including:

- the subjects were adults who discussed their own learning because in order to get into the subjects' minds it is necessary for them to describe their own mental functioning – there is no other way to understand it; and
- the emphasis was on the process rather than on product.

At the same time, this might be seen to be a fundamental weakness in the research since Kolb's model predisposed the subjects to use his four elements of learning and this may have meant that the respondents omitted elements in their stories, or aspects of their learning, that would have been significant. In addition, I did not seek to categorise the learners by age or gender and so on in order to try to see if different learning processes were related to different categories of person. Rather, I combined the different learning incidents on the assumption that given a sufficient number of subjects I would be able

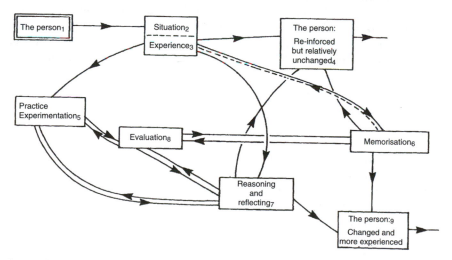

Figure 1.2 The process of learning (Jarvis 1987: 26).

to record the different learning processes themselves. On reflection, I still feel that trying to discover the different processes by getting adults to discuss their own learning is the correct way of seeking to understand learning, although I might have prompted the respondents in their discussions to draw out other points not mentioned by Kolb. However, I am not sure that I would have actually discovered a relationship between different categories of person and learning processes, although we shall return to this discussion when we examine learning styles.

It was, however, possible to detect a number of quite different routes, or types of learning, through the diagram shown in Figure 1.2 and I originally suggested nine, but it is a categorisation which I can no longer accept in its entirety, although it is necessary to outline it below before I extend it:

- *Presumption* (boxes 1→4): individuals presume upon the situation and do not learn from it.
- *Non-consideration* (boxes 1→4): for a variety of reasons the individuals do not consider the situation and do not learn from it.
- *Rejection* (boxes 1→4): for a variety of reasons the individuals reject the opportunity to learn from the situation.
- *Pre-conscious* (boxes 1→3→6→4 or 9): individuals experience situations, albeit with low awareness, which they do not really consider them but from which they have learned something.
- *Practice* (boxes 1→3→5→8→6→4 or 9): individuals learn basic skills without thought.
- *Memorisation* (boxes 1→3→6→8→4 or 9): individuals remember the information which they were given.
- *Contemplation* (boxes 1→3→7→8→6→9): individuals reflect upon a situation and either accept or change it.
- *Reflective practice* (boxes 1→3→5→7→5→8→6→9): individuals think about the situation and then act upon it, either conforming or innovating upon it.
- *Experimental learning* (boxes 1→3→7→5→7→8→6→9): individuals think about the situation and agree or disagree with what they have experienced.

The first three of these I called non-learning, the second three were non-reflective learning and the final three were reflective learning. At the same time, it will be seen that there are some quite profound differences between the two cycles, with mine being much more complex than Kolb's. But then Kolb omits, amongst other things:

- the person, so that he fails to note the way that the person is changed;
- the bodily sensations of experience;

- the influence of the social situation and, therefore, the social construction of experience;
- the process of reason and, therefore, of planning;
- the possibility that we may not always universalise our experience;
- emotional and practical learning.

These weaknesses constitute a fundamental flaw in Kolb's model of learning. At that time, I defined learning as 'the transformation of experience into knowledge, skills and attitudes' (Jarvis 1987: 32). Over the following twenty years I have conducted this workshop on many other occasions, discussed my work with many people, studied and thought deeply about the processes and amended both my model and my definition on numerous occasions. However, I do not think that it is necessary to trace this rather tedious process here so much as to use the conclusions of this initial study, and their weaknesses, as a springboard to illustrate the current outcomes of my research into human learning. At the same time, there are considerable strengths about this model, since about two hundred adults and their own understanding of their learning processes constituted the basis of this research, and many more adults have subsequently worked through similar workshops and recorded similar outcomes. There is, amongst other things, for instance:

- an emphasis on the learner as a person;
- a recognition that the learners know the way that they learn better than someone (a researcher) who is external to them;
- a recognition of the complexity of the human processes;
- an understanding of the interaction between the person and the social world as being significant for learning to occur;
- the centrality of experience in learning;
- an important emphasis on the possibility of non-learning from social living;
- a recognition that we both learn through thought and practice;
- an understanding of pre-conscious learning;
- an understanding of the nature of the changed and more experienced person.

In precisely the way that I criticised Kolb, I have criticised my own work and I now point to the following problems about it and I will do this under three headings: my understanding of the learning process, my types of learning and my definition. At the same time, I will not discuss all the detail of my criticisms here as some of these will become much more obvious in the following chapters and I will refer back to this chapter at the appropriate points.

The learning processes

While I am confident that learning is a combination of processes, I now think that I did not:

- manage to capture its complexity;
- depict the person-in-the-world, rather in relationship with the world;
- recognise how the person is changed incidentally through experience and so two of my forms of non-learning actually contain the possibility for incidental learning;
- relate reason and the emotions;
- fully understand the place of memory in relation to the learner and the learners' experience and life history;
- successfully depict the continuous nature of learning, since this diagram referred to only one learning incident with arrows entering and leaving the process to try to illustrate the continuity of learning;
- include evaluation within the reflection process;
- examine planning as well as reflection.

In addition, a major weakness was only in looking at what happens to the person rather than what happens to the content of the experience as well. Both need to be looked at simultaneously in order to understand learning.

Types of learning

I always recognised that my typology was too neat and that, while it clearly underlined more of the complexity of the learning processes than other models at the time, there were other forms of learning that needed to be recognised. I now think that:

- I needed to recognise that in both non-consideration and rejection there is the possibility of incidental learning and of the learner being changed;
- the distinction between cognitive and practical learning is over-simple if not false;
- learning through the emotions is much more significant than I originally realised (see Chapter 6).

Definition of learning

While I am very confident that learning begins with the transformation of experience, I no longer think that 'into knowledge, skills and attitudes' tells the whole story about the learning processes and so I have transformed the definition. Moreover, I had assumed the definition of transformation, whereas this process underlies some of the most profound quesions about learning it, as we shall see below. At the same time, I claimed that we will perhaps never fully understand human learning, and as more research has been published which affects our understanding of the learning processes I am more convinced that this remains true.

Many of the points that I have summarised here can be found in the numerous books and papers I have written about learning since the above was published nearly twenty years ago. At the same time, I am also aware of other criticisms that I could make and that other scholars have also made about my work,[2] but I do not think it is necessary to rehearse any others here. It is, to my mind, important that we should always be prepared to revisit our own work, acknowledge its strengths and weaknesses and incorporate more research findings from our own and others, and other disciplines, into our understanding of our work. Jarvis and Parker (2005) have endeavoured to illustrate something more of this multi-disciplinary perspective in their edited volume looking at learning from an holistic perspective.

Current understanding of the processes of human learning

I realised from the outset that it is impossible to capture the complexity of all the processes of transforming experience and so I have had to forego the endeavour to depict the learning processes per se and to produce a number of simple diagrams to draw out the essentials. At the same time, I have had to recognise that my understanding of the processes of learning was too simple and so I have produced a much more complicated definition of learning. I now regard human learning as *the combination of processes whereby the whole person – body (genetic, physical and biological) and mind (knowledge, skills, attitudes, values, emotions, beliefs and senses): experiences a social situation, the perceived content of which is then transformed cognitively, emotively or practically (or through any combination) and integrated into the person's individual biography resulting in a changed (or more experienced) person.*

We will return to the matter of definition later in this volume when we examine other definitions and theories of learning. However, at least five elements in the above definition require further discussion: the person-in-the-world; the person experiencing the world; transforming the content of the experience; transforming the person experiencing the world; and the changed person in the world.

The person-in-the-world

In the following discussion, we need to understand the nature of the person – body and mind. Learners are whole persons rather than a body or a mind; they are both material and mental. Personhood is at the heart of our understanding of learning and although psychologists, e.g. McAdams (2001), have been focusing upon personhood, the study is ultimately multi-disciplinary. Apter (1989 in Harré 1998: 6) suggests that the person has distinctness, continuity and autonomy and Stern (1938: 70) suggested that the person is both open to the world and capable of having an experience in it (in Harré 1998: 77). In a sense, this discussion is about conscious experience that necessarily takes us beyond psychological studies of personhood into the realms of philosophy, upon which we will concentrate below and in the following chapters. Persons are both responsive to the world and sources of activity in it. We will discuss the mind–body relationship in the next chapter but its significance here is that philosophers do not agree on the relationship between the two, so that we have to discuss this relationship in some detail if we are to reach an understanding of human learning. In addition, it is not possible to separate reason from passion, so that the person is a thinking, feeling, acting individual. There is more to the human being than the physical; the person is in some way a combination of the material and the mental, or the non-material.

From the foregoing discussion it is also clear that in order to understand this process it is necessary to understand individuals' relationship with their world; it is their world – life-world rather than *the* world – but the world is space and time. Few theories of learning have tackled time, although many have discussed certain aspects of space. The life-world, however, is not a static phenomenon – it changes over time in relation to the changes that occur both in the wider world in which it exists and to the individual's involvement in it, and so we cannot depict a simple relationship with it in respect of learning. But the person exists in a 'flow of time' within the life-world. However, there is a third element that we must include in this discussion of the person's relationship with the world, and that is culture. It is within culture that the self is born (see Mead in Strauss 1964) and, paradoxically, the culture is incorporated into our self-identity (Bruner 1990: 29) as we acquire language. As we shall discuss later in this volume, it is through narrative that we organise memories so that they can become life stories about the self.

Indeed, there are at least three forms of relationship within the life-world that need to be considered, which also relate to the present and the future. In the present there are two ways in which people act with the external world: through relationship with other individuals (I–Thou) and through an awareness of phenomena (things, events and so on – I–It) (Buber 1959).[3] Even so there is also an envisaged relationship with the world, which occurs when individuals think about the future while they are still in the present; they have desires, intentions and so on. In a similar manner we can think about the past, or about an idea – we can contemplate, muse and so on, and thus relate to ourselves. This reflecting upon our past results in our own awareness of our life history and educational biography (Dominice 2000). The way these may be depicted are shown in Figure 1.3.

Person to Person	I ↔ Thou
Person to Phenomenon (Thing/Event)	I → It
Person to a Future Phenomenon	I → Envisaged Thou or It
Person to Self	I ↔ Me

Figure 1.3 The person-in-the-world.

The double arrows represent a two-way relationship and the unbroken ones indicate that there is harmony between my biography and my experience of the situation: I am able to cope with the latter without forethought, as Schutz and Luckmann (1974: 7) write:

> I trust that the world as it has been known by me up until now will continue further and that consequently the stock of knowledge obtained from my fellow-men and formed from my own experiences will continue to preserve its fundamental validity ... From this assumption follows the further one: that I can repeat my past successful acts. So long as the structure of the world can be taken as constant, as long as my previous experience is valid, my ability to act upon the world in this and that manner remains in principle preserved.

This relationship is an interpersonal one, so that when we are in agreement with those with whom we interact there is a sense of harmony between us. We are in harmony with our knowledge of the world in which we are acting, as well as with the emotions that we share – when we know that we can repeat our past successful acts, we feel 'at ease' in the world. It should be noted here that this sense of being in harmony means that fundamental both to the learning process and to life itself there is an 'in-built' conservatism. But there are times when this harmony does not occur and we then experience disjuncture; this can be a situation in which we are not sure how to act, or even experience a 'magic moment' that just stops us in our tracks. It is something out of the normal – abnormal or supra-normal – and it gives rise to astonishment, wonder or some other emotion. It is at times like this that we become aware of our world. We will explore disjuncture more fully in a later chapter, but we can see immediately that it relates to consciousness and awareness, and I want to keep these two concepts separate throughout this study. In addition, there is an emotive dimension to disjuncture – 'unease' may be one way to describe it.

There is a sense in which the I ↔ Me relationship also occurs to some degree in the first three, although in the fourth one, unlike the others, it might also be an end in itself. At the same time, it is at the heart of desire, like and dislike, and other emotions that result in planning, thinking and, maybe, action. It is here, in the memories of previous experiences, that I interact with myself and learn and grow.

Additionally, during these processes there is an almost hidden element: time. Being-in-the-world automatically implies existence in time as well as space, and that it is impossible to step outside of either. Time is contentious phenomenon. It is something that knows no boundaries and in which there is always emergence of newness, a sense of becoming. We are always becoming, but learning is an element in our being; it is always a present process. Time is, in a sense, external to us and is a flow of ever-changing reality which Bergson (1998 [1911], 1999 [1965], 2004; Lacey 1989) called *durée*. However, we are not always conscious of its passing and when we do suddenly become aware of it, we often express it as 'How time flies'. Nevertheless, there are instances when we are thinking about the future and we have the opposite experience of time: 'Isn't time dragging?' When time drags we become very aware of the world in which we live, and this is important to our understanding of our own experience. When time flies, our biography is in harmony with our situation and we may not consciously learn. While we are acting in the world, we are not aware of the world beyond our actions, although our body continues to age through the ravages of time. However, frequently we are confronted with novel situations in this rapidly changing world, so that we cannot remain in harmony with the world and it is almost as if time stops and we experience the present situation (Oakeshott 1933).

The person experiencing the world

It is this moment, when time seems to stop, that I have called 'disjuncture'. Disjuncture occurs when our biographical repertoire is no longer sufficient to cope automatically with our situation, so that our unthinking harmony with our world is disturbed and we feel unease. We have a tension with our environment. We become very conscious of our situation in the world – what Habermas refers to as a relevant segment of our life-world (1987: 122). Indeed, we either problematise it or have it problematised for us. Potential disjunctural situations are depicted in Figure 1.4.

This awareness is not only a segment of our life-world upon which we

Person to Person	I ←//→ Thou
Person to Phenomenon (Thing/Event)	I –//→ It
Person to a Future Phenomenon	I –//→ Envisaged Thou or It
Person to Self	I ←//→ Me

Figure 1.4 The person experiencing the world.

focus, it is also an episode in time; it is an experience – we will discuss the nature of experience below. We need to distinguish this meaning of the word 'experience' from that of total experience or life-history, and we do so here by calling it *an experience* – an episodic experience. Episodes are not a fixed moment in time, although many of them are short and immediate. This is the elusive present. Now we think, feel and maybe do something about the outside world. We are aware of our world and have a sense of consciousness about it. The interaction between 'I' and 'the world', however, is itself a multi-faceted phenomenon. For instance, our experience of the world varies in intensity, in formality and in mode. It can, amongst others, be spoken, written or non-verbal communication; formal, non-formal or informal; emotional, sensitive or cold; oral or silent; visual; tactile; something we like or approve or vice versa and so on. The sensations we have of the world are what are also transformed. It is about the whole person.

It is at the intersection of us and our world that we are presented with the opportunities to learn. Nevertheless, the world is also changing rapidly. It is itself episodic. Our life in the world continues, but through frequent changes and continuity has become instability and frequent, if not constant, disjuncture. We are constantly exposed to learning opportunities. Naturally, we will expand upon this discussion later in this volume.

Transforming the content of the experience

Previously, I concentrated on the transformation of the person rather more than I did on the transformation of the content of the experience. Now I want to rectify this. I have also argued that learning occurs as a result of the person-in-the-world and in Figures 1.3 and 1. 4 I have discussed the four different relationships between the person and the world: person to person; person to phenomenon (thing/event); person to a future phenomenon; person to self.

In the first two, all five senses are operative and individuals may have an experience as a result of any of them, or any combination of them – hearing, seeing, smelling,[4] tasting[5] and touching and feeling. (I have treated touching and feeling together but the former refers to touching something exterior to the body, whereas the latter refers to the sensations that are generated as a result of bodily conditions, such as pain.) Their transformation can occur through thought, action or emotion, or any combination, and as we shall see in Figures 1.5 and 1.6, learning occurs after the experience, even though the time lapse may, but need not, be very short. Consequently, we can talk of:

- hearing as a way of learning;
- seeing as a way of learning;
- smelling as a way of learning;
- tasting as a way of learning; and
- touching and feeling as ways of learning.

This approach is very similar to that of by Locke in his *Essay Concerning Human Understanding* when he distinguished between sensations and reflections, although he was not concerned with the whole person in quite the same way. It is clear, however, that once we make this distinction, we open the way to at least two basic questions that require considerable discussion: the nature of sensation and the relationship between mind and body. Indeed, we can ask the question as to whether the sensation is a cause of or a correlation with the meaning and emotion that we place upon the experience, which we will address below and in the following chapter. Our understanding of learning theories depends to some extent upon the answer that we reach to this question.

In everyday life, these ways of experiencing all operate towards our learning even though we may not be aware of many of them, since we tend to take for granted the way our senses operate. Consequently, we learn preconsciously in both purposeful and incidental learning. Indeed, it would not be possible for us to be consciously aware of every detail of every experience that we have. Nevertheless, formal education has tended to restrict understanding of learning to hearing and seeing, although this is very gradually changing. I remember asking a group of nurse educators to write down their definition of learning and to leave it aside for a moment. I then asked them if, when they were working on a hospital ward, they could recognise a condition by its odour and they all affirmed that they could. I then asked them how they had acquired that knowledge, and they replied that they had learned it. Then I asked if any of them had included smell in their definition of learning and, naturally, none had. Their formal education had omitted a major way of learning significant to their work!

Learning through the senses does not only result in being able to identify smells and so on, but also in attitudes, beliefs and values. In addition, different intonations on words enable us to interpret them differently, so that each of the senses can affect the type of experiences that we have and from which we learn. Even so, we can also see that the three ways of transforming the experience are also ways of learning, and each of them can occur in any combination, so that we can also talk of:

- thinking as a way of learning;
- doing as a way of learning; and
- feeling (experiencing emotion) as a way of learning.

Any combination of these three latter ways can assume many different forms of learning, so that we get critical thinking, problem-solving learning, reflective learning, action learning and so on – all of which will be discussed later. At the same time, thinking, doing and feeling are not only reactions to previous experiences, but they can also look to the future. Hodgkiss (2001) suggests that there is evidence that consciousness is also intentional and, therefore, in some way future-orientated, so that being conscious can lead to thought about some form of action – although we have to remember that there is no logical relationship between thought and action, and it is perhaps through the emotions that thought can be transformed into action. However, either of these two can dominate in the process of learning and a number of different types of learning can occur: contemplation, rational thinking, desiring, planning, action learning and so on. In addition, the emotions can have a considerable effect on the way that we think, on motivation and on beliefs, attitudes and values.

What we actually transform, besides our selves as persons, is the sensations that we have, which are the content of our experiences (Crane 1992). It is these that are initially transformed in the learning process by thought, action or emotion, or by any combination of them. We will look briefly at the three dimensions in the following diagrams and we will return to these in considerably more detail in a later chapter.

However, the point of issue here is how do these sensations become the content of our experiences? For some scholars, as we shall see in the next chapter, the sensations are what happens in the brain and so this is a meaningless question. But we reject the equation of mind and brain – as will be discussed in the next chapter – and so we need to explore how these sensations of sound, smell, taste and so on become meaningful in the mind. This is a complex process of learning; the type of distinction that some scholars have drawn between children's learning and adult learning has some validity, but it is only partially correct. I want to suggest that we can make a distinction between initial learning, which is predominantly non-reflective and happens in children, and post-initial learning that is more often reflective, although skills learning can be both. This is the only distinction I want to draw between adult and children's learning. Figure 1.5 depicts the process that occurs within people in their life-worlds, in which sensations are transformed: this is initial learning.

Following Schutz and Luckmann (1974), we take our life-worlds for granted (box 1), though we recognise that very young children may not be in a position to do this as they are in a continuous state of learning. But in novel situations throughout life we have new sensations, so that we can rarely take the world for granted; we enter a state of disjuncture and implicitly we raise questions What do I do now? What does that mean? What is that smell? the sound? and so on. Many of these questions may not be articulated in the form of question – there is a sense of unknowing (box 2). Through a variety of ways we give meaning to the sensation and our disjuncture is resolved. An answer (not necessarily a correct one) may be given by a significant other, a teacher, incidentally in the course of everyday living, through self-directed learning and so on (box 3). Once we have acquired an answer to our implied question, we have to practise it in order to commit it to memory (box 4). The more opportunities we have to practise the answer to our initial question,

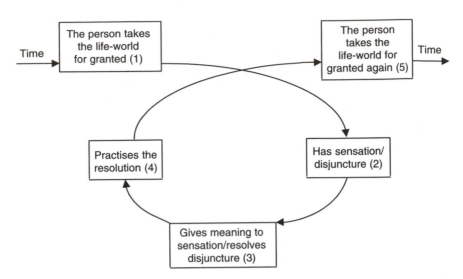

Figure 1.5 The transformation of sensations: initial and non-reflective learning.

the better we will commit it to memory. Since we do this in our social world we get feedback, which confirms that we have got an acceptable resolution or else we have to start the process again. As we become more familiar with our socially acceptable resolution and memorise it, we are in a position to take our world for granted again (box 5). The significance of this process is that once we have given meaning to the sensation and committed the meaning to our memories, then the significance of the sensation itself recedes in future experiences as the meaning dominates the process, and disjuncture occurs when we cannot understand the meaning, we do not know the meaning of the word and so on. It is in this process that we incorporate culture into our very early learning experiences and in a sense this also reflects basic stimulus–response theories of learning.

Another simple example of this process is if we meet some people for the first time and we do not know their names. We experience a sense of unease because we do not know how to address them, but when we are introduced to them and learn their names our disjuncture is resolved. However, we are not in a position to take our life-world for granted because we have not yet committed those names to memory. Consequently, we use them when we talk with the individuals until we can take their name for granted. We soon know if we have used them wrongly since we will get the appropriate feedback, and when we have committed the names to memory we are once again in a position to take our life-world for granted. We may go through this process many times before we have really mastered all the names of the people whom we meet. In this repetition another element of learning occurs: it is through repetition that we are able to generalise. Generalisation is an element in Kolb's learning cycle but one that I did not find occurring in my own research into learning. But then I only asked my respondents to discuss one learning episode, although as they discussed their four learning episodes in the groups they were generalising about learning. The more often we repeat the same phenomenon, the more likelihood that we begin to generalise about it, and it is a short step from generalisation to thinking in the abstract.

This process occurs frequently in our lives when, for instance, we are confronted with a situation which we do not understand, even a word the meaning of which we do not know, hear a sound we do not recognise, touch a material that is strange to us and so on. In these disjunctural situations we are very conscious of the sensation itself, but we then have to acquire the meaning of the words, the name of the material that we are touching, the sound, smell or taste that we do not recognise (box 3). When we have resolved our disjuncture we have to practise what we have learned until we have committed to memory the meaning of the word, the origin of the taste, touch, smell, sound and so on. Once this has been done we can take our life-world for granted again.

There are a number of significant things about these processes that we need to note: first, our experience depends to a great extent on the accuracy and proficiency of our senses. In other words, our learning is ultimately dependent on our body, and biology is a significant factor in the learning process – not just because of our genes but also because of the way that our senses function. Second, even though we are aware of the sensations in the first instance, it is not the sensation that is committed to memory but the meaning of the sensation – the identity of the type of material that we were feeling and so on. The sensation has been transformed. Third, what we have been unaware of during the whole process is the neurological and other physiological processes that go on – from body to brain to mind – as we have these experiences and which have to occur if the transformation from sensation to information is to be achieved. This is natural, since we are most often unaware of the functioning of our bodies in the processes of daily living (see Jarvis and Parker 2005, where there are discussions on some of these points).

In young children the progress between boxes 3 and 4 is extremely complex (Vygotsky 1988) since the children have to develop both thought and language and have to relate them to each other in the processes of daily living. This is part of the process of early development and primary socialisation. Only when these have been achieved can children begin to take their life-world for granted (box 5).

In precisely the same way we can learn skills: we know that when we cannot perform an action (box 2) we experience a disjunctural situation. Either through teaching, imitation or some other method, we begin to acquire the necessary techniques to perform the skill, but when we first do it we are still novices. With a lot of practice we can become competent and eventually we might become experts (box 4). It is in these later stages, from competence onwards, that we can feel confident of our ability to perform the required tasks and then we are in a position to take our world for granted again (box 5).

These processes, however, do not occur in the absence of emotion. When we are in harmony with the world – at peace with the world, as it were – we have a sense of contentment, confidence and harmony with our life-world. But when we are confronted with a novel situation we feel unease, disharmony and may lack self-confidence and so on. The process of resolving our disjuncture and practising our solutions may take motivation, perseverance and a lot of effort. Finally, when we re-establish the taken-for-grantedness we might have all the original emotions but also a sense of self-achievement. We cannot go through this process free of emotions.

This, then, is the basic process of non-reflective learning. It is also the process of rote learning, and we will return to this below. This corresponds to the non-reflective learning discussed in Figure 1.2 above and in my original research into learning. The significant thing is that the original sensations have been transformed into knowledge, skills, attitudes, values, emotions and so on. However, there is another stage in this process, for having learned the knowledge, the skill, the attitude, etc. we become less aware of the sensations themselves in the process of daily living, since we have committed them to memory and now take them for granted. We are now more aware of the knowledge, skill, attitudes, beliefs and values than the senses. In future situations, it is in these that we may experience disjuncture, and it is upon these that we can reflect and continue our learning and get new knowledge, skills, attitudes and so on.

However, as our previous research has argued, it is not just the sensation that is changed, but as we have indicated in this diagram, the person is also changed and so it is now necessary to examine the person who is experiencing the world. Indeed, Figure 1.5 should never be taken in isolation from Figure 1.6, since these two depict the same process but from different perspectives.

Transforming the person experiencing the world

At the heart of all my models of learning has been the process of transforming episodic experience and internalising it. This may be seen in Figure 1.2 above. Both in this figure and in subsequent diagrams I failed to capture this transformation as clearly as I would have liked, but in Figures 1.5 and 1.6 I have endeavoured to depict it more clearly. At the same time, the word 'transformation' contains the mystery of human learning, since the bodily sensations of experience have to be transformed into mental meanings by which we explain our personal experience, as referred to above. This underlies the importance of a fuller discussion on the body–mind relationship. It

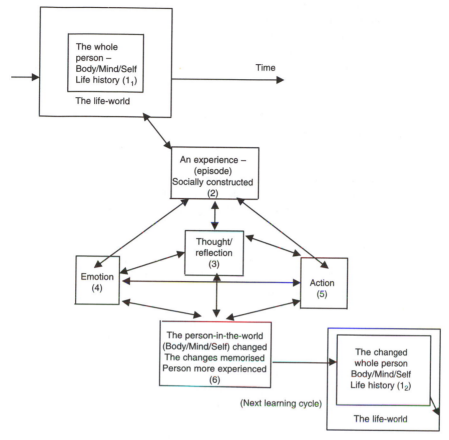

Figure 1.6 The transformation of the person through learning.

is this process of experiencing that is a matter of both mind and matter (Bergson 2004 [1912]).

Within the Confucian tradition education is truly meaningful when it leads to a perfection of the self (Lee 1996: 33), but I would want to argue that it is learning that leads as close to the perfection of the self as it is possible to get and this would find agreement in the neo-Confucian tradition. Learning, however, comes with great effort and diligence and, significantly within the Confucian tradition, it is more likely to occur when the persons are freed from the 'cult of restraint' (Lee 1996: 33) – that is when they change their societal context and can act with individual autonomy.

As individuals are thinking, feeling and acting beings, we transform our experiences through all three dimensions, often simultaneously although on some occasions we may not use all three simultaneously, e.g. contemplation, and so in Figure 1.6 we depict these as one process acting through any combination of the three dimensions simultaneously. There is a significant point that we have to take into consideration at this stage, since having the experience in itself is no reason for doing anything about it. There need be no logical connection between the experience and the action, but it is the pressures exerted by the disjuncture between life history and experience or the affective element in the experience itself that provide the motivation or the pressure to act upon the experience.

Significantly, Illeris (2002: 19) also discussed three dimensions – cognition, emotion and society – and it is with the last that I disagree. For him the learning person is cognition and emotion and these occur within society – he omits the individual activity through which we also learn. Consequently, he fails to discuss behaviourism within his framework. I certainly include the social dimension, but it is the whole person who is in the world, so that cognition, emotion and activity are all affected by the social context.

However, we can now depict the processes by which the person is changed in the learning experience (see Figure 1.6).

Figure 1.6 contains many similarities to my last attempt to depict learning in a single diagram (Jarvis and Parker 2005), but in this I have tried to capture the continuous nature of learning by pointing to the second cycle. However, this diagram must always be understood in relation to Figure 1.5, since it is only by combining them that we can begin to understand anything of the complexity of human learning. Nevertheless, it does make an important point about repetitive learning – it is always the changed person repeating the learning, so that even rote learning may be about continuous change and not mere repetition. Indeed, Simpson (1995: 57) makes this point clearly, although he might over-state it for our purposes:

> Repetition is not a mere 'repetition of the same', abandoning itself wholly to the past. It is, rather, a matter of being a *new* application of already existing possibilities, a unique appropriation of tradition.

Repetition can be repetition of the same when we merely go through the motions and do not learn from it. It is like the maxim of having fifty years experience or one year's experience fifty times. We shall return to this when we examine Chinese learners later in this study (Kennedy 2002: 433ff.).

However, the experiences that we have may not always be ones that we intend or are even aware of, and so it is necessary to distinguish between those that are intended and those that are not. I have deliberately chosen the term 'incidental' in order to distinguish it from 'unintended', which is the opposite of intended, and it will be used in this manner here. Self-learning is lifelong but it is incidental and we learn it pre-consciously. Through such learning we acquire such attributes as self-confidence, self-esteem, identity, maturity and so on. We shall return to this discussion again in the following chapters. These encounters occur in social contexts such as education and the work place. Intentional learning, by contrast, occurs when we have an experience, an encounter with the world in which we live, through which we are changed in some way as a result. It cannot occur without self-learning, although we may not be conscious of the latter. Often it occurs in unintended ways. For instance, we may not always be entirely unaware of everything in a situation and we may unconsciously sense the world and memorise a sensation, like the face in the crowd or the smell that we associate with certain places and so on. In these situations, we acquire tacit knowledge. This is *preconscious* and it can occur at any time and in any situation. In a similar manner, experts can adjust their skilful actions without necessarily being conscious of it and have preconscious skills learning. It is very hard for experts to explain how they have adjusted their actions, as Nyiri explains: experts 'rarely have the self-awareness to recognize what it [practical knowledge] is. So that it must be mined out of their heads painstakingly, one jewel at a time' (1988: 20–1). This is the same type of process we all experience in everyday life (Heller 1984), where so much of our behaviour is based on the presumption that the world has not changed, and also on our tacit knowledge.

However, there is a problem here, which is with what I initially called non-learning but which I now recognise that the processes that I included here might also be transformative, and so I want to make a brief reference to them below.

The changed person in the world

The person is changed in at least three different ways. First, the person's self is changed both by the acquisition of all the things we have discussed mentally, emotionally and in expertise (Figure 1.5), but also in terms of identity, self-confidence, esteem and so on. Additionally, the learner may place a new meaning on the world and events and so on transforming the former one. This might be *incidental learning*, but Polanyi (1962: 74) regards it as latent learning, and it is a direct consequence of being alive and conscious of the world, although the learning may be pre-conscious since the individual is probably unaware that it is actually happening.

Second, through *purposeful learning* the person acquires a combination of new knowledge, skill, attitude, emotion, value, belief and appreciation of the senses and the person is changed. Purposeful learning is what is most frequently defined as learning. This learning may be either intended or unintended, but it is always accompanied by incidental learning. Later, we will discuss the distinction between intended and unintended learning, but when we speak of learning throughout this book we are always referring to the combination of purposeful and incidental learning.

Third, the changed person is more experienced, more able to cope with similar situations and problems because of the learning that has occurred, that is to say that the learner has become more intelligent. Not all intelligence is biologically-based, as Cattell (1963) showed us many years ago. He distinguished between fluid and crystallised intelligence: the former relates to biologically based intelligence, whereas the latter refers specifically to experiential. In other words, some of our intelligence is learned and we become more intelligent as a result of our learning experiences.

Learning changes us. In the same way, other people with whom we interact are also being changed through their learning, so that the interpersonal relationships between people in the world are always dynamic; there is always the potential for disjuncture and, through interaction, learning will keep on occurring. Similarly, the wider world is always changing, what Bauman (2000) calls 'liquid modernity', and so individuals will continually suffer disjuncture and need to keep on learning in order to re-establish harmony with it. Lifelong learning is a social necessity. However, if individuals disengage from the wider world so that their life-world changes less slowly than the wider world, they lose potential learning opportunities. They are harmony seekers (Jarvis 1992). In the third instance, planning, desiring and thinking about the future will continue, but each time it does it will be a new experience since some learning, both purposeful and incidental, might well have occurred through the processes of living and thinking since the last time this planning was undertaken, and also during the planning process.

The rapidity and continuity of change gives rise to questions of stability and continuity. I (Jarvis 1999) tried to respond to this by suggesting that every event is new since time does not stand still. In a much more profound way, Bauman (2000, 2003 inter alia) has captured this sense of rapid change by describing modernity, society, love and so on as 'liquid'. The essence of society may not change rapidly but its form is no longer, if it ever was, static. Nevertheless, the individual's sense of being a person is held together by memories of previous experiences that can be linked together through language into a life story. The ever-changing person still has a sense of continuity and distinctiveness since that person's life story, or story of learning and remembering, is unique.

I have used the words 'changed' or 'developed' and I have tended to favour the former since the latter term tends to contain a value-bias, as it is often used to refer to the process of changing people in the direction that society or the persons' employers wish, as in human resource development. Yet we can see immediately that individuals' changes are not dependent upon stages of biological maturation, as Piaget (1929) argued, but on their experience that is, itself, dependent upon their relationship with the world in which they live, and consequently with their own life-world. This was a position also adopted by Vygotsky (1978) through his adherence with dialectical materialism in respect of children's development. At the same time, learning is not synonymous with change, since biological maturing can occur without learning taking place automatically, e.g. when someone is in a coma.

Types of learning

In my previous work I was able to isolate nine distinct types of learning and indicate how the processes of learning proceeded through my diagram. Incidentally, Marton *et al.* (1996: 70) isolated six distinct conceptions of learning: increasing one's knowledge; memorising and reproducing; applying; understanding; seeing something in a different way; changing as a person. However, they did not really expand the domains of the emotional and practical, and neither does changing as a person occur in all their types of learning. Even so, this typology points to the complexity of the learning processes and in what follows all of these approaches to learning are included. I wrote at the time of my earliest work that I thought that my typology was over-simple, and I now have a much more complex understanding of learning and yet it is still necessary to discuss different types of learning here. The starting point for such a discussion must be the point at which learning begins, which is experience: the intersection of the person with the life-world. There are a number of ways through which we relate to our world. They revolve around the fact that either we are in harmony with that world or there is disjuncture between our biographies and our consciousness of that world. These were depicted in Figures 1.3 and 1.4 above. These relationships include:

- harmony;
- disjuncture – when we at ease with our disjuncture;
- disjuncture – when we feel that the outside world is putting pressure on us;
- disjuncture – when we wish to change our world in some way.

Each of these relationships might lead to a different type of learning. Indeed, we have already pointed to the first two of these.

HARMONY

Basically, harmony is a non-learning situation and I have called it 'presumption'.

Presumption   In situations where we are in harmony with our world (Figure 1.3) and we take it for granted, time flies; as Schutz puts it, 'when I immerse myself in my stream of consciousness, in my duration, I do not find any differentiated experiences' (1967: 47). In fact, society generally has been structured on presumption – that we always act in the same way as we have previously done because the world has not changed from what it was like the last time we performed a similar act. Consequently, cyclical ideas of time have also emerged – time goes round in circles, history repeats itself and so on. Without this form of stability, however, there could be no society. The concept of society is of a stable phenomenon and learning is merely learning to find out how to perform in it and then to conform to its patterns and once this has occurred we can take the environment for granted so that there is no further need to learn in that situation! This is a rather crude description of the social process of socialisation, which is also a form of learning.

Non-learning also occurs in other common situations. Unfortunately, for instance, we see many images of suffering on television but because we see so many images we are no longer able to be surprised or angered at some of them. The familiar becomes taken-for-granted, whatever it is, and we merely observe it without learning anything more about it. Because there is harmony between our biographies and our experience, there is no disjuncture. Consequently, there is no conscious learning – we call this *non-learning*, although incidental learning might also occur.

Pre-conscious learning   I am including pre-conscious learning here, discussed above, since it occurs before we have a conscious experience of a situation. We are apparently in harmony with our world, but images get imprinted upon our minds or we hear but apparently do not remember words, for instance, which we recall at a later time when we do have a relevant experience that enables/demands that we recall that image or the information that we were given. In addition, we learn emotional responses to situations and experiences and often these are pre-conscious.

DISJUNCTURE – CAUSED BY EXTERNAL CHANGES

Disjuncture is usually a cause for learning, but there are two situations where we have an experience but from which we do not learn from an external input, although we may learn something more about ourselves in the process. We note from both Figures 1.5 and 1.6 that the processes whereby we transform our experiences are not simple and direct; in all cases emotions and practical aspects might, but need not always, occur simultaneously with the cognitive.

Rejection and non-consideration   In both of these responses we may be sufficiently at ease with our external world to recognise disharmony but do not need to seek to rectify it immediately. They are both apparently non-learning situations in which incidental learning might occur. In both, disjuncture occurs but, for a variety of reasons, individuals may not wish to learn from their experience. For instance, we probably all have had the experience of not knowing how to do something and yet knowing that we should learn about it, but also knowing that we just do not have the time. We are frequently too busy, often this is in the workplace, and this means that we tend to do things the way that we have always done rather than to learn a better or a different way. We just do not have the time to consider it – but this does not mean that we not learn something incidentally, and we are changed. In precisely the same way, we may be aware that someone we are listening to on the television (a politician, for instance) is trying to change our attitudes, beliefs or values, for instance, and we do not want these changed so that we turn the television off – and we reject an opportunity to learn. Yet we might still learn incidentally from the experience. In this sense we still transform our experience, albeit pre-consciously, and are changed by it.

There are other situations, however, where the disjuncture might result in other different types of learning.

Non-reflective learning   In order to re-discover harmony we accept the outside stimulus and learn it so that we conform to the external world. What we learn might be cognitive as a result or oral or written words; but it could also be olfactory, tactile, taste and so on. We have to recognise that non-reflective learning occurs both in initial and post-initial learning and, therefore, is the one common form of learning that occurs both in Figures 1.5 and 1.6. We might also learn non-reflectively as a result of seeking to copy somebody else whom we observe. 'Sitting by Nellie' has been a traditional way of learning skills from experts, but we all do this during socialisation and even as adults: when we go into a new situation, we often seek to imitate the way that we see others behave. Additionally, we all learn through imitation when, for instance, we are in new situations and are unsure of correct procedures and so on. In other words, we learn to conform in our behaviour, learn our mathematical tables, we accept that a certain taste is associated with a specific food or drink, smell of a certain flower or illness and so on. We learn skills in the same way – observing the expert and copying those practices that have gained widespread approval and so on. In these instances, we do not seek to question them in any way; we merely accept them and re-establish a sense of harmony with our external world because we have learned an external fact, action, value or belief. In my previous studies, I referred to these as memorisation and skills learning (see Figure 1.5). We will discuss these fully when we discuss authenticity in a later chapter.

This is the way that learning has been perceived until very recent times, and to some extent it still is. Education was considered to be a process whereby the best knowledge, values, beliefs and practices were to be passed on to the succeeding generations, who were expected to learn what they were receiving and continue the tradition. We will, of course, return to this traditional perception of learning throughout the pages of this study.

Thoughtful and reflective learning   In other disjunctural situations, we might wish to consider carefully what the knowledge, belief, values, skill, etc. with which we have been presented. In these cases we think or reflect carefully and decide whether to accept them or not, and practise them or not – as the case may be. We will discuss thought and reflection as the same or different processes later in the first part of this volume. Clearly, when our reflection does not lead to a practical outcome, we can see it as contemplation, meditation and so on. But, if we are in the practice situation, then we are the reflective practitioners about whom Schön (1983) wrote. In the former case, we learn new knowledge, appreciation of new sentiments and art forms and so on, but in the latter we learn practical knowledge and new skills.

In thoughtful and reflective learning, we may not accept the input that we have received. For instance, we may not agree with the information, we might not like the sentiments or the values inherent in what we are given and so on. Consequently, we read or hear the input with an expectation that we will reflect upon it, disagree with some of it and that we will arrive at new knowledge and so on that will be integrated into our biographies, but it will certainly not be the same as the input. Nevertheless, it would be quite wrong to assume that all thoughtful and reflective learning will produce negative reactions in the learners. We might, having given careful thought to the input, agree with it and so we will learn the content of the input to our experience.

DISJUNCTURE – CAUSED BY INTERNAL CHANGES

In all of the types of learning discussed thus far, the learning process follows the disjuncture that we, as learners, experience as a result of the changes in the exterior world.

We may also experience disjuncture as a result of our learning, beliefs, values or changed aspirations and so on. In this case the disjuncture causes us to desire change. In planning, we think rationally and reflectively and this might be seen as thoughtful and reflective learning – even contemplation. However, once we put plans into action, we begin to learn in a different way. In one sense, we turn 'knowledge how' into the confidence of being able to do something and in this sense our learning experience results in considerable changes to the self-image as well as the practice of new skills and knowledge. Ryle (1963) criticised the dualism of mind and body by claiming that action is a single exercise of practical knowledge and not two distinct ones from the mind and the body. However, his weakness lies in the fact that these actions are phenomenological since the experience of performing in this way is totally different from the action itself and irreducible to any physical skill or even to practical knowledge.

Indeed, this phenomenological experience is something that we have every time we are conscious of interacting with the exterior world. There are, however, some situations in which we learn when this does not occur: these are the pre-conscious learning situations that we discussed above.

Conclusion

Our concern, in this introductory chapter, has been with exploring some of the fundamental aspects of human learning itself, but we can see from the outset that learning is a very complex process and it is no wonder that different theorists and researchers have emphasised different elements of the whole. During the remainder of this first section we will explore in greater depth the main elements in the learning process, and in the second we shall see how many different theorists' work fits into this overall picture, although the approach will be different from that of Illeris (2002). The critique of the second section of the book will enable us to ask the extent to which it is possible to have a comprehensive theory of learning.

From the outset, however, it is clear that it is the whole person who learns and the nature of the person is problematic, so that the following chapter will begin the explore some of the issues about the person that relate to learning.

Chapter 2

It is the person who learns

We have probably all heard teachers saying, 'I teach mathematics, or education, or whatever'. Perhaps we have said it ourselves, and we know precisely what we mean – our subject is mathematics, or whatever. It is easy to say that this is what we teach and everybody understands us because we take for granted that we teach individuals. But mathematics cannot learn! Neither can any other subject! This is one of the problems of talking about teaching and learning, we leave out the most important element in the processes – the learner. We actually teach individuals mathematics. In order to understand learning we do need to understand something about the nature of the person. Rogers (1983) was keen to emphasise that it is the whole person who learns – which is true, but there are different ways that we can begin to understand personhood within this context: we can look at biographies (Houle 1984) and autobiographies, life histories (Alheit *et al.* 1995) and educational biographies (Dominice 2000), or we can try to analyse something of the constitution of personhood (Harré 1998; McAdams 2000) in order to see how this affects our understanding of the processes of learning. In my earlier work (Jarvis 1987) I opted for this last approach and I want to expand it here as I have continued to think about it within an even broader context (see Jarvis and Parker 2005) and recognised its significance for learning theory.

However, it is necessary to understand what we mean by personhood. McAdams (2001: 691–5) suggests that personology – the study of the person – emerged from the Harvard Psychology Clinic in the mid-twentieth century and that the study of lives:

- is shaped by a multitude of forces;
- is complex, lifelong and never-ending;
- requires a close examination of mental life;
- is multi-disciplinary;
- includes living, historical and fictional;
- entails a wide range of concerns from local to global.

Harré defines the person as 'a unique, embodied being, rich in attributes and powers of many kinds, having a distinct history and, importantly, being morally protected and liable to be called into account as a morally responsible actor' (1998: 71). This definition follows that of Charles Taylor in *Sources of the Self* (1989) where he argues for a moral basis of selfhood.

The whole person consists of body and mind and so the first part of this chapter will briefly examine the philosophical debates about the relationship between body and mind. Thereafter, we will look at the body and then the mind, the self and identity and in the final section we will begin to relate this discussion to different types of learning.

The mind–body relationship

From the earliest philosophical studies the relationship between the body and the mind has constituted a problem which, although rarely discussed in the literature on human learning, has influenced the way that some scholars have understood learning. Even so, we noted in the first chapter that an existentialist position does not accept the crude mind–body dualism, whereas other scholars have maintained its validity. There is, indeed, no agreement between scholars about the nature of this relationship and Maslin (2001) suggests five main theories:

- dualism;
- mind/brain identity;
- logical or analytical behaviourism;
- functionalism;
- non-reductive monism.

We shall discuss briefly each of these in turn before we look at body and mind separately.

Dualism

By rejecting Descartes' well known dictum 'I think, therefore I am', we did not reject the classical dualist position which states that the human person is a composite of two completely separate entities: body and mind. However, we will reject the more extreme dualist position that starts from the assumption that mind is not dependent upon the body. Plato, for instance, considered that the soul also actually exists before birth (see Crabbe 1999), which reflects the type of belief that everybody is created individually by God, or a god. But we will not deny that the person's mind is the possessor of experiences and consciousness. Consequently, the mind might be related to a faith position that human beings possess a soul, something which can continue to exist after the body dies and considering the time when Descartes actually wrote, it is not surprising that his theory reflects such a belief system. Although not adopting such a position does not automatically rule out the possibility of some form of existence beyond life itself. This discussion, however, is beyond the remit of this study. There are, however, a number of major problems with dualism, such as the existence of the brain itself – if there is a mind that has all the experiences and so on, why do human beings have such complex neurological mechanisms that we call brains? We also know from scanning the brain that when the mind is active, so is the brain, but this may reflect a correlation rather than a causality. In addition, it is clear that when we act it is our body as well as our mind that performs in unison rather than each act being two distinct elements: the thought and the action. Ryle (1949 [1963]), from his weak behaviourist position, forcefully criticised the idea that there were two distinct phenomena in every action. Yet we argued in the first chapter that there is a dualism of body and mind when it comes to sensations and experiences, and this position we must maintain here even though we do not accept the idea that the mind and the body are two separate entities. In addition, we know that learning is more than just a mental act and so adopting a dualist position opens up questions about many contemporary theories on learning, such as information processing and experiential learning from different perspectives.

Mind/brain identity

This is a monist theory which claims that only physical substances exist and that human beings are just part of the material world; therefore, mental states are identical with physical ones. This raises fundamental problems about the nature of culture and meaning. But we know, for instance, that when we think brain scans reveal increased neuron activity; Greenfield (1999: 124) writes:

> . . . there is no magic ingredient for consciousness. . . . the issue is a quantitative one, depending on the degree of recruitment of neurons: the extent of recruitment will determine your consciousness at any one time . . .

Unlike dualism this is a reductionist position in which there is little or no room for a separate mind, let alone a soul, but it is one which points the way forward in terms of how we can understand learning a little better since it helps us understand how the brain operates. It also helps us understand something more about the mechanism of thinking (see Jarvis and Parker 2005). If we can affect the functioning of the brain, we can affect the way that we think. Consequently, if we can speed up the brain we might be able to increase the rate of learning and so on.

Nevertheless, there are a number of problems with this approach, such as being able to locate in the brain where a thought is occurring does not explain the meaning we give to that thought, or any intentions or plans that we might have as a result of it, or even rationality itself. Indeed, thoughts are different in type from neurological activity and Bruner (1990: 34) rightly, in my view, suggests that it is culture rather than biology that shapes human life, although I would not claim that biology has no influence at all. Maslin also raises other difficulties, but these are sufficient to demonstrate that while the theory has certain attractions, it also leaves many questions unanswered. Consequently, while we can begin to understand how the brain functions, it does not overcome all the problems of how the mind operates, nor of the relationship between the two, and so it does not answer all the problems we have about understanding human learning.

Behaviourism

A great deal of theory and policy about learning has been couched in behaviourist terms ever since the time of Pavlov. Maslin summarises the behaviourist position thus: 'behaviourism maintains that statements about the mind and mental states turn out, after analysis, to be statements that describe a person's actual and potential public behaviour' (2001: 106). Indeed, we have already seen the claim 'I act, therefore I am' – and this can, in some circumstances, be regarded as a behaviourist statement. Behaviourism does explain some of the outcomes of the learning process which can be measured, so that in an age where quantification is important, it is not surprising that behaviourism retains its attractions. Nevertheless, there are major problems with it theoretically, such as whether behaviour is the driving force of human being or whether there are other forces, such as meaning or even thought itself. It seems to me that none of the objections to the mind/brain identity theory are overcome by postulating that everything can be reduced to behaviour. Indeed, it appears that behaviourism is a weak theory since it almost completely denies the common sense assumption that I can actually think my own private thoughts and do not have to reveal them to anybody. To put it crudely, a good poker player could hardly be a convincing behaviourist. While behaviourism can point to the outcomes of the learning processes, it is incapable to explaining the processes themselves.

Functionalism

This approach regards the mind as a function of the brain, so that if we can understand all the inputs and outputs and also the state of operating mechanism, we account for our understanding of mental states. In other words, the brain is seen as a complex computer – a picture that has become rather common in recent years. This theory has gained a great deal of currency recently because of the analogy with the computer appears credible, especially now that we can also talk of artificial intelligence. But we might ask, is the human being no more than a sophisticated computer – especially one that has been programmed to 'think'? If we were to accept this, then learning could be reduced to a computer program. Indeed, Searle (1992) makes the point that thoughts have meaning and intentionality – something that a computer program performing its functions cannot have. Not only this, but computers are thoroughly rational machines from which they cannot deviate from their programmed logic, but human beings are not totally rational! It was a computer specialist who invented the term 'fuzzy logic' to describe the way that we behave in contrast to the way computers function. In my own research into superstition many years ago, I discovered that all my respondents were in some way or another superstitious, or less than rational in their behaviour (Jarvis 1980). Freudian psychology also points us beyond the bounds of rationality. Lowe argues that one of the problems with 'the computational approach is that it seeks to throw light on human visual cognition *without* invoking general intelligence' (1992: 99; italics in the original). Maslin also raises a number of other objections and, despite the popularity of the analogy, this theory is not at all convincing. Nevertheless, it is one which has assumed a certain prominence as we have learned more about neuroscience, but if we reject it then information processing theories of learning must automatically be seen as weak.

Non-reductive monism

This theory is also dualistic in terms of properties but not substances. Maslin (2001: 163) describes it thus:

> It is non-reductive because it does not insist that mental properties are nothing over and above physical properties. On the contrary, it is willing to allow that mental properties are different in kind from physical properties, and not ontologically reducible to them. It is clusters and series of these mental properties which constitute our psychological lives. . . . property dualism dispenses with the dualism of substances and physical events, hence it is a form of monism. But these physical substances and events possess two very different kinds of property, namely physical properties and, in addition, non-physical, mental properties.

The relationship between the physical and mental properties might be described in terms of supervenience, which is 'the idea that one set of facts can fully determine another set' (Chalmers 1996: 32). There are, according to Maslin, three elements in supervenience discussions: irreducibility, co-variation and dependency. Chalmers also makes the crucial distinction between logical and natural supervenience. A problem, then, with mental properties is that they cannot be located like physical substances – in this sense they are not a physical site and neither are they the processes that can be seen in brain scans. Consequently, Chalmers, therefore, argues that consciousness per se cannot be logically reduced to a physical condition, that is, it is not logically supervenient upon the material, but he does not rule out the idea that the mind is naturally supervenient on the natural. He has, therefore, ruled out the most common approach, as have others before him (see Bergson 2004 [1912]), he does not deny some form of dualism. This is something to which we will return later in the book on a number of occasions, when we examine the concepts of the 'self' and consciousness – and its nature. It is this position that is accepted here.

Having examined five different ways of looking at the mind-body relationship we can find no simple theory that allows us to explain it. Exclusive claims should not logically be made for any single theory, although they are made quite widely in contemporary society. Some of the theories, however, appear to be much weaker than others, such as mind/brain identity, behaviourism and functionalism. This is unfortunate since these are the ones most widely cited in contemporary society. We have accepted a form of dualism that may best be explained as a form of non-reductive monism, although we are less happy with dualism per se. Yet we have to acknowledge that none of the theories can claim universal allegiance and in each there are problems that appear insurmountable. Nevertheless, we feel that non-reductionist monism is a relatively strong position, which we will utilise in this volume and to which we shall return later when we look at the 'self' and consciousness. Indeed, we agree here with Harré that the human being is both physical and mental, but the mind–body relationship remains an unanswered problem. We will now look at the body and the mind separately.

The body

From the above discussion, it is clear that for some theories the body is all that there is: we can only be known by our behaviour since there is nothing beyond it. We are our bodies. Nietzsche (1969: 62, cited in Hodgkiss 2001: 155) captured this:

> Behind your thoughts and feelings, my brother, stands a mighty commander, an unknown sage – he is called Self. He lies in your body. He is your body. There is more reason in your body than in your best wisdom.

Yet in statements like this it does appear that Nietzsche has to revert to a dualistic form of language to communicate his ideas, which might be no more than a cultural reflection but it might also be an indication that there is something beyond the body which we can call a mind, or a self. Nevertheless, the body is something rarely studied for many years outside of the fields of art and the physical sciences, although more recently social scientists have turned their attention to it (Falk 1994; Schilling 1993; Turner 1996). It is not surprising, therefore, that learning theorists have not recognised its significance to learning, although it has long been acknowledged that bodies have drives and needs which underlie the individual learning process. Now it is beginning to be recognised that the physical sciences have a contribution to make to our understanding of human learning (see Jarvis and Parker 2005, especially chs 2–4) and the biology of learning is beginning to emerge as an arena for study. There is also a place for a pharmacology of learning since we know that the brain can be affected by different drugs. In the previous chapter we acknowledged that we exist-in-the-world and that the world is impregnated with us and we develop as individuals as a result of our being in the world, which pointed us to a non-reductive monist type of position. There is a dialectic relationship between us and the world and in some ways our body is that element through which this relationship is conducted. Consequently, we will first look at the way that we experience the world through the senses. Thereafter we will look at our body including our genetic system, and finally we will look at the nature of the brain.

Senses

Locke (1993 [1690]) separated our understanding into two elements: sensations and reflections. Sensations are how the external world impinges upon us and then we reflect on our sensations, or experiences. But we are not just recipients of sensations since we transform them into meanings – see Figure 1.5; we also have intentions and externalise our reflections. Being-in-the-world is, therefore, being conscious of it through our senses and so we experience it, although our perception of it is coloured by our memories of previous experiences. We shall return to this when we look at the nature of experience later in this volume.

Consequently, provided our physical bodies are normal and all of our senses operate, we are able to experience the world and therefore learn through what we hear, see, smell, taste, feel and touch. But normality is a problematic concept which does not imply sameness. As we watch young children growing we are also conscious that they are actually learning to put names to things and colours, to learn different tastes, sounds, smells and tactile experiences. We can see, therefore, how the mind is developing through experiencing and memorising as a result of early experiences of the world beyond the body. We know that some people develop better vision, hearing and so on than others; we know that artists, for instance, can communicate through sophisticated pictures and musicians through music so that they can employ their senses to a much more highly developed degree than the remainder of us. They also appreciate and perceive the world differently through these highly developed senses. In addition, we can see how our perception of the world is being shaped by our life-world and the continuity of our being-in-the-world is carried through memories (see box 6 in Figure 1.6). By contrast, as we age some of the physical attributes of the body decline and our senses are less highly responsive to the world; we see less well, become deaf, forget things and so on. In these instances our bodies process the sensations less effectively and our experience of the external world is less precise. We are also aware that during times of physical illness we are less likely to be motivated to indulge in concentrated studying, so that the state of our body affects our motivation to learn. Nevertheless, the world is full of stories of people whose extraordinary will-power has helped them overcome the state of their body and achieve tremendous feats of learning – Helen Keller is frequently cited as an example. Indeed, lives such as these demonstrate most clearly the weaknesses of some of the theories cited in the first section of this chapter.

Body

We are our bodies, whatever position we adopt about the body–mind relationship, but we are also more than our bodies. In the next section we will suggest that there is a mind/self which is learned as a result of experiences. Yet this is no place to develop a biology of learning but rather to point in the direction that it might develop. In this section we will focus briefly on four aspects of the body only: genetic make-up, circadian rhythms, bodily conditions and blood pressure.

Following Parker (Jarvis and Parker 2005: ch. 2), our bodies are programmed in the genetic material (deoxyribonucleic acid or DNA) of our genes which is passed on from one generation to the next in an egg and a sperm when they fuse to produce a human embryo. This contains information (coded in its inherited DNA) about how to grow and develop into a new human being. She points out that 'there are no genes for (say) a bundle of behaviour patterns that could be regarded as "feminine behaviour" (whatever that may be!)'. The DNA can be regarded as a recipe rather than a blueprint because the information it contains will be manifest only if the external environment in which it develops is enabling. If the DNA is, in fact, only a recipe, then the pursuit to reduce everything to a genetic basis is crudely reductionist and omits other elements that affect behaviour, although understanding our genetic constitution will certainly help treat certain physical conditions. However, genes neither determine our intelligence nor our ability to learn, although they might have some effect on some of those abilities. Nature without nurture is an incomplete picture of human growth and development.

Gardner (1993) has studied how the nervous system develops and he shows that there is a normal process of biological development given the fact that it receives sufficient stimulus, indicating its genetic nature. Indeed, he says that even the brain acts along certain developmental paths – canalisation

– while still retaining flexibility. He (1993: 40–45) suggests that there are five principles of flexibility, or plasticity, related to:

- the degree of flexibility encountered in early life;
- the importance of critical periods during the time of development;
- the region in the nervous system, those parts of the system that develop latter are more malleable;
- the need to have certain experiences;
- the level of 'wholeness' or injury of the system.

In addition, we know that the level of nutritional intake affects the functioning of the body and so it can be postulated that the diet will also be significant to our understanding of learning. Moreover, our bodies all have periodicity which is not dependent to a great extent on the changes in the external world; we all know that some people are 'morning people' and others nocturnal and so on. We also know little at present about the way that our learning is affected by our circadian rhythms, although there may well be quite a significant relationship. Our senses are also affected by our bodily conditions; for instance, we experience pain, hot and cold, and physical stress, and while we give meaning to these conditions, they certainly have some affect on the way that we learn. Finally, we do know that our brains are affected by blood pressure and that if the body is physically fitter and the blood flows around the body in a more natural manner our brains function better. This is important in our understanding the relationship between ageing and learning and Cusack and Thompson (1998) have demonstrated that intelligence levels can be affected by physical exercise in elderly people, so that we can see that in some way the brain, and therefore the mind, is affected by the level of physical exercise we undertake – learning is affected by our activity! In addition, Cattell (1963) distinguished between fluid and crystallised intelligence; the former is biologically based intelligence and the latter relates to experience. As we age the former may well decline but the latter continues to develop so that the great majority of us retain our ability to function in the world and learn throughout the life span. The brain, however, is part of the body and so it is necessary to look briefly at it now.

Brain

Stein (2005) writes:

> The brain is made up of one hundred thousand million (10^{11}) separate cells, 'neurones', that gather information from diverse sources through their 'dendrites', integrate them in the 'cell body' and send the outcome of their processing to be passed on to the next neurone via their elongated axons which make 'synapses' with the next neurone in the chain.

The most rapid period of brain development occurs during development of the foetus in utero from the 6th week to the 6th month of pregnancy. During this time a million million (10^{12}) new neurones are generated; in fact an amazing 250,000 new neurones are added every minute. However only 10% (still 10^{11}) of these neurones are destined to survive after birth. The other 90% are programmed to self-destruct ('apoptose') because they fail in a lethal competition with other neurones to make useful functional connections. This is an example of a general principle of brain function that persists throughout life: 'use it or lose it'. The main function of each neurone is to communicate with other neurones via synapses made with its dendrites and axons, either close by or at great distances. In an adult the axons of neurones connecting touch receptors on the toe with the brain, are up to 2 metres in length. But unless a connection or contact serves a functional purpose, it will lose out in a cut-throat competition and be removed.

This long quotation explains clearly how the brain develops and gives us a basis to understand how it functions during learning. In addition, it must be recalled that the physical development in the cortex continues after birth and is most active during the first three years of life, so that this is development is affected by early experiences of daily living. During learning there is some alteration in the synaptic connections, both in creating new ones and in strengthening those which already exist.

In addition, we also know that different parts of the brain perform different functions:

in 97% of people, including two thirds of left-handers, the left hemisphere is relatively specialised for speech and language whereas the right is more important for visuospatial analysis and emotional expression. These differences are not absolute; the right hemisphere is important for some aspects of language, such as its emotional tone, and the left hemisphere plays a part in some visuospatial functions such as helping to determine the relative position of letters in a word.

(Stein 2005)

Gardner (1993: 54) also suggests that while the brain can be divided into different regions with each important for certain tasks, no region acts exclusively in respect to one specific task. Yet his (1993: 54–5) almost resigned comments on the way that scholars in fields other than neuroscience have responded to our knowledge of the brain is quite revealing:

Now even if localization proves to be the most accurate description of the nervous system, it remains possible that there may still be very general problem-solving devices as well as considerable 'horizontal' structure – with perception, memory, learning, and the like cutting across heterogenous [sic] contents. Nonetheless, it would seem high time for psychologists to take seriously the possibility that the molar – and even the molecular – analyses of the nervous system may have definite implications for cognitive processes.

So much for the inter-disciplinarity of contemporary academia! Gardner, however, goes on to suggest that the brain is rather like a computer, but as we pointed out earlier in this chapter we do not accept that the mind is no more than a computer-brain. Even so, the fact that it is possible to localise brain functions has given rise to his understanding of multiple intelligences so that as we consider human learning we need to recognise that our different experiences of the wider world largely activate specific areas of the brain, although if one or more of them have impaired functioning then other areas will try to compensate for the malfunctioning area. As we age, however, this compensatory activity will not occur so frequently and our brain cells will be less effective or else atrophy completely. Consequently, it is a matter of using or losing the use of these specific areas of the brain and their corresponding attributes of the mind. Having briefly looked at some of the elements and the way in which they contribute to our understanding of learning, we must now examine the concept of the mind.

The mind

All the theories of body–mind relationship, with the exception of dualism, assume that the mind – if we have one – is in some way contingent on the body. However, Gergen (1994: 129–30, cited from Newman and Holzman 1997: 29–30) claims that:

> It is a revolution that extends across the disciplines and which replaces the dualist epistemology of a knowing mind confronting a material world with a *social epistemology*. The locus of knowledge is no longer taken to be the individual but rather patterns of social relatedness.
>
> (italics in original)

But this does not overcome the question of the mind since we still have to be aware of these patterns. In my original study (Jarvis 1987) I, in common with many others, argued that mind develops as a result of experiences of the world external to the body, either a dualist or a non-reductionist monist position fit this argument and while there are objections to these positions as there are to every other one, they still remain the more convincing to me – especially the non-reductionist monist position. Indeed, the mind, and therefore the self, are learned in the same way as all learning takes place, through experiences that are then stored in the brain and which later develop into minds and selves.

Chalmers (1996) suggests from the outset that no single concept of mind solves all the problems with which we are confronted but rather we need two concepts: a phenomenological one and a psychological one. The former is the mind of 'conscious experience and a mental state as a consciously experienced mental state', whereas the psychological one is as 'a causal or explanatory basis for behavior' (1996: 11). Clearly a great deal of our thinking here points to the ideas underlying the phenomenological mind, although we recognise that a number of the theories of learning are based upon the psychological conception of the mind.

The very earliest sensations the body experiences are in the womb – the heartbeat being universal. I recall being told by a pregnant North American First Nation person when I was in Alaska that, 'My people teach us to talk to unborn babies in the womb'. They recognised the significance of the experiences of the unborn creating preconscious memories in the brain. Nevertheless, the very use of the word 'preconscious' presupposes that there is something called 'consciousness' which will emerge. Bergson (1998 [1911]: 111) argues that consciousness actually exists in any living organism in relation to its power to move freely, that is to act in the world. Hodgkiss (2001) suggests that there are a number of dimensions of consciousness: self, emotion, will, memory, imagination and language, which we would argue are components of the mind and can be seen to a greater or lesser extent in the theory of learning outlined in the previous chapter. We will now use this theory, but also following Mead (Strauss 1964), to illustrate the way in which mind emerges from these earliest experiences.

From the moment of birth children experience the material world beyond them through primary experience. This occurs directly in two forms: with people (I↔Thou), the basis of interactionism, and through their other sensations (I↔It). But people also mediate their own experiences and understandings of the world, thus providing secondary experiences to other with whom they interact in an I↔Thou relationship. The people with whom children interact are the significant others in the immediate life-world; in the first instance this latter relationship is a one-way relationship (I←Thou), although it soon changes to I↔Thou as they develop and interact. But children also interact with inanimate objects in the external environment, from which they also have experiences. Whatever the understanding and perception of those early experiences it is stored in the brain through memories, so that children develop a stock of knowledge and experiences about the world. Following Vygotsky (1978), we would argue that this is rarely a direct stimulus-response since from very early children perceive their world and act upon it as well as respond to it. In addition, both Vygotsky and Mead place considerable emphasis on signs and gestures which aid the memory and, from early days, they help orient perception so that their experiences are not 'of the world' or 'of the social world' (interactions with significant others) but are constructions of that world. But, from early on, even in the womb, we have experiences about which we are incapable of thinking – especially before we have developed language. Some of these are conscious experiences but others are stored in the mind without being considered – they are preconscious. Often these preconscious experiences occur through senses other than the one about which we are aware at a given time, and so from early childhood a great deal of our learning about ourselves and our world is not entirely conscious learning.

These sensations are received through all five senses and so visual images, tactile sensations, odours, sounds and tastes and are transformed cognitively, emotively or behaviourally and they are then all stored in various parts of the brain and develop a stock of memories. However, the transformation from the sensation to the meaning (from the body to the mind) lies at the heart of the mystery of learning (see Figure 1. 5). These sensations also cause pain or pleasure, satisfaction of bodily need or leave the need unfulfilled and so on – from which emerge likes and dislikes and other attitudes towards things and people. Memory is different from the sensation that caused the experience: 'it is an inversion of historical time [it] is the essence of interiority' (Levinas 1991: 56). In a sense, the memory is itself a reflection on the experience and it contains knowledge, attitudes, values, beliefs and emotions that we have gained as a result of the experience. This is where mind differs from the computer – the computer carries data and then information which needs to be transformed into knowledge and so on, and while the brain is the repository of the sensations the mind is the storehouse of the knowledge. The person is the one who utilises these memories and they are wider than cognitions.

Freud pointed out that some of these memories do not remain in our conscious minds but reside in our unconscious; they are actively repressed and kept from our consciousness. He postulated a variety of reasons for this repression, including aggression and sexual problems, but they still affect our thinking, feeling and acting. Consequently, our experiences are also affected by our unconscious in ways that we cannot always determine and may not be able to control and so, consequently, are both our learning and any subsequent behaviour.

From before birth, but most certainly from the moment of birth, that store of memories in the brain increases with every experience and children are changed – they grow and develop – but, more significantly, it is from within this ever-changing store of memories that self-consciousness emerges. Herein we experience the growth of the mind. Moreover, this store of memories becomes one of the bases for our self-identity: I am the store of memories of my experiences and learning in the world – I am, in part, a learned being. My other base is the physical body. Consciousness is the continuing response to the early experiences – not just of the objective world but of the interactions with significant others within the social world, or the life-world. There is, consequently, a sense in which the quality of this initial environment, the nature of the life-world, is quite fundamental to the formation of the mind and, therefore, to the ability to process future experiences. With the passing of time, this store of memories grows and increasingly it affects the way that children perceive their world; in a sense their consciousness of the world, and therefore the way that they perceive it, is shaped by their previous experiences of it. We are all children of our time and place. Gradually, children also become conscious of themselves as active players in the world – 'I am, therefore I do' or 'I do this and therefore I am this person' – but the sense of 'I' is at least not well developed at this early stage, so that Mead differentiates between 'I' and 'Me' in the first instance. This is the way by which children experience themselves as they develop a sense of identity – an 'I'. They are objects of themselves before they become subjects. Indeed, Luckmann (1967) has suggested that it is as children's stock of knowledge grows it enables them to transcend their biological beings and become selves. But it is this private stock of knowledge, which nobody else can ever know, that predicates the sense of self. Significantly, in this process of developing a self, children both see themselves within their life-world and they also individuate themselves. Nevertheless, the significance of play is vitally important at this time – play is a form of auto-didacticism in which children endeavour to understand and give meaning to their world and to themselves as actors in it. This meaning is entirely their own, it is a part of the private self.

At the same time, the development of language is important since it is through language that we can both store memories and recall them. While the store of memories need not necessarily be only a linguistic phenomenon, language is a symbol of things experienced and reflected upon, but also of the abstract content of experiences – of knowledge, attitudes, beliefs, values and the emotions. As language develops so children are able to have more secondary experiences and enrich the interpretations they place upon all their experiences of the world. The knowledge is not contained in the language but it is the medium through which the experience is understood and communicated to others.

Mead (Strauss 1964: 218) recognised the significance of the life-world in the development of the self although he called it the 'generalized other', which he considered to be a cohesive and standardised social group which would form the basis of the developing unified self. Even when he wrote, the idea of a generalised other was problematic and as the world has diversified this concept has lost its credibility. Nevertheless, the recognition that the self is a social phenomenon, something learned from the exterior world, is extremely significant. However, Bauman (1995) can talk about *Life in Fragments* – for the unified community has disappeared and in its place we have fragmented and individualised society. From our earliest days we are made conscious of the complexities of society so that the idea of a self reflecting on a common culture may actually be problematic and social difference and individuality may be reflected in the emerging personal self, which seeks to provide some form of unity for these diverse experiences and memories. Indeed, Loevinger claims that this seeking to make sense of experience is not what 'the ego does, it is what the ego is' (1976: 5). This is a lifetime project. Loevinger actually traces the stages of ego's development (see McAdams 2000: 590–601). This sense of unity is one of the three elements in the 'I', the other two being agency and identifying with oneself, according to Blasi (1988 in McAdams 2000: 592).

The self and identity

Mead considered the self to be a unity but Harré (1998: 4–5) actually suggests it has three elements:

- Self 1: the sense one has of possessing a unique set of attributes.
- Self 2: the shifting totality of personal characteristics.
- Self 3: the totalities of impressions that individuals make on other people.

Clearly self 1 is the self of self-identity, whereas self 2 recognises the changing human being over time and self 3 is the social identity. Self 1 is, I think, the self which Mead described as emerging within the mind. Self 2 emerges over time as we develop and become self-aware, whereas self 3 is experienced from babyhood and as such may help determine the other two elements. This is akin to 'Me'. The person is, for him, a combination of all three senses of self and these can be seen through the distinctness, continuity and autonomy of the person, following Apter (1989: 75). This unified self is a product of social processes. Harré (1998: 3) writes:

> . . . the self as the singularity we each feel ourselves to be, is not an entity. Rather it is a site, a site from which a person perceives the world and a place from which to act.

True! The brain is the neurological phenomenon in the body and as a result of experiences we learn and store our memories and develop our minds, in which we acquire our sense of selfhood. Luckmann (1967: 47) focused on this remarkable process whereby we learn to transcend our bodies and claimed that when this occurs a religious phenomenon has happened. Being able to identify with ourselves means than we can also ask ourselves who we think that we are, and who do others think that we are. In a sense, becoming Me is the start of the process of identity development and throughout our lives we are always confronted with this as we interact with our wider world and reflect upon our experiences. Belenky et al. (1986: 31), in their study of 135 women, also illustrate this process and demonstrate how it continues throughout people's lives; some of the women suggest that the 'source of self-knowledge is lodged in others'. Erikson's (1963) eight stages of life depict this process. While we have criticised Mead's 'generalised other', O'Neill (2003) has recently shown that teenagers living in a residential school develop a personal identity that emerges from their family background while they acquire a second one as a result of living in a closed community. Indeed, as we go through life so we all learn new identities and learn to discard old ones. But we not only learn new identities and also continue to have identities thrust upon us – if we do not, then we become socially excluded, outcastes, in a network society. And as Erikson pointed out, we have our identity crises, but not only in our adolescent years as more and more people seeking psycho-therapy demonstrates! In liquid modernity, however, Bauman (2004: 89) points out:

> In our fluid world, committing oneself to a single identity for life, or even for less than a whole life but for a very long time to come, is a very risky business. Identities are for wearing and showing. Not for storing and keeping.

One identity that does seem to have considerable permanence, however, is ethnic identity. Learned within our own life-world during primary socialisation many of us acquire this very potent identity, which symbolises us as a people in whatever nation we might live. As we have seen in recent years, its preservation has led to ethnic conflict, ethnic cleansing, civil war and so on. In a real sense the ethnic boundary is socially constructed and maintained and in many countries in the world and where there is a scarcity of resources or a wide divergence in religion and history, ethnic identity helps maintain the divisions in wider society. The fact that the 'Other' lies beyond the boundary helps maintain and strengthen the boundary which in its turn, paradoxically, reinforces the sense of identity.

However, we can see how we learn both our sense of selfhood and our identity. If we look back to our theory of learning, we see in Figure 1.6 that at the end of every learning process we have memories, which we integrate into our biography. It is through this process that in the first instance, in our early years, we build up a store of memories that enables us to develop this sense of self – initially self 1. Many of these learning processes are affected by how significant others see us, in our babyhood (self 3), and how they treat us. This determines the types of experiences from which we are going to learn which, in turn, affects the development of self 1. Since all of our early learning experiences are embedded with the culture of our life-world, we are going to incorporate many of these dominant elements both in our selves and in our identities. Clearly as we grow and develop (and begin to develop self 2) we can choose more of the experiences from which we learn, and this leads to a reinforcing of self 1 and so on.

We are all co-authors of our own biographies now, able to choose our occupation, domicile, partner and interests and so on. We are what we think and do but we are also what we have learned and remember. But what we do affects the way that others identify us and it is this that allows them to identify us, which, in its turn, affects our self-identity. Our minds are the storehouse of our memories of the complexities of the lives we have led and are leading, so that our identities are a complex interplay of self and social – what I see myself to be, what I do and the person others see me to be. As this process continues, we learn a sense of self-identity. However, our identity is not just our store of memories, it is also about the way that people treat us as persons and what we learn about ourselves from this and, additionally, it is about our own perception of our body. Finally, our identities are affected by the spaces that we occupy, a point to which we will return in a later chapter. Not only do we learn about ourselves, we also learn to be ourselves – we learn our own identity. Significantly, our selves and our identities are learned phenomena. All of our experiences, experiences that we as persons have, are transformed through cognitive, affective and practical processes and we become more experienced people and the experiences themselves and their outcomes become memories that we can recount as we interact with other people.

Mind, self and identity are learned phenomena. While we can locate the neurological processes in the brain, we are more than our bodies but not distinct from them. The learning processes are processes whereby the whole person (body and mind) constructs an experience that is transformed into something partially beyond the body and yet contained within it. But experience itself is problematic and later in this volume we will begin to explore the diverse meanings of the concept of experience. Before we do this, however, there are certain implications from the above discussion that need briefly to be focused upon.

The person

The person is both body and mind, not just personality in the psychological sense. Identity is a matter of both the body and the mind and we know ourselves through both, and others recognise us first by our bodies and then by our actions. Our actions are also driven by both biological and self needs, as Maslow (1968) highlighted many years ago. His 'hierarchy of needs' moved from the physiological through safety to the need for love and belonging and then progressed to self-esteem and self-actualisation. Maslow argued, however, that the needs at one level have to be partially satisfied before we can move upwards to the next, but we would dispute that this is a hierarchy or even that the order is significant. What is clear is that needs stem from both body and mind – the person's needs arise from the whole person.

Motivation to act, and to learn and enrol in educational courses, has a whole person basis, although theories of motivation tend to be more than this as Maslow made clear in his distinction between A-values (self-actualising characteristics) and B-values (being-characteristics). McAdams (2001: 446) suggests that together these characteristics make for a unity of consciousness.

There are many theories of motivation, although this is not the place to expound these in detail. Suffice to note that most of these stem from the need to self-actualise, although Rogers argued that there is an inherent tendency 'to actualize, maintain and enhance the experiencing organism' (1951: 487, cited in McAdams 2001: 41). Basically, his concern is that the whole person should be maintained and developed. In contrast, Freud argued that a great deal of human behaviour stems from two opposing groups of instincts: life and death instincts. He then argued that sexual instincts tend to be repressed, so that human behaviour is often driven by unconscious motivation. This is crudely the basis of psychoanalysis, and while this will not be discussed here it must be noted that his theories do not find universal assent – but they do stand as an important criticism of rationality and of rational behaviour.

These theories all stem from an understanding of the whole person. When these drives are activated disharmony is generated within the individual that leads them to act in order to re-establish both internal harmony. In precisely the same way, the external world changes and generates disharmony between the individuals and their world, which also acts as a social driving force for action and the re-establishment of harmony. In both of these cases, the disharmony is a driving force for learning and change. It is this disharmony, however it is caused, which I have called 'disjuncture' – the gap between the individual's biography and perception and construction of the experience of the external world. It is a moment of potential for learning, whether it is cognitive, emotional or behavioural.

Conclusion

A great deal of education, teaching and learning have focused upon knowledge and, therefore, upon cognition, mind and the nature of theory and argument. In a sense, we can see the influence of Cartesian thinking on the body–mind relationship and of the Enlightenment with its emphasis on rationality in these developments. However, with the recognition that mind and body are not related in quite the way Descartes argued and that the body also plays a significant part in human learning, we are beginning to recognise that learning should have life-wide connotations, or perhaps more significantly that we need to look at whole person learning in life-wide contexts. Since the whole person learns, a great deal of learning occurs in all our social living that is unrecognised, incidental, unintended and often discounted – some of this learning falls within the ambit of what I have called 'pre-conscious learning'. Much of it is recognised long after it has occurred, as autobiographies and biographies (Houle 1984) note how certain events occurred which changed people's lives are only recognised long after they have occurred: this is also one of the strengths of the life-history research approach to learning.

Ask people to describe an experience in which they have learned something because they have been taught and this is relatively easy, but ask them to describe how they have learned to be themselves and they will find this much more difficult. This is because throughout our lives we have experiences of the external and social world and we transform these and remember them almost without thinking. This is part of the process of everyday living. In education, we are taught and might learn knowledge and, to some extent, skills but we are rarely taught smell or taste, unless we learn to be a wine taster or a perfumier and so on, so that formal education not only artificialises or restricts our experiences. On more than one occasion when I have taught trainee nurse teachers I have conducted a little experiment: I have asked them to write down their own definition of learning – most write one that is about behaviour or cognition – and then I have said we will come back to this later. I have then asked them whether, when they are working in the hospital wards, they can recognise an illness as a result of the smell that comes from a bed. All have said that they can and all have recognised that they have learned to associate a certain aroma with a certain condition – but no one in my little experiment has ever included smell in their definition of learning! This is also true for learning from other senses.

Indeed, nurses can be taught to perform the role of nurses but they have to learn to be a nurse – their identity of nurses grows upon them as they play their role. In the first instance there is a sense of 'playing' but this is gradually transformed into an ontological state and while the end-product is recognised the process of learning that state rarely is. In precisely the same way, it dawns upon us that we are ageing and while there may be specific instances in our lives, like retirement, which make us aware of the social condition, the maturing process in which we are constantly learning is continuous and often totally unrecognised. Learning is to a great extent incidental to daily life but it is both a constituent element and the basis from which we can continue to learn. I learn to be me – we all learn to be ourselves through the process of living. It is paradoxical that we learn to be ourselves incidentally! The wider our experience of life and the more we learn to reflect on it and not take it for granted, the more we learn and the more we become whole people.

Here, then, we are confronted with one of the paradoxes of our existence: it is the whole person who learns and without learning we could not be people, but we often reduce learning to behaviour or cognition and provide reductionist explanations that remove the inexplicable from the whole and explain it functionally. The inexplicable mystery of learning is in transcending our biological bodies and becoming selves, in turning stimuli into meaningful experiences, in being both bodies and minds and in thinking and acting. Often, especially, in official policy documents on learning, the whole-ness of the person is downplayed. But learning is not just an individual phenomenon – not just the preserve of the philosopher and psychologist – learning always occurs in social situations, in relationships, in our life-worlds – learning occurs in social context, as the title of my first book on learning asserted, and so it is to the social context that we must now turn before we return to the relationship between the person and the context when we examine the complex nature of experience.

In drawing this chapter to a close it is important to make clear the relation-ship between the self, even the embodied self, and the person. Perhaps Jenkins summarises this most succinctly when he writes: 'The self is the individual's private experience of herself or himself; the person is what appears publicly in and to the outside world' (2004: 28). However, time does not stand still and the self that emerges in early childhood grows and develops throughout life, and so it is necessary for us to recognise the develo-ping self, but in the next chapter we look at the social setting in which this process occurs.

Chapter 3

Learning in the social context

In the opening chapter we had already recognised that because we exist, we are 'in-the-world'.

We are born into the world and humankind's reaction to it has always been to master it, which is to understand it, and to make it meaningful – in other words, to learn about it. We can see from the outset that learning is at the very heart of our human essence. But also 'we-are-with-others-in-the-world'; we all live in relationships, which we depicted as inter-personal (I↔Thou) and the impersonal (I↔It). In other words, we live in the physical world but also in social relationships. No person is an island, but we are individuals. We experience the world phenomenologically – it is our pre-eminent reality, our life-world. It is bounded by our experiences – but these have been expanded by mass media to a world beyond our daily experience, transmitted to us from around the globe. In this sense our life-world has been globalised and has become extremely complex, and one of the main aims of this chapter is to illustrate its complexity. By so doing, we will show that it is virtually impossible to specify the wide variety of social factors that contribute to the social context of our learning.

A great deal of the material contained in this chapter[1] has a sociological basis and this has two implications for this study. Initially, it means that we cannot divorce our philosophical or psychological thinking about learning from the sociological, so that all learning theories must be inter-disciplinary – despite discipline-specific claims. Second, the sociological orientation will form the basis of the second volume of this work on lifelong learning and the learning society, but it will build on the conclusions of this volume.

Nevertheless, our life-world is not only a world of space, it is also one of time, so that we can see immediately that it is situated in a world that precedes us and exists beyond our temporality – it transcends us. In addition, time is continuous and so we can make sense of our life-world experiences through our memories and interpretations of our experiences. But in this sense, it is about our own consciousness, what Schutz and Luckmann refer to as a 'stream of consciousness' (1974: 51). But much of our life-world we take for granted and time, since we are unaware of its passing, is what Bergson called *durée* – duration. When we exist in the flow of time, living is self-evident and non-problematic. But, on occasions, there are interruptions in our flow of experiences and we have to stop and think, and we become aware. This is what I have previously referred to as disjuncture. Even so, in contemporary society our experience of both time and space has been re-aligned. But now it is necessary to examine this social context – this is the life-world.

There are a number of dimensions to the life-world, each of which has a multitude of sub-divisions so that it is impossible to examine all of them, even though they may all be relevant to our understanding of experiential learning. In this chapter we will explore some of the wide variety of social contexts within which learning occurs. In the first instance, we will discuss the concept of the life-world itself. Thereafter, we will look at the three major dimensions: culture, time and space, and within each we will examine a number of significant sub-divisions on order to understand something more of the complexity of human learning and also to demonstrate how our learning is affected by the context within which it occurs.

The nature of the life-world

Williamson (1998: 23) makes two very valid points about studying life-worlds, both of which we have already met in our discussions:

- People live their lives in and through others, so that their understanding of themselves is inter-subjective.
- People strive to live meaningful lives.

It will be recalled that in the first chapter we noted that Habermas (1981: 119) said that he regarded societies as both systems and life-worlds. He regarded life-worlds as relating to social groups whereas Schutz and Luckmann start with individuals and suggest that the 'everyday life-world is the region of reality in which man [sic] can engage himself and which he can change while he operates in it by means of his animate organism' (1974: 3). Nevertheless, they highlight the point that individuals do not have perfect freedom in their life-world since there are a variety of obstacles and many other people inhibiting our spontaneity; we only have a relative degree of autonomy. It is within this context of everyday life that we have experiences in which learning occurs.

But our learning is often unintended and frequently unnoticed, since we are often so familiar with our life-world that we take it for granted, live within the flow of time and just adapt our behaviour – almost unthinkingly – to changing circumstances. Each adaptation means that we also gradually alter our knowledge of the situation, although we are not always aware of it. This can be seen if we ask people to describe their learning experiences, as

I did in my research, and they found it tremendously difficult to describe precisely how, or even when, they learned unless they describe formal learning in which they have a teacher. In addition, it can account for the discrepancy between the espoused theories of action and the theories-in-use that Argyris and Schön (1974) discovered in their study of theories of action. Only when there are sudden changes or novel situations are people stopped in their tracks, as it were, because they do not know automatically what to do or how to respond to a question and so on. This is disjuncture; it is one that teachers try to create in formal educational settings – the teachable moment.

The life-world, however, is contained within the wider society and consequently it is not independent of the social forces generated by globalisation.[2] This means that the global pressures of the advanced capitalist market and information technology permeate the life-world so that individuals grow up and develop, learning to take for granted the culture generated by global forces. Their learning about the wider capitalist world is unintended and often pre-conscious, but this occurs because these forces have colonised our life-world. Consequently, our life-world is also about people's life-worlds. Not only is the life-world contained within a wider society, there is a total mixture of institutions and groupings within it, such as the family, formal and non-formal institutions such as school and work and informal meeting opportunities during leisure and so on. Each contains its own sub-culture and normally we adjust our behaviour automatically to fit into the organisations and groups with which we are familiar. It is for this reason that both incidental and pre-conscious learning are important forms of learning, although they are less frequently studied than some other types, but social organisation is dependent on them. At the same time, when we join new groups we have to go through a more conscious learning process during which we actually learn the sub-culture so that we can fit into that new group, whether it be a work group or a leisure one. The learning processes might not be very different but the settings in which we learn are: herein lies one of the linguistic problems with some terminology about learning. We are apt to talk about formal learning or non-formal learning and so on, but what we should actually be talking about is learning in formal situations, in non-formal situations, etc. The linguistic shorthand is misleading! Different people may react to and learn in a variety of ways in similar situations.

However, our life-worlds are not only about culture and our positions within the different sub-cultural groups, but they are also about time and space. For instance, the process of joining new organisations and learning their sub-culture takes time, social time and body time. But even more, each new learning experience occurs in time and so it is never a static phenomenon – change is endemic. It is, therefore, necessary to recognise the significance of time when we look at learning in social situations; it is even more important when we recognise that there is a sense in which disjunctural situations are ones when we become aware of time and its passing, so that at the heart of the experiences from which we learn are episodes of time.

At the same time as there is process through time, space is another major dimension of the life-world. Not only is the life-world for most people situated locally, although as Gouldner (1957–8) highlighted many years ago there are a few – more now than there were then – whose life-world is cosmopolitan. Our life-world has also been expanded through globalisation and especially the exposure we all have to the information media, so that we become aware of ourselves within, say, Europe or America, our own country or state, our region and so on. These all contribute to our multiple identities. But space is not only geographical, we all live in social space, at the centre of some institutions and at the periphery of others, and during socialisation we move from the one towards the other. Where we are situated also affects the experiences we have from which we learn.

In the remainder of this chapter we will first explore culture and relate it to identity and experience, which is at the heart of learning. Then we shall do the same for space and time. Having examined these, we will be in a position to discuss the nature of experience, which lies at the intersection of persons and their world and from which we learn.

Culture

Culture is a word with a multitude of different meanings, but from an anthropological perspective culture may be contrasted with nature. Gehlen (1988: 29) writes:

> In order to survive, he [humankind] must master and recreate nature, and for this reason man must *experience* the world. He acts because he is unspecialized and deprived of a natural environment to which he is adapted. The epitome of nature restructured to serve his needs is called *culture* and the culture world is the human world . . . Culture, therefore, is 'second nature' – man's restructured nature.
>
> (italics in original)

But unlike animals, humans have minimal instincts and so they have to learn this second nature and pass it on from generation to generation, so that children's education is often seen as transmitting the most worthwhile knowledge from one generation to the succeeding one. In this sense, education is 'from above' since the dominant forces in the older generation decide what should be included in the curriculum – one way of viewing curriculum is that it is a selection from culture. Culture is all the knowledge, skills, attitudes, beliefs, values and emotions that we, as human beings, have added to our biological base. Culture is a social phenomenon; it is what we as a society, or a people, share and which enables us to live as society. In order for humanity to survive, it is necessary that we should learn our culture. Learning, then, becomes necessary for the survival of societies and in the process we, as human beings, learn to be. This learning occurs, as we have already pointed out, through personal interaction (I–Thou) with significant others (Mead: see Strauss 1964) in the first instance, and then within the wider life-world.

However, it is clear that globalisation and rapid social change have affected the nature of society and that our life-world is now multi-cultural. Perhaps we should now to recognise that all of us live in multi-cultural life-worlds which are gradually reflecting the locality. Consequently, we learn a diversity of interpretations of reality from the outset, especially through the mass media. This might well result in some persons not acquiring the same sense of security, sense of community membership and self-identity as people did in previous generations which, in turn, has given rise to identity-crisis, what Giddens (1991) refers to as 'existential anxiety'.

But the learning is not just embedded in the present, it is always future-orientated in order that humankind should master the world and survive:

> The acts through which man meets the challenge of survival should always be considered from two angles: They are productive acts of overcoming the deficiencies and obtaining relief, on the one hand, and they are completely new means for conducting life drawn from within man himself.
>
> (Gehlen 1988: 28–9)

These actions are communicative and manipulative. But for Gehlen, the common root of knowledge and action lies at the heart of the human response to the world or, in other words, experiential and situated learning, as opposed to the instinctive behaviour of animals. Instinctive behaviour is repetitious and reproductive, as indeed is patterned behaviour in social living, but in the latter we know that we could have done things differently. Learning, then, is a social necessity and through it human beings learn to be.

Experiential learning begins with response to our life-world and it is within this that our learning takes place and we will briefly examine a number of learning processes that occur within the life-world, including socialisation and role making, developing self and identity, and acquiring language, knowledge and meaning. In a real sense these are all inter-related and any separation here is for heuristic purposes only – we will deal with them in the following sub-sections: primary socialisation, secondary socialisation, brainwashing and indoctrination and, finally, cultural and social capital.

Primary socialisation

Culture is an ambiguous concept that functions both externally and internally. When we are born into the world we have no cultural awareness, although we have learned a number of phenomena pre-consciously in the womb. At birth then, culture is external to us but internal to our significant others and through interaction with them we internalise (learn, often non-reflectively and unintentionally in the first instance) it. Once they have shared and we have learned the relevant knowledge, values, beliefs, etc. the culture becomes our own subjective reality and as such helps determine the way that we perceive and experience the world, and consequently we learn in it and from it. This is the process of socialisation which Berger and Luckmann (1966: 150) sub-divide thus:

> Primary socialization is the first socialization an individual undergoes in childhood, through which he [sic] becomes a member of society. Secondary socialization is any subsequent process which inducts an already socialized individual into new sectors of the objective world of his society.

Crucial to this process is learning the language of the people since it is through language that meaning, knowledge and so on, are conveyed. Language is at the heart of the greater part of our conscious learning and it will always reflect the culture of our life-world, as many childhood educators have demonstrated. Language, as such, is arbitrary and symbolic; no word, thing or event has intrinsic meaning, and it only assumes meaning when meaning is given to it, which occurs through narrative that unites the disparate episodic events in our lives. Consequently young children grow up to learn the meaning of words, but the process is more complex than this. Let us assume that my young grandson is looking at the computer on which I am writing this chapter but he does not know that it is a computer, nor does he yet know the word 'computer', although he can see the object/instrument that I am using. In fact the computer has no meaning for him. As he looks at it, the sensations on his retina are transmitted to his brain and so he is aware of the image of the computer and he still has to learn the word. At the same time he has to learn to associate the word 'computer', a sound which is transmitted to his brain as sensations generated by the sounds he has heard. Eventually the visual and the sound sensations are linked in his mind and the object becomes a computer. He can then take the meaning of the word for granted – he has learned it non-reflectively, and it is almost as if there is no longer a separation between the word and the instrument. Even this non-reflective learning process is complex, associational and takes time before it becomes a subjective reality. Once we have accomplished it, we shortcut our language by saying that the instrument is a computer, not that members of our culture call the machine a computer (see Figure 1.5). Naturally, in other languages the word denoting 'computer' may be very different. But once learned, the word 'computer' has two realities – an objective reality and a subjective one. This is true of all the language that we learn in early childhood, and without that language we would find it almost impossible to give meaning to phenomena in our life-world. Once we have language, it helps to organise our experience and give it meaning. But the meaning we give anything is a social construction since it reflects our culture that we have learned from others during our primary socialisation. Traditionally, as Mead demonstrated, this socialisation was affected by interaction with significant others, but in more recent times the media, especially television, have also become very significant and they assume a more dominant role in the lives of most people, especially the young.

However, once we have language, we can express ourselves, share our thoughts and become functioning members of our social group. We can also expand the breadth of our thinking, develop our own meanings of things and interpretations of events within our own purview, and we can become creative and innovative. This ability to think independently gives a second strand to our individuality – the first coming from our biological and genetic inheritance – so that we can see how our conception of our selves, as persons, is enabled by the development of language and meaning. With it, we develop self-confidence and this is another unintended and incidental facet of our learning. As we develop this sense of individuality, self-identity and selfhood, so we have a growing store of memories upon which we can assess new experiences and new learning and so we can engage in negotiation of meanings and interpretations with others within our life-world. In other words, we can develop our critical and creative faculties, and these are relatively independent of our biological base. Consequently, the ability to learn reflectively develops with our growing ability to use language and, perhaps, our preferences for the way that we learn are also developed at this time.

Clearly some learning styles are culturally based, as recent research into Chinese learning styles has shown. Lee Wing On (1996: 35–6) cites Zhu Xi:

> Generally speaking, in reading, we must first become intimately familiar with the text so that its words seem to come from our own mouths. We should then continue to reflect on it so that its ideas seem to come from our own minds. Only then can there be real understanding. Still, once our intimate reading of it and careful reflection on it have led to a clear understanding of it, we must continue to question. Then there might be additional progress. If we cease questioning, there'll be no additional progress.

There is a cultural tradition here going back to the thoughts of Confucius himself: that memorising, understanding and reflecting should precede questioning, which is different from the Western tradition where questioning comes more rapidly in the order of things.[3] At the same time we must recognise that Confucian thinkers located learning within the context of teaching and so learners were expected to respect the master, learn his words, understand them and then to question. In the West, we have been influenced by the more 'natural', romantic and liberal connotations stemming from Rousseau's *Emile*. Learning, then, assumes a cultural form and we acquire some, but maybe not all, of our approaches to learning this way. The success of Chinese learners illustrates that this approach needs to be understood more thoroughly in the West, and we will return to this in the concluding paragraphs of Chapter 5 (see also Jarvis 2005). In becoming aware that we are Western or from a Confucian heritage country, our self-identities are also expanded for not only do we have a sense of self, we can also locate that self within a wider context, e.g. Western or Chinese and so on. Western cultural beliefs and practices have also been learned in the same way and, as Keddie (1980) showed many years ago, Western individualism is learned in a similar socialisation process and reinforced by traditional education classes. In a similar manner we can see that authoritarian and democratic cultures will affect both the manner in which we learn and, perhaps, also the relationship between our learning and our behaviour.

In precisely the same way as we are affected by our ethnic cultures, so we are affected by the manner in which each culture treats gender. Whilst we are born with sexual differences, Parker (2005) points out that culture plays a larger role in learning our gender differences than do our genes. Consequently, we learn to be boys and girls and women and men. There are many studies which demonstrate the way by which masculine and feminine behaviour is acquired in different cultural and sub-cultural settings and Belenky *et al.* (1986) illustrate just how significant is this process to the creation of women's sense of self.

In addition, we are socialised into our socio-economic class position in society, acquiring the language, sense of self and identity, and sub-culture relevant to our position in our social milieu. The fact that Western society is structurally now much more open means that it is possible to move to different socio-class positions as we develop. The same phenomenon is, naturally, not true for either our ethnicity or our gender. In all of these situations, however, the significance our early socialisation in the development our own lifelong learning should never be under-estimated.

Culture, then, is far from value free. Whilst we can look at the processes of human learning and recognise what actually happens, it does not mean that we need to accept the values that are contained within the cultural practices. All cultures have values and, therefore, the ethics of the culture needs to be recognised, as I have shown elsewhere (Jarvis 1997) and to which we will return later in this study. O'Sullivan (1999) has shown quite convincingly why education needs to be transformative and learning critically aware of the environment in which we live.

Secondary socialisation

As we grow and develop, so we enter other groups having their own sub-cultures, such as schools, leisure clubs and work, and in each of these we go through a process of secondary socialisation. We learn to be a student, a club member and a worker; in other words, we learn specific behaviour associated with our position. However, as Turner (1962) showed, the process of secondary socialisation is not merely a process of imitating the behaviour of other role players; that is behaviourist learning. He showed that 'role behavior in formal organizations becomes a working compromise between the formalized role prescriptions and the more flexible operation of the role-taking process' (1962: 38). It is interactive rather than merely imitative, as has been often assumed, pointing to a more complex interaction between 'ego' and the generalised or selected other in learning to perform organisational roles. Moreover, the fact that 'alter' validates the role behaviour indicates that the role player is an accepted member of the organisation and that the role behaviour is likely to conform to certain norms and social expectations. In each status change and personal development there is social identity transformation, although our personal identity remains a continuous and a less frequently changing phenomenon.

None of us remain in the same social position and play the same role throughout the whole of our life span (see, for instance, Erikson 1963), so that we change both roles and statuses – and with it social identities and so on. When the change is gradual it is possible for both the individual and society to cope with it in the normal course of things, but when it is sudden or dramatic then both the individual being changed and the immediate social group have to be prepared for it. Consequently, status change is often ritualised by the social group through rites of passage, initiation rituals and so on. From the work of van Gennap (1960 [1908]), these in-between periods in status change have been regarded as liminal periods. Victor Turner (1969: 81) described the ritual process whereby young people were initiated into adulthood amongst the Ndembu people in central Africa:

> Liminal entities, such as neophytes in initiation or puberty rites, may be represented as having nothing. They may be disguised as monsters, wear only a strip of clothing, or even go naked to demonstrate that, as liminal beings, they have no status, property, insignia, secular clothing indicating rank or role, position in the kinship system – in short, nothing that may distinguish them from their fellow neophytes or initiands. Their behaviour is normally passive or humble; they must obey their instructors implicitly, and accept arbitrary punishment without complaint. It is as though they are being reduced or ground down to a uniform condition to be fashioned anew and endowed with additional powers to enable them to cope with their new situation in life.

Here, then, we see that the initiands were treated as if they had to have their old culture removed and a new 'second nature' provided for them, so that they could fit into society in their new position. Their new learning had to be free from the influences of previous learning. These teaching methods might be regarded as immoral, but they were totally symbolic of 'unlearning' a previously learned culture. This might be seen as a form of brainwashing, an endeavour to remove the effects of a culture upon a person through physical and psychological techniques. Our status rituals are by no means so harsh or as clearly structured since we live in a more open society, but they likewise symbolise the new position and therefore the new learning that has to occur in such social change. Indeed, such writers as Lave and Wenger (1991) borrow the language of anthropology when they discuss situated learning, which in their study is basically a description and analysis of secondary socialisation as a learning process.

Once we have internalised the external culture and made it our 'second nature' it becomes a basis for our own interpretation of our experiences and for our giving them meaning. In other words, this is the psychological consciousness. This consciousness is both learned and validated within the culture and points us to the way that our own interpretation of our own experiences is socially constructed. Thus we can begin to see the significance in understanding the culture into which the learners are born and within which they live if we are to understand their learning processes, but we have already pointed to the significance of space in this process since we have indicated how globalisation affects local cultures.

However, socialised individuals also continue to learn, albeit within a more restricted framework. The Club of Rome Report *No Limits to Learning* (Botkin *et al.* 1979) illustrates this by dividing learning into two types: maintenance learning, which is 'the acquisition of fixed outlooks, methods and rules for dealing with known and recurring situations . . . and is indispensable for the functioning and stability of every society', and innovative learning, which is 'the type of learning that can bring change, renewal, restructuring, and problem reformulation' (1979: 10). In other words, innovative learning results in changes in the way individuals act and ultimately change in culture. We are continually doing both in our own learning, and the more that we seek to maintain the patterns of behaviour with which we are familiar, the more we will tend to resist learning. Therefore, rejection and failure to consider learning opportunities – discussed in the opening chapter – become a feature of our daily life and experience.

Brainwashing and indoctrination

The socialisation processes imply that we learn what is expected of us in morally acceptable situations, but there are many situations when undue pressure is exerted upon us to learn what is expected of us. Wilson (1972: 18) defines indoctrination thus:

> indoctrinated beliefs are those which a person may think that he has accepted freely, for good reasons, but which he has in fact accepted when his will or reason have been put to sleep or by-passed by some other person, who has some sort of moral . . . hold over him, by virtue of his authority or some other power-bestowing psychological factor.

Wilson goes on immediately after this quotation to say that this is a state which Sartre would call self-deception. Throughout our socialisation and education we may well be exposed to this type of social pressure, which, naturally enough, results in both social and culture reproduction so that our learning might be seen as no more than maintaining the status quo. Whilst frequently applied to religious belief situations, it might be more true to claim that within this so-called learning society that indoctrination is much more prevalent, and secular, than it is religious. Indeed, one of the problems with indoctrination is that we may well be unaware that we have been indoctrinated; for instance, in the way that we accept the ethos of consumer society generated through the media at the behest of advanced capitalism. Indeed, we do not always realise just how profoundly changed we are by the ethos of the organisations within which we work, or just how they are affected by the social pressures of advanced market capitalism.

While the exterior forces producing indoctrination might be quite gentle and not very intrusive, there are other situations where these pressures are much greater and forced upon the recipient. The removal of overt freedom might be the distinguishing feature between indoctrination and brainwashing. The latter (Lifton 1961) might be regarded as thought reform or re-education and has been practised by oppressive totalitarian political regimes. The process is designed to make individuals feel that their previous learning is wrong and so they are forced through manipulative psychological techniques to confess to this, and having done so, they open themselves to re-education. However, the process does not produce a façade of change but a genuine sense of self-change, which, as Lifton discovered, has lasting effects even after the process has been completed and the brainwashed person freed.

Both of these are generally regarded as being morally unacceptable, although it would be true to say that less concern is expressed about the former since there is a sense in which the indoctrinated person has a greater degree of freedom to reject the pressures than does the brainwashed one. Even so, the latter know that they have been brainwashed, whilst the former might not be aware that they have been indoctrinated, and perhaps there is little worse than being imprisoned behind the bars of our own minds!

Cultural and social capital

Culture is, therefore, most significant in both the creation of the self and in our understanding of human learning. It is perhaps not surprising that its value has been translated into the concept of 'capital' in the West, which in itself demonstrates the power of the global sub-structure to colonise language and social thought with the riches of the human and personal being translated into economic concepts, and judged as economic value. Bourdieu (1973) was amongst the first to use the term in this way, although it has subsequently been as widely, and as influentially, used by Coleman (1990) and Putnam (2000). Each, however, has used it in different ways: Bourdieu in relation to a materialist conception of culture; Coleman in relation to education and inequality; Putnam as a combination of networks, norms and trust that allows participants to achieve their desired goals. This distinction is nicely discussed by Schuller *et al.* (2000), although it is not necessary to pursue it further here. We are treating social capital here more like the way that Putnam does in as much as it refers to the wealth of resources inherent in the culture of the life-world, all of which affect and contribute to human learning and, in fact, to every learning episode. But we do not accept that this should actually be translated into economic value. In this anthropological sense, we can relate it to discussions of community and association (Toennies, 1957), which themselves reflect the way that culture changes from more closed to more open society and the differing personal relationships that have occurred in different forms of society. As Bauman (2000) has shown in his discussion of liquid modernity, society is now even more open and changing more rapidly than ever before and we might now say that association has continued to change in the direction of individuation. Human learning is, therefore, profoundly affected by all of these changes since we are-in-the-world and we share its culture through relationship and narrative.

Space

Space and time have been re-aligned by globalisation, as we have already seen. Even so, it is possible to mention briefly some ways in which space plays a part in affecting the experiences which we have of the world from which we learn. Space can be seen both in terms of physical and social distance.

Physical space

To a considerable extent it is physical distance that has been re-aligned through global forces. Through the mass media we can experience instantaneously scenes from every part of the globe. I am actually writing this paragraph during the tragic period of the Asian tsunami disaster, and wherever we are in the world at this time we are confronted on television with the horrendous suffering of the people and we are able to understand just a little more of their sorrow and suffering than we could have done a few years ago if the disaster had only been reported by wireless, or even earlier by telegraph. We cannot experience their suffering at first hand, but at least we can share just an extremely small part of their experience a little more. We can learn – perhaps more of the emotion – as a result of the media.

The physical environment is also a major constituent factor in all of our learning experiences since we learn through our senses. Much of the effect of the environment results in both pre-conscious and unintended learning since we take our environment for granted for much of the time. It is only when we enter novel situations that we become aware of the significance of our environment – when we suffer from natural disasters such as the Asian tsunami or when we want to take photographs when we travel and so on – and then we become more conscious of our physical space and try to learn more actively from it. Nevertheless, our perceptions of the environment are generally structured within the social context within which we live, which, as we have already shown, are given meaning within a cultural context that has been colonised by the forces of globalisation. Our experiences of our environment are socially structured and we need to be aware that we do not just perceive it as a camera taking a photograph but as a culturally meaningful environment. Much of the time, however, our learning from our physical environment demands the same critical awareness, as O'Sullivan (1999) has called for in his *Transformative Learning*.

Social space

At the start of this book we focused on the I↔Thou relationship, and it is this that is changing quite fundamentally in many ways. While the significance of others in primary socialisation may not have changed tremendously, the nature of many of our other relations has changed greatly – now we probably relate to more people throughout the world than most of our ancestors ever did, but the nature of that relationship may be less intense or less intrusive in our everyday lives. This has, therefore, changed the nature of many of our inter-personal relationships and of the way that we both experience and learn from other people. But we are still individuals-in-relationship with others; we still share and narrative has become a major feature of contemporary society – as was the telling of stories a major way of teaching and learning in traditional society.

Social space also has its own cultural meanings so that, for example, when two people stand close to each other they are regarded in Western cultures as being intimate, but this is not universal. Social space is culturally meaningful and we interpret our experiences of social space from the perspective of our own cultural understanding, which, in its turn, means that our learning from our experience of social space is never free of social implications.

We have already alluded to social class in the first section of this chapter, but social space is about a wider variety of situations, such as: structures of the group's organisations and networks of which we are a member; power and authority that we can exercise within each; the role and position we play in the organisation or network and so on. Since we live in liquid modernity, in Bauman's terms, very few of these factors are static, which basically means that we are more often confronted with new, or disjunctural, situations than were our ancestors. This means that our experiences in many of our everyday contexts change with great rapidity but that we also change our position within such organisations more frequently, so that we can take fewer situations for granted. Hence there are fewer opportunities to presume upon our world and more to learn from it; failure to recognise change and learn may relate to ageing or even to our position within the organisation and so on. It is not that organisations are learning organisations but that individuals within those organisations learn and then endeavour to implement that learning in their social context. But today we have more opportunities to learn. One of the problems that we discovered in many forms of vocational education is that when individuals were sent on education and training courses, they did not necessarily learn the political or organisational skills necessary to implement their learning within the organisation and often they did not have the power or authority to influence their managers or to implement changes themselves, so that change was often not effected. In these situations, it is hardly surprising that we meet with such terms as 'learning organisations' and bureaucracies are being replaced by looser networks. Indeed, information technology and rapid social travel has made the establishment and maintenance of these networks feasible. But it is not only space that has been re-aligned, time has also been similarly affected by the changes in contemporary society.

Time

Time, like culture and space, has been colonised by globalisation; in this case again the technological sub-structural force plays a major role. We live in an instrumental society, the need to achieve certain ends, usually within a given timeframe is paramount so that we only have the time to do so much! We have executive summaries of books, reports and papers because the executives have not got the time to read the whole – in this way, their learning is constrained by the value they, and us, place upon time. Time is, in this sense, linear and irreversible. Not only can we not go backwards in time, we cannot unlearn what has been learned, even though we can continue forward and correct our learning. Likewise, just as the same water does not flow under the same bridge twice, we cannot repeat the same action in the same time – it is always a different action in a different time.

Time, or our awareness of time, then, structures our experiences in the same way as does space and, in conjunction with it, time has been re-aligned by contemporary changes. Naturally, we do not have the time or the space(!) here to expand our understanding of time and its relationship to experience and, therefore, to learning to the extent that we would like, but in this section we will demonstrate a few of the most significance points for our understanding of learning.

We have previously referred to Bergson's concept of *durée*, which he (1999 [1965]: 30) described thus:

> There is no doubt that for us time is first identical with the continuity of our inner life. What is this continuity? That of a flow or passage, but a self-sufficient flow or passage, the flow not implying a thing that flows, and the passing not supposing states through which we pass; the *thing* or *state* are only artificially taken snapshots of the transition; and this transition, all that is naturally experienced, is duration itself. It is memory, but not personal memory, external to what it retains, distinct from the past whose preservation it assures; it is memory within change itself, a memory that prolongs the before into the after, keeping them from being mere snapshots and appearing and disappearing in a present ceaselessly reborn.
>
> (italics in original)

Elsewhere he describes time like a melody in which we hear the whole in order to appreciate it, but the individual notes played individually do not comprise the melody. When we can take our situation for granted, and presume upon it – see again the idea of presumption as non-learning in the first chapter – then our inner life is in harmony with the flow of time but, paradoxically, it is when our biography (past) is not in harmony with our construction and interpretation of our experience (present) that we suffer disjuncture from which we can learn – perhaps the motivation for this is so that we can re-establish this harmony once again (future). Disjuncture is a present experience and it is only in the present that we can learn. Learning is a present process. In a sense, the past is dead – we can learn from the past, regret it, resent it and even interpret it differently and thus re-write our biography or our history, or, alternatively, we can accept our past and try to change the external in the present to conform to our perspective, or their can be a mutual sharing – fusing of the horizons. While we can learn from the past, and from our memories of it, our learning from the past always occurs in the present. Learning is about being: human being. Human leaning is about human being. Being is ever present, but it always contains in its presence the potentiality to learn and is, therefore, always becoming. We are potentially always becoming and, therefore, always learning – for learning is literally being in the present; whether it is being in the present and living for the present or being in the present and living for the future is another matter, however.

There is a sense that when disjuncture occurs we not only become aware of our situation in time and space but we also become aware of ourselves as actors in temporal situations – even aware of our own temporality. We experience ourselves in time, something which Kirkegaard (1959) suggested had two aspects to it – an external and an internal history. Simpson describes the former as something 'through which we must move in order to achieve a goal or realize a moment of significance' (1995: 50–1), whereas with our internal history we do not move closer to goals for there is a sense that they are already in our possession and time is itself a constitutive feature and in our doing and repeating we do not seek to overcome time but come to terms with it. Immediately we can see how distinct are these two understandings of time become significant when we think of theories of learning.

External history

With external history, time stands between us and our goal and the moment of satisfaction is the moment when we can achieve our goals – the quicker we can do it the better, and so efficiency has become a watchword in contemporary globalised society. We can conquer time, albeit momentarily! It is the product of the learning rather than the process that is important – the end is important irrespective of the means. Hence the executive summary and so on, typifies this approach to life. The type of behaviouristic theory of learning that focuses upon the end of the process – 'the result of experience' – is the key issue. The more that we can control the means the better, and here we are confronted with technology which, as we have pointed out in the opening chapter, is one of the driving forces of the sub-structure of society, offers us the opportunity to control the means and, therefore, to control time itself. We can be autonomous and self-sufficient and with the introduction of more refined technology we can take even greater control of time – and, perhaps, we are not far from introducing drugs that will speed up the functioning of the brain and make our learning quicker and more efficient (?). Paradoxically, we can become entrapped by the technology which we employ in order to help us control time.

Internal history

Within internal history, we recognise the passing of time so that we can never repeat precisely the same actions, although we can come very close to it through what Simpson (1995: 50ff.) calls 'repetition'. But he (1995: 57) makes the point that:

Repetition is not mere 'repetition of the same', abandoning itself wholly to the past. It is, rather, a matter of being a *new* application of already existing possibilities, a unique appropriation of tradition. The temporality of *praxis* effects a fusion of the horizons of the past and the future.

(italics in original)

In repetition, we do not aim at an end-product so much as to advance beyond the present state and to dig deeper, as it were. It is through this repetition of things in life, in the fusion of knowledge and skill, in *praxis* that we discover that knowledge turns into wisdom and skill into expertise. In many situations, these are unintended outcomes of daily living, but in training repetition assumes an external historical perspective – the expertise is the goal of mastering the skill or technique. In this sense, what we might call expertise might be little more than a matter of competent performance since we do not have the time for constant repetition but, as such, we call it expertise and in a sense we 'dumb' down standards. Even more so, if we can replace the human performance by a technological one since the human performance is repeated, then we will do so as it is cheaper, quicker and may be more reliable. We can never master the technique of acquiring wisdom, we can only learn it experientially and pre-consciously through the process of living and in the sheer professionalism of the practitioner who only seeks to practise, then the expertise grows with the practice in such a way that it is hard, maybe impossible, for expert practitioners to articulate it since they have never been aware of learning it. As Nyiri (1988: 20–1) puts it:

> One becomes an expert not simply by absorbing explicit knowledge of the type found in textbooks, but through experience, that is through repeated trials, 'failing, succeeding, wasting time and effort, . . . getting a feel for a problem, learning when to go by the book and when to break the rules'. Human experts thereby gradually absorb 'a repertory of working rules of thumb, or "heuristics", that, combined with book knowledge, make them expert practitioners.' This practical, heuristic knowledge, as attempts to simulate it on a machine have shown, is 'hardest to get at because experts – or anyone else – rarely have the self-awareness to recognize what it is. So it has to be mined out of their heads painstakingly, one jewel at a time'.[4]

It is this latter approach to life – pre-conscious learning of wisdom and expertise – through the living and experiencing in the 'now' that contemporary globalised society seeks to overcome the uncertainly of life through control of the processes of production.

In addition, we can begin to see how both motivation to learn and the assessment and evaluation of learning have begun to acquire such significance in contemporary society. We can begin to see how the idea of the 'meaning' relates to our understanding of internal and external history, and this is something to which we will return in the following chapter.

There are, of course, other ways of looking at time (Adam 1990, *inter alia*), but for our purpose in seeking to understand the place of time in our life-worlds and in human learning we have begun to open up yet additional variables in our seeking to understand both experience and human learning.

Conclusion

We live in a complex world and we have seen how difficult it is to isolate individual factors within it, but living in the world means that we have to interact with it in a variety of ways, and this is the nature of human experience. In the following chapter we will again point to the complexity of this phenomenon, but it is from experience itself that we learn.

Chapter 4

Experience – from which we learn

Being, and therefore becoming, lay at the heart of our thinking about learning – and thinking per se is but one element in it. Being-in-the-world means that we have to experience it, and so it is necessary to understand what experiencing it means and this is a much wider discussion than that which is contained in the idea of experiential education, or even experiential learning. Dewey (1938) was one of the earliest twentieth-century philosophers of education to place emphasis on the notion of experience, although for the most part his discussion was limited to certain forms of experience that could be planned within an educational setting. Indeed, on many occasions, but not all, he appears to see experience as something quite limited and bounded by the demands of education – something which is continuous but bounded by time, so that individuals move from one discrete experience to another in a series of situations. It is this notion that is limited, as we shall see below, but he also notes correctly that an 'experience is always what it is because of a transaction taking place between an individual and what, at the time, constitutes his environment' (1938: 43). Other philosophers extend the discussion as, indeed, we must as we regard experience as being at the heart of learning, which is at the heart of conscious living itself. But then we are not discussing experiential learning here but the nature of learning itself, which must always stem from experience. Indeed, Kant (1993) recognised that we need to relate space and time to our capacity to experience things and that we could not know them by pure reason. And so we might ask, what precisely is experience?

There is a sense in which we take for granted the idea of experience; it is self-evident that there is a world out there and that during our conscious life we apprehend it in some way. Perhaps it is this taken-for-grantedness that has sometimes prevented us from recognising that we actually use the term in a number of different ways. Examine an ordinary dictionary definition (*Collins Dictionary* 1979) and we find a multitude of meanings, such as:

- a particular incident;
- a feeling;

- accumulated knowledge;
- an impact of an external phenomenon;
- life history;
- an emotional or aesthetical moment.

All of these definitions have one thing in common – they refer specifically to the internal world, as it relates to the external one. But there is a fundamental difference between those interpretations; some imply that experience is a continuous whole and lifelong, whereas others suggest that it is episodic, some emotive, whilst others cognitive and so on. However, I recognise that biography spans the whole of my life's experience and that experience itself must be more than a sequence of episodes. From this, I want to suggest that there are at least four ways by which we can understand this concept: consciousness, biography, episode and sensation, each of which will be discussed in the first part of this chapter. In the second part, we will expand our discussion by examining awareness and disjuncture, the construction of experience – perception, the meaning we give to our experiences, and different types of experience.

The nature of experience

Four totally different ways of understanding the idea of experience are discussed here; each is relevant to our understanding human learning. In addition, there is a brief fifth sub-section relating experience to virtual reality since we also learn in simulated situations.

Consciousness – the ability to be able to be in the world and 'know' it

Chalmers opens his book *The Conscious Mind* thus: 'Conscious experience is at once the most familiar thing in the world and the most mysterious' (1996: 3). Indeed, he (1996: 5) suggests that it is a surprising phenomenon:

> If all we knew about the facts of physics, and even the facts about dynamics and information processing of complex systems, there would be no compelling reason to postulate the existence of conscious experience. If it were not for our direct evidence in the first-person case, the hypothesis would seem unwarranted; almost mystical perhaps. Yet we know, directly, that there is conscious experience. The question is, how do we reconcile it with everything else we know?

In his 'mystical', we find echoes of Luckmann's (Luckmann 1967) assertion that when human beings transcend their biological foundations a religious phenomenon occurs. Conscious experience is something of a mystery. In any full-length study of experience, we would now be forced to ask how experience has itself come into being, but for our purpose of trying to understand human learning, we can accept our own evidence that it exists and that we are aware of our experiences through our sensations, feelings and thoughts.

As we discussed in the opening chapters about there being two forms of mind, so Chalmers argues, quite convincingly, that there are two forms of consciousness – a phenomenological and a psychological. The former is about 'what is *means* . . . to feel a certain way, and what it means for a state to be psychological is for it to play an appropriate causal role' (1996: 12). Clearly, in some of the more recent studies recognising the emotional, educationalists are beginning to recognise the difference between the two. Chalmers (1996: 8–11) suggests some forms of phenomenological experience, such as emotions, sense of self and pain; he (1996: 26–7) also indicates some forms of psychological experience, such as awakeness, introspection and knowledge. Consequently, he offers two definitions of conscious experience:

- Phenomenological: the concept of mind as conscious experience and as a mental state as a consciously experienced mental state.
- Psychological: the concept of mind as a causal or explanatory basis for behaviour.

(1996: 11)

However, Chalmers is careful not to separate these too much, asserting that many of the different psychological forms of consciousness can also be associated with phenomenological states. We will see this quite clearly when we discuss conscious experience in relation to awareness later in this chapter.

There is a sense in which Chalmers reflects something of Bergson's discussion on *durée* in this distinction. For Bergson, we live in the flow of time which is a continuous coming and passing, rather like a cinema film projector, which is an image he uses, whereas when we stop to think about something within it, it is rather like a single frame. The continuous is rather close to Chalmers' phenomenological, whereas the psychological is closer to Bergson's stopping and reflecting upon something within this stream, which below we call episodic experience. However, the analogy of the camera is extremely misleading when we think of experience, for while we can think of an episodic experience rather like a frame of a film, our experience is not a mirror image of the external world; we perceive the world and thereby select from it those things that are relevant to our biographical development. Perception is a major part of the process of constructing experience and we will discuss it in more detail below.

Biography – the outcome of a lifetime

Experience is seamless and relates fundamentally to our conscious awareness of the external world throughout our lifetime. Oakeshott (1933: 10) expressed it thus:

> the view that I propose to maintain is that experience is a single whole, within which modifications may be distinguished, but which admits to no final or absolute division; and that experience everywhere, not merely is inseparable from thought, but is itself a form of thought.

The seamlessness is a view shared by other thinkers (Dewey 1938: 37; Schutz 1967: 45–53, *inter alia*). Indeed, this is how Knowles (1980) viewed it in his discussions of andragogy – learners bring their lifetime experience to the learning situation. But for Oakeshott experience is subjective and cognitive. He argued that experiencing is always a 'world of ideas', whereas we are suggesting that the person is more complex and that our biography comprises bodily and emotive, as well as cognitive, dimensions. When we act upon the external world, we are also thinking and feeling about it – we might know how to do a thing and also have the ability to do it (practical knowledge), but we also usually have feelings about it, which may actually be a significant motivation for us to act. We also are aware, for instance, that sports people train their bodies and musicians their arms and fingers to act in an almost instinctive manner. Bergson (2004 [1912]) also recognises this when he discusses two kinds of memory, which he relates to motor mechanisms and independent recollections. Consequently, the body acts, sometimes apparently almost without the mind, or in response to an external stimulus, so that experience is more than just the ideas – it is cognitive, emotive and physical.

This understanding of experience as biography is also very significant in life history research and, indeed, when we look at studies, such as *Women's Ways of Knowing* (Belenky *et al.* 1986), we can see the value of using it in this manner in seeking to understand human learning, since it becomes clear how the accumulation of previous experiences affects their current ones.

Episode – the moment of contact with the world

An episodic experience we have may be a direct encounter with the external world or it may be mediated to us. However, the significant point is that at a moment we become conscious and aware of the external world – which I have called disjuncture – when my biography and my interpretation of the immediate world are not in harmony and I cannot take my actions for granted, then I am forced to ask questions – why? how? and so on. It is at this moment we become aware of the world and have an episodic experience.

This is the 'now' when we have a subjective understanding of the world and an awareness of time. While this is a widely used way of understanding experience and, indeed, it is one of the ways used in this book, it is conceded that it is an artificial construction since the continuous flow of time can never be stopped and so we can never isolate 'the present from the past' and once we try, the future has already arrived. At the same time, it is necessary to postulate a present for the sake of recognising that we do focus our attention on specific objects or events during certain moments in our life. It is, therefore, not time that has changed but it is our awareness of our being in the world that has been heightened (Bergson 2004 [1912]).

We can experience that world through our senses, albeit through a process of perception so that the extent to which that experience is direct is itself debatable. But we can interpret the sensations that we are having, and this constitutes a primary experience. However, most of our experiences of the external world are mediated: we are told about a phenomenon, we see pictures on the television and we are taught theoretical ideas by teachers, although we have not had the opportunity of experiencing these for ourselves – they are secondary experiences, albeit within the context of a primary experience since the process of receiving the sensation is primary even though the content of the experience is often secondary.

It is this episodic experience that I have depicted in Figure 1.6. This is at the heart of our learning episodes and the length of the episode will be fairly short, although if we have good powers of concentration we might be able to string together a number of episodes into something of a unity. However, the episodic experience begins with those bodily sensations, which we experience in a given social situation at a specific time.

Sensation – the ability to be able to 'sense' the world

We all have our basic senses from which we are able to learn about the world: hearing, seeing, smelling, tasting, touching and feeling. In the final category, or two categories, we can begin to see the problem that we had with the phenomenological and the psychological since touching and feeling are profoundly different. But the first five also give rise to an interesting issue, e.g. when we hear something it sets off sensations in the ear that are transmitted to the brain – as impulses, but how do these impulses acquire meaning since they have no meaning in themselves, for words are arbitrary symbols? The same might be asked of the sensations transmitted by our eyes, our nose, our taste buds and the nerves at our finger tips and so on. Consequently, we can see that there is a real sense in which these sensations are mediated to the brain through the body, which again points to the significance of our understanding the relationship between the mind and the body. Initially, we have to learn both the sensation and the meaning in our childhood, so that our meanings reflect our culture – but we can see immediately that the external world we appear to experience is not the immediate cause of the meaning that we give it – there is a correlation between the two, but not a causal relationship. Therefore, our experience of whatever it is, is always socially constructed and bodily mediated (Figure 1.5).

In earlier times, it was widely believed that we were born with innate ideas and it is this that Locke endeavoured to refute when he started to write his *Essay Concerning Human Understanding* in 1690 (1993). In this Locke (1993: 23) recognised that there are no innate principles in the mind, or other innate skills:

> The senses at first let in particular *ideas* and furnish the yet empty cabinet; and the mind by degrees growing familiar with some of them, they are lodged in the memory, and names got to them. Afterwards the mind, proceeding further, abstracts them, and by degrees learns the use of general names.

While we do not accept that we are born with 'an empty cabinet', since we claim that pre-conscious learning occurs in the womb, e.g. the heart-beat of the mother and the regular beat that most of us enjoy in music and so on, we do accept the principles that Locke outlined in a more general way. We actually have sense experience to which we give meaning as a result of our previous learning experiences, albeit these experiences are themselves perceived.

Experience and virtual reality

Increasingly simulation is becoming a learning tool and its object is to recreate the actual reality through technological means. It is now possible to create situations in which the visual, aural and even tactile dimensions of experience can be recreated. Basically, these dimensions of a real situation become artificial aspects of information, allowing us to experience something approaching reality. Clearly, the subjective experience is different for a number of reasons, including the artificiality of the surroundings (including the place in which we are located, the attire that we may have to wear and so on), but also because we are aware that we are not in the actual situation. We know that we will not experience precisely the same combination of colour, touch, smell and so on. In short, virtual experience is another form of experiential learning, in as much as it is either the trainers/teachers or the providers of the leisure experience who are creating a situation that will give the learner or subject an 'experience' which might approximate crudely to the actual reality. The more impersonal the reality, the greater the chance there is of approximating to it. A flight simulator might provide a more realistic experience of an actual situation than would a simulation of an eerie, dank-smelling dungeon of an ancient castle on a stormy night. It might be claimed that virtual reality technology is still in its infancy (Simpson 1995: 155), but no simulation can create the actual experience of the interaction of the person (body/mind) with the multifarious dimensions of a complex social situation. That we can focus on the major elements of specific types of experience, like learning to fly a plane, is a tremendous technological advance and a genuinely innovative tool for learning the skill, but the trainees still know that they are in a simulated situation and their bodies will not be recipients of the same sensations as they would in an actual situation. Hence, virtual experience does not alter our understanding of experience itself, although it does provide opportunities for learning that are more difficult to produce in reality.

We have now examined five different ways of understanding the concept of experience – each of which is relevant to our understanding of learning. In our relationship with the external world, we are at specific moments conscious, and aware, of it and are recipients of sensations about it which are frequently associated with previous learning experiences which may be cognitive, attitudinal, skills-based, belief-based, ethical or even new sensations. In a sense the idea of experiential learning seeks to incorporate all of these to some extent, but we will examine this more fully in the second part of this book. In our learning these experiences are transformed through cognitive, emotive or behavioural processes and integrated into our biographies. But our understanding of these processes is also dependent upon our understanding of the body–mind relationship since the sensations are physical and the biography is mental and also a combination of the psychological and the phenomenological.

Having reached some basic understandings of the complex word 'experience', it is now necessary to expand these and to examine some of the implications of our discussion in order to understand human learning a little better.

Expanding our understanding of experience

Each of our interpretations of experience is relevant in our quest to understand human learning, but it is necessary to relate these conceptions of experience more closely to our own experience of learning in the world. As we have pointed out, experience occurs at the intersection of our selves and the world in which we live, so that it is necessary to explore the notion of awareness and relate it to experience. Similarly, we have made the point that we do not experience the world like a camera taking a photograph of our field of potential experience, so that we need to see how we perceive the world and construct our experience. But no object or fact has intrinsic meaning and so we then need to understand the meaning-making process and, finally, we all have different types of experience and some of these are quite fundamental to our understanding of learning, so that the second part of this chapter begins to explore these aspects.

Awareness and disjuncture

When we live in the flow of time and presume upon our world, we are always conscious of the external, but we might be less than aware of all its elements all the time. For instance, when we are driving along a familiar road, we may not be aware of the fact that we are passing familiar side-roads and so on, but we can be helped to recall these if at a later date it becomes necessary to have our memories jogged. We might claim if we were asked that 'we were not aware' of something that occurred at the periphery of our vision in a taken-for-granted situation. Awareness, then, seems to be used in a slightly different manner to consciousness here, although Marton and Booth (1997: 99) say that they use the two terms synonymously in their book on *Learning and Awareness*. Chalmers, however, is clear that he uses them differently, although he recognises that there is considerable proximity between them, but he suggests that 'a subject is aware of some information when that information is directly available to bring to bear in the direction of a wide range of behavioral processes' (1996: 225). For him awareness is psychological consciousness as opposed to phenomenological consciousness, and Marton's and Booth's study is limited to the former.

Awareness, however, is much closer to my use of disjuncture, although disjuncture can also occur with phenomenological experiences. In living in the flow of time and taking my world for granted, I can have experiences which I take into my mind – which I called pre-conscious learning in the first chapter – about which I later have to have another experience so that I can call to mind the pre-conscious and only then can I learn from it, as my illustration above of driving my car down a familiar street demonstrates. I can have many other experiences of which I am aware but from which I do not learn because my interpretation of them is in accord with my stock of knowledge or level of skill and so on. The important factor here is that when my interpretation of the situation in the life-world and my life history (biography) are in harmony, then it can continue to live in the flow of time. But when my interpretation of my experience is not in harmony with my memories, or I am unable to interpret the situation at all – experiences that are disjunctural – I am certainly aware of them. Disharmony becomes a motivating factor driving me to learn so that I can re-establish that harmony through new learning. Indeed, harmony with their social world, or more significantly with their life-world, may be amongst the most important motivating factors for most individuals to learn – it may be an even greater motivating factor than those specified in Maslow's (1968) hierarchy of needs. Maslow started his analysis from a more individualistic perspective than the one adopted here and for Maslow 'love and belonging' is in the middle of the hierarchy rather than the most basic. Yet we are born in an I ↔ Thou relationship with our mothers and we need to remain a member of the family group until we achieve a certain level of independence. A feeling of disharmony with the life-world – a sense of disjuncture – remains the greatest learning need that individuals have so that they can return to the original state of harmony. Indeed, through my behaviour I might even endeavour to create such situations so that this will be possible.[1] However, when no harmony exists I am consciously aware of it; I do not know the answer to the situation, neither do I know what to do. This is disjuncture, but it is one of the fundamental paradoxes of the human condition – the possibility to learn begins with the awareness of ignorance. This is precisely the reason why it is necessary to contrast learning with instinct since when I live within the flow of time and act presumptively upon the world, it is as if I act instinctively.

Disjuncture, then, whether it is created by the rapid changes in society or because I have new desires, aims or hopes and aspirations for my life, is always a motivating factor.[2] It is a driving force making me act, think, plan and so on. There is something fundamental to the human condition that indicates that we all endeavour to live in harmony with our social and cultural environment, and this may well reflect and be an extension of our pre-conscious learning from our earliest experiences within the womb and the way that we were nurtured in our earliest childhood when we were totally dependent upon the Other within our life-world.

Interest and perception

Our experiences in the world can be other-induced, or self-induced, but the manner in which we respond to them might depend to a considerable extent upon our interests. Hence, we noted in the first chapter that there are experiences that I called non-learning, in some sense: they were non-consideration and rejection. One of the reasons for these is certainly lack of interest: interests, therefore, form a major factor in our quest to understand human learning better. Schutz (Wagner 1970: 112–13) conceptualised our interaction with the world in terms of zones of relevance. For him there are four concentric circles of interest:

- that within our reach that can be observed and partially dominated;
- fields that cannot be dominated but connected to our primary zone;
- fields that are not currently connected with our primary zone of interest; and
- those having no relevance at all to us.

We are, consequently, going to focus on those things of relevance and interest to the exclusion of those that do not impinge upon us specifically, so that we will see and recognise more precisely those things within our purview that are relevant to us. In the same way, we are less likely to perceive things in a certain way if that way is beyond our immediate concerns, although we are all aware that in psychological experiments we may perceive some shapes hidden in a picture differently from others, but I do not feel it necessary to pursue this further at this stage.

If we do focus on certain things in our life-world to the exclusion of others, then there is a sense that this leads us both into process of focused learning, or specialisation, and this enhances our own individuality. The more we learn, the more we become individuals and different from others, although this has usually been understood to be within the context of primary socialisation in which we learn a common language and culture, though learning always has the potential to individuate. At the same time as we appear to focus on the specific we are confronted with a paradox since it is through this same process that we also develop. This focusing is also learning and expanding (Engeström 1987). Inspired by Vygotsky's idea of a proximal zone of development, Engeström (1987: 144) has recognised that part of the process of individuation leads to expansion and development and that human learning is in some ways 'a contradictory unity'. In a subsequent study Engeström (1990) focused on development in terms of imagination and creativity.

Indeed, we can see that specialist interest is focused and it is upon this that we focus, but at the moment when we capture it, it expands. Once more we can see the paradox of learning played out within the framework of time, as Figure 4.1 shows.

However, this paradoxical process is confronted with another problem: how does interest arise in the first instance? Vygotsky (1978: 33) linked this to the development of language in children, through which we are linked to the socio-cultural group within which we live:

> A very special feature of human perception – which arises at a very young age – is the *perception of real objects*. This is something for which there is no analogy in animal perception. By this term I do not mean that

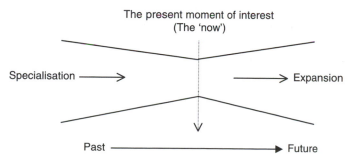

Figure 4.1 A paradox of interest and time.

I do not see the world simply in color and shape but also as a world of
sense and meaning.

(italics in original)

For him, all human perception is categorised rather than isolated perception;
in other words, from an early age we focus upon phenomena in our world
and concentrate upon them since they are relevant to us. Significantly,
because we are born into a socio-cultural world we are going to learn the
language and perceive phenomena in a similar, but not the same, way as
others within our world. We are, likewise, going to be influenced by significant others and those who exercise hegemonic influence over our culture.
Human learning, therefore, must always be influenced by our interests and
by those of our significant others, but while there is some reproduction
within the process, there is always change and development within the continuity of the culture. But events and phenomena have no intrinsic meaning
and so it is necessary now to turn our attention in this direction.

Interpretation and meaning

Fromm (1949: 44–5) highlights clearly this human problem of neither events
nor phenomena having intrinsic meaning:

> Man can react to historical contradictions by annulling them through
> his own action; but he cannot annul existential dichotomies, although
> he can react to them in different ways. He can appease his mind by
> soothing and harmonizing ideologies. He can try to escape from his
> inner restlessness by ceaseless activity in pleasure or in business. He can
> try to abrogate his freedom and to turn himself into an instrument of
> powers outside of himself, submerging himself in them. But he remains
> dissatisfied, anxious and restless. There is only one solution to his prob-
> lem: to face the truth, to acknowledge his fundamental aloneness and
> solitude in a universe indifferent to his fate, to recognize that there is no
> power transcending him which can solve his problem for him. Man must
> accept responsibility for himself and the fact that only by using his own
> powers can he give meaning to life. But meaning does not imply cer-
> tainty. Uncertainty is the very condition to impel man to unfold his
> powers. If he faces the truth without panic he will recognize that *there is
> no meaning to life except the meaning that man gives his life by the unfolding
> of his powers, by living productively*: that only by vigilance, activity and
> effort can keep us from failing in the one task that matters – the full
> development of our powers within the limitations set by the laws of our
> existence. Man will never cease to be perplexed, to wonder, and to raise
> new questions.

(italics in original)

Naturally, built into Fromm's own analysis lies his own understanding of the meaning of existence and one does not have to accept it, but the point of fundamental importance is that all meaning must stem from our own response to the questions of our being since there is no intrinsic meaning in creation or existence. As Husserl claimed, 'I live in my acts' and so meaning must lie in my action or in its intentionality, i.e. I mean to do something, or I meant to do it and so on. In this sense, meanings lie both in reflection on past experiences and reflection (planning) of future actions and experiences. That is, I must find my meaning in my being. As Fromm rightly points out, there is no meaning in life, or at least no apparently intrinsic meaning, and so this leaves us with ultimate questions: in this sense being itself is disjunctural. Being means that we have to live in a state of uncertainty, life is a living question, and now we are confronted with the same issues that we were when we discussed time – an internal and an external history: the former is about the meaning of being in which we just come to terms with time, and the latter is about the meaning of ends which is about the reasons why we seek to master time and achieve specific ends in our actions.

But within the framework of experience per se, meaning is always a matter of looking back:

> Because the concept of meaningful experience always presupposes that the experience of which the meaning is predicated is a discrete one, it now becomes quite clear that only a past experience can be called meaningful, that is, one that is present to the retrospective glance as already finished and done with.
>
> (Schutz 1967: 52)

But in order to give that past experience meaning or in order to provide a rationale for a future action, we need to be able to step outside of the frame of duration and reflect and become aware of the passing of time. Reflection, however, may actually distort the original meaning (motivation) underlying the action, as we rationalise our own biography. But our intentionality (the meaning underlying a future action, i.e. motivation) may be just as specific as was the original motivation behind a previous act/experience. But we see that meaning, in the sense of motivation, is being used here differently from meaning in the sense of being, or living in duration. The latter may be more metaphysical/religious (we ask questions about 'why?') and so on, while the former may be more technical and specific (what I wanted to achieve was), but both will reflect the culture of our life-world. It is the latter, however, that dominates in contemporary global society. Meaning, then, can be social in the sense that it is cultural, but it can also be individual. Often the two will be similar but there are occasions when an individual subjective meaning system might be seen to be profoundly different from that of the group and this might serve to marginalise the individual whose learning from experiences will differ from that of others in the group.

The meaning that we give experiences may be fairly constant over time since in some ways they reflect our philosophy of life, although we do undergo considerable changes from time to time, such as in religious conversion which is a profound change in meaning schemes. Nevertheless, it is this concept which Mezirow (1991) sees meaning at the heart of his understanding of transformative learning. He (1991: 5–6) defines meaning schemes as being:

> made up of specific knowledge, beliefs, value judgments, and feelings that constitute interpretations of experience, become more differentiated and integrated or transformed by reflection on the content or process of problem solving in progressively wider contexts.

Basically, Mezirow sees meaning schemes as personal belief systems, or ideologies, whereas he uses the term 'meaning perspectives' to refer to 'the structures of assumptions within which one's past *experience assimilates and transforms new experiences*' (1991: 42). For him, 'Meaning schemes are the concrete manifestations of our habitual orientation and expectations [meaning perspectives] and translate these general expectations into specific ones that guide our actions' (1991: 44). In a sense, we can see that meaning schemes, used in the way that Mezirow does, relate to our sense of self-identity, for they contain aspects that are peculiar to our self. For Mezirow (1991: 11), making meaning is central to what learning is all about, but while we can agree with a great deal of his understanding of meaning, and even meaning making, we can see that within the context of study of human learning he has focused upon the cognitive to too great an extent and limited his analysis of the learning process: this is something to which we will return in the second section of this book.

But not all experiences might be meaningful. For instance, as I write these words I have a very stiff shoulder that is affecting the way that I am using the keyboard and the pain is a phenomenological experience, in the way that Chalmers used the term 'phenomenological consciousness' (see Chapter 2), but in itself the pain is not meaningful. However, if I reflect upon the stiff shoulder then I can perhaps explain it, and in this sense I give it meaning. The explanation that I give it may be medical, or historical, in the sense that I try to explain why it has occurred, or I might merely try to laugh it off as an everyday occurrence and nothing to worry about. In this sense the meaning of experiences 'is nothing more . . . than that frame of interpretation which sees them as behavior' (Schutz 1967: 57). I now have a cognitive experience, which relates to Chalmers' psychological consciousness.

The experience of pain may be an experience that I have which in itself requires no explanation or meaning, although I can endow it with one or more meanings. The meanings that I give it might depend on the context within which I am, or my mood and so on. It might also depend upon my own approach to my daily living. Different people suffering pain might approach the whole experience differently. Marton and Säljö certainly found that different students approached their reading differently since some 'students *focused on the text itself* [while others focused] *in what the text was about . . .*' (1984: 39–40; italics in original). The former were less likely to understand the author's intention in writing the text but only understood the words, and this has been called a surface approach, whilst those who sought the author's meaning had a deep approach. Hence, we see emerging here another learning style and in other work they found a relationship between the approach to learning and the understanding that the learner had of learning per se. Those who considered learning to be either a quantitative increase in knowledge or memorisation adopted the shallow approach, while those who related it to understanding the meaning or understanding reality adopted a deep approach (Marton and Säljö 1984: 53). Consequently, we can see that the readers' style was related to a wider meaning system and if they change their understanding of the purpose of learning, then they might change their approach to learning. In this sense, learning style might not relate only to personal attributes such as personality, but to their own meaning scheme.

However, there may be other experiences we have to which we just cannot give a meaning – we may just have to be agnostic about them even though we try to provide an explanation. In a sense we may be content to live in this types of disjunctural situation because we know that in this complex world there are others, experts, who can explain them. Ignorance of this nature may be an inevitable outcome of complexity – there are situations in which we have experiences from which we just cannot learn, apart from the phenomenological consciousness we have of these experiences. This may be because the gap between our biography and our perception of the experience is just too big for us to grasp. In that sense, we are confronted with non-learning situations.

I am, consequently, confronted with something of the complexity of the concept of meaning and we have already discussed a number:

* the meaning of being;
* the meaning attributed to the ends of an action;
* the meaning of given to events and phenomena;
* phenomenological meaningless experiences; and
* cognitive meaningless experiences.

However, in employing different approaches to explaining the pain in my shoulder leads to another major question – do the different explanations provide me with different experiences of the pain, and do different explanations given to different people provide them with different experiences?

Varieties of experience

Since we experience the world through our senses, we naturally have experiences that are predominantly in the domain of one or other of the senses. However, it would be false to say that in the ordinary course of events experiences occur in one domain only. For instance, when we hear something, we sometimes respond emotionally, when we smell something there might well be a cognitive response as well and so on. However, experiences through our senses are predominantly primary ones; they are, as it were, us 'touching' the world directly. But in themselves they are meaningless. Primary experiences are more that just the sensations, however, since through reflection and interaction with others we give them meaning, so that we know that a certain odour comes from a flower in the garden or the factory in the town, etc. Living in the life-world, our daily lives consist of primary experiences to which we respond in a wide variety of ways.

Living, and therefore doing, is a primary experience. I live through my acts. Consequently, in the course of daily doing (and living) we acquire many skills and the exercise of skill is always a primary experience. It is not surprising, therefore, that in preparing people for occupations practical placements have become an increasing necessity as we re-discover the need for apprenticeship and mentoring since the apprentice-master cannot learn the skills for the apprentice. Learning the skills must be done through the act of doing and, therefore, experiencing. But doing something is not just an act, it has a cognitive dimension as well and the inter-relationship between knowledge and skill emerges. We acquire practical knowledge, and we will return to this below.

Since our lives are lived a great deal of time in the same vicinity, many of our primary experiences are common and similar to each other, so that we tend to take them for granted. These are our norms and expectations and, as such, we tend to presume upon them and take them for granted, to the extent that the level of our awareness of our immediate world is often very low. These are either non-learning or pre-conscious learning situations. But the unexpected often occurs. We can be stopped in our tracks by something we consider beautiful, such as a lovely flower display in a local park, and have an aesthetic experience. In a similar way a beautiful sunrise over a waterfall can give rise to a sense of wonder and awe that might be called by some a religious experience. Interestingly, this experience occurs within time and the person who has this experience might want to return to the same place in the hope of having a similar experience again – and so the place becomes a 'holy place'. We can see, immediately, that reflection upon the sensation begins to enable us to categorise experiences according to our response, or the meaning that we give it. For instance, the beautiful sunrise might be awe-inspiring to two people, but the meaning that they give it differs – one categorises it as religious and the other as aesthetic and so on. At least two things emerge from this immediately: that these categories are to a very great extent determined by the culture in which we live and, second, it is each person who is having the experience and each person's biography is unique, to their interpretation of their experience must be their own. While the two may differ in response to the experience, neither can say legitimately that the other is wrong because there is no absolute table of classifications, nor is the experience empirical. Consequently, they can only beg to differ! But this is also where power and hegemony enter in because one of the pair may be in a position to enforce upon or influence others about one perspective of the situation to the exclusion of the other. We are now confronted with a fundamental point about experience, for while these two persons are categorising their experiences differently, they are not having the same experience and the one cannot have the primary experience of the other. We cannot have another person's experiences. Experience is always subjective and, therefore, so must be our learning.

Throughout our discussion so far we have insisted that it is only through interaction and sharing that we can develop our own selves. In precisely the same way, culture is shared. It is through interaction that we experience other people, and this is a primary experience. But it is not just the person whom we experience; in the interaction we share our narratives and even listen to each other's discourses. The content of the narrative or discourse is also experienced, and this is a secondary experience. Most of what we learn about the world comes from secondary experience and much of what we are taught in college or university, often called theory, is also secondary experience – it is the interpreted experiences of others that is transmitted to us, about which we always need to be critical. The process of providing secondary experiences is what Knowles called 'pedagogy' and, for many educators, this has become to be seen as insufficient and so they provide primary experiences, through role play, simulation and so on, in order that the learners experience cognitively, physically and emotionally. The relationship between theory and practice may also be seen as a relationship between primary and secondary experience. It is this provision of primary experiences that has come to be known as 'experiential' teaching and learning. Experiential learning, in this limited sense, is also existential, but all existential learning would not be considered experiential.

We would argue that this distinction between primary and secondary experience is crucial in differentiating learning per se from what has been called experiential learning or experiential education. All learning is from experience, but experiential learning is more concerned with the primary experience.

Conclusion

It is through the memories of our experiences that we acquire our sense of self-identity and so it is not surprising that within adult education and life-long learning research has developed using life-history methods. But our quest to begin to understand learning has not yet been completed, for having had the experience we need to transform it, and this is the subject of the next chapter.

Chapter 5

The transformation of experience

'Transformation' is a term frequently associated with education and learning (Cranton 1994; Mezirow 1991; O'Sullivan 1999), but rarely is it used in association with experience. To transform something is to alter either its form or its function and in a sense this is precisely what learning is – transformation through two processes, altering first the sensations of the external world into an experience and then changing the experience into an element of our biography, which could be knowledge, skills, attitudes, values, beliefs, emotions or the senses – or any combination of them.

We have already argued that sensations are transformed into conscious experience through the natural processes in the body and that this process contains a considerable mystery in respect to the phenomenological, whereas the transformation in respect to the psychological can be explained through understanding the way that we learn to associate different sensations as a result of our early learning. Learning is, as we have seen, at the heart of human living. Every time we learn – the transformative outcome from our experience – we add another story to our expanding biography. Whilst we still remain the same self, the self is also changing and developing. We are both being and becoming simultaneously and this continues throughout our lifetime. The being is the sense of human identity – I am Me. Paradoxically, I am the same and I am different at the same time. But this is also true of our bodies – they are also transformed through the ravages of time. Neither should they be regarded as something entirely separate from our learning since our brain, as a physical and neurological mechanism, is part of our body and it is affected by both our physical condition and our mental functioning, which, in its turn, can also affect our physical functioning. In addition, we learn to associate our self-identity with the changing body. In this sense, the whole person is continually undergoing transformation – in both body and mind – and yet in another sense the self remains the same.

However, as children grow and develop, their attitudes towards other people change and so, therefore, does the nature of the I↔Thou relationship. This change is itself a form of learning from experience and relates to a number of other developmental learning that we all undergo. This process is pre-conscious and unintended and it does not happen in isolation. For instance, Selman (1980) showed (see Table 5.1) that as children mature they move through three stages of perspective taking in relationships (see Habermas 1990)

We see here that attitudes towards the other change both in terms of moving from a self-centred perspective to one in which we learn to stand outside of ourselves, but also our understanding and experience of relationship changes from a subjective and self-centred one to a mutual one. We do not move automatically through these stages, neither is there evidence to suggest that in adulthood persons are able to step outside of themselves and 'see themselves as both actors and objects, simultaneously acting and reflecting upon the effects of an action on themselves, reflecting upon the self in interaction with the self' (Habermas 1990: 143). Nevertheless, as we mature, the way that we construct experiences will necessarily be changed and so, therefore, will our learning.

Our concern in this chapter is to explore these processes further, through which experience is transformed and which underpin the learning process itself. In Figure 1.6, however, we argued that there are three processes, either individually or more likely together, that contribute to this: the cognitive, the emotive and the practical. However, for the purposes of this discussion, the cognitive occupies more of our attention than the other two, so that the chapter will be divided into two parts, the first dealing with the cognitive.

The cognitive dimension

There are at least two major aspects to this dimension: knowing and thinking. I want to deal with each separately in two separate sections, but we before we do so it is important to recognise that initially we have to learn in order to develop our thinking, and it was Piaget (1929) who pioneered research into this. He suggested that children go through a five-stage cognitive developmental process and the level of development will affect children's understanding of their own experience. He suggested that this process is

Table 5.1 Selman's stages of perspective taking

Stage 1: Differentiated and subjective perspective taking (about ages 5–9)
        Concepts of person – differentiated
        Concept of relations – subjective

Stage 2: Self-reflective/second person and reciprocal perspective taking (about ages 7–12)
        Concepts of person – self-reflective/second person
        Concepts of relations – reciprocal

Stage 3: Third person and mutual perspective taking (about ages 10–15)
        Concepts of person – third person
        Concepts of relations – mutual

related to biological age, although his sample was much too small for him to demonstrate this clearly. What we do know, however, is that children develop cognitively and his findings may be summarised as in Table 5.2.[1]

Apart from the size of the sample, Piaget's work, while widely accepted and quite ground-breaking, had a number of other weaknesses. Obviously we do not pass from one stage to another and leave the former behind, but our own level of thinking varies from situation to situation. But our conceptual development cannot be reduced to biological development, and neither is there evidence to suggest that the two are interlinked. In addition, we do not know the relationship between conceptual development and culture or ethnicity. Indeed, the experiences that children have within their life-world rather than their biological age may be a major factor in conceptual development. Finally, our conceptual development does not stop when we reach the abstract level and Riegel (1973) highlighted the fact that adults think in what he called 'dialectical operations' terms, which is the ability to tolerate problems and contradictions (Allman 1984: 76).

It is through our experiences that we learn and continue to learn and develop the art of thinking, which, in its turn, affects both our knowing and the ways in which we go about thinking. We are now in a position to examine knowing.

Knowing

I have used the word 'knowing' here rather than knowledge, since knowledge gives a sense of something static, an object, something that we have. Additionally, subjectively, we might not distinguish between knowledge and belief – they are both known to us, so that the distinction made below is much more an objective one than subjective. Indeed, we might claim that 'we believe our knowledge is true', but we might also claim that 'we know that our beliefs are true', and they might actually refer to the same item of know-

Table 5.2 Piaget's stages of cognitive development

Stage 1	Sensori-motor	0–2 years	Infant learns to differentiate between self and objects in the external world
Stage 2	Pre-operational thought	2–4 years	Child is ego-centric but classifies objects by single salient features
Stage 3	Intuitive	4–7 years	Child thinks in classificatory way but may be unaware of classifications
Stage 4	Concrete operations	7–11 years	Child able to use logical operations such as reversibility, classification and serialisation
Stage 5	Formal operations	11–15 years	Trial steps toward abstract conceptualisation occurs

ing. The point of the distinction between knowledge and belief is a matter of justification or legitimation in relation to truth, as we shall see below. At the same time, in the learning diagrams I have used the term 'knowledge', but I have also included 'belief' in order to convey both aspects. Knowing is about being and becoming, but it is also about having knowledge and holding beliefs[2] – knowing reflects the dynamic nature of being, which is that we live in time – in duration. It is about change – transformation itself. Knowledge is an outcome of learning and I have used it here in relation to other ways of knowing, such as having beliefs, values and attitudes. I want now to examine each of these in turn.

Knowledge

Knowledge has been defined by some as something objective and outside of us as well as something internal and personal – part of us (Popper 1979: 73). But this is a confusion between information and data on the one hand, and learned knowledge on the other. Interestingly, the Chinese word for knowledge has two characters – one is *xue*, to learn, and the other is *wen*, to ask (Cheng 2000: 441) – and as Kennedy, citing Cheng, says, the 'action of enquiring and questioning is central to the quest for knowledge' (2000: 433). Knowledge is 'a belief' that something learned that can be shown to be true/valid by legitimate arguments. But Popper suggests that objective knowledge is published in books, stored in libraries and so on. However, we want to argue here that knowledge per se must be something known, so that it must be personal and subjective. Consequently, the content of the books is the authors' knowledge but not the readers'; it is data and information to readers. Until such time as data and information are learned by individuals, they remain data and information: learning transforms information into knowledge and belief. In this discussion I want to use the concept of 'knowledge' to refer to beliefs that can be justified as truth and 'belief' to refer to those thoughts that we store in the minds that cannot be justified as truth. In both, however, we can say that thinking is the major process by which they are gained, which we shall examine in greater detail below. Data and information are always external to the person but knowledge and belief are internal. Naturally we can then debate the nature of knowledge and we can say that there are at least three different types: it can refer to knowing information – 'knowing that', to 'knowing how' and 'knowing people'.

The extent to which all of our knowledge is consciously in our minds is questionable. Freud has certainly highlighted the significance of the unconscious and Polanyi (1968) has pointed us to the tacit dimension. This appears in two forms: first, it occurs when we take for granted the situation within which we are and then act in a taken-for-granted manner. Additionally, it can be detected in the manner by which we perform our actions, as we will discuss below, when we look at theories of action (Argyris *et al.* 1985). However, we also learn pre-consciously, as we discussed in the opening chapter, and the knowledge that we gain is only tacit knowledge until such time as we call it into our conscious mind and reflect upon it. However, it might rightly be asked whether tacit knowledge is actually knowledge or only potential knowledge. If knowledge is something personal and conscious, then it is potential knowledge at best.

Indeed, what makes knowledge knowledge? I can justify and legitimate my own knowledge in at least three different ways:

- by the power of my logic I can argue from basic premises to conclusions and that for so long as the premises are accepted and the logic is sound, I can regard my conclusions as true;
- through my experiences and sensations, I know that certain phenomena exist and these I can demonstrate empirically. Any meaning that I place upon the empirical fact, however, does not have the validity of knowledge since the fact cannot contain its own meaning; and
- through my experiences of living, my knowledge of the world 'works' for me – every time I use my knowledge and it works, it is true because it works, then it is pragmatic knowledge.

Each of these three are legitimate bases for knowledge, but we can see immediately that even these justifications of knowledge contain within themselves a degree of temporality since: my premise may later be found to be false; my logic may not be as powerful as I assumed; my actions do not always allow me to presume upon the changing world; or the empirical phenomena that I know are only known for as long as I exist in time. Knowledge, then, is not eternal or unchanging and may only contain a 'truth' within these given parameters.

However, there is at least one other significant way of thinking about knowledge. Most knowledge is learned directly as a result of an experience and that is a posteriori, so that, for instance, I know that the floppy disc lying on the desk beside my computer is rectangular in shape. Seeing the disc, i.e. experiencing it, enables me to know that the floppy disc is rectangular in shape. But I cannot know by the same experience that all floppy discs are rectangular in shape – I cannot experience them all. But I know that if they are all to fit my computer they all need to be the same shape, so that by reason I can conclude that all floppy disks that will fit my computer have to be rectangular in shape. This is a priori knowledge – it is learned by reason. The fact that I had to use my reason and that my conclusions are drawn, even though I cannot experience all of the discs, shows that this form of knowledge is based on logical thought rather than directly on experience. Nevertheless, it could be argued that ultimately the basis of this form of a priori knowledge is experience about which I have used my reason and drawn conclusions – that is learned.

Once we have knowledge about the everyday things of life, there are two further ways of moving beyond it. The first we have suggested is that we presume upon the situation, act upon it, take it for granted, and live within the flow of time and not learn from it. Presumption is the almost instinctive behaviour that we all have when we can assume that the world has not altered and we can act upon it in precisely the same way this time as we did the last when we were in a similar situation. The second way, however, is that even though we believe that we know the 'truth' of the situation we still need to treat the 'truth' as questionable and recognise that more questions lie beyond the 'truth' to which we need to continue to seek answers. Perhaps approaching life this way demands a certain degree of humility since it always assumes that we do not 'know it all'. Socrates, at times, describes wisdom as 'not knowing'. Wisdom has at its heart the sense of humility about daily living (Stikkers 1980: 11). Scheler (1980: 91) writes:

> in all Asian cultures it was *the 'sage'* and *a metaphysical* mind that won over religion as well as science. This, it appears to me, is the *most significant difference between Western and Eastern cultures*. In the East metaphysics is *self*-cognition and *self*-redemption, . . . For this reason also we find in the beliefs of the peoples of China, India, and even Japan, the predominance of the *ideal of the sage* in contrast to the Western *ideals of heroes and saints*.
>
> (italics in original)

The persons who continue to seek knowledge gradually grow in wisdom, but this might not always be recognised by the sages themselves. Even so, it will be recalled that in our discussion about time we differentiated between internal and external history. In the latter, we seek to master time and achieve given ends effectively and efficiently, but in the former we seek to come to grips with time and live in the present. As human beings we live in the present, seeking always to understand the present, and learning is a way of living and one of the outcomes is to know profoundly – being wise. Nevertheless, one person's wisdom remains information to those who read wisdom literature or who listen to the words of the sage, and only if it is learned does it becomes the learners' knowledge, but not yet the wisdom. There are no short cuts to wisdom and neither can it be taught – it can only be learned through life. But 'the wisdom of the fathers' is something that Western culture has either neglected or rejected, with the rapid speed of social change and relevant knowledge – what Scheler (1980: 76) would see as the artificiality of scientific and technological knowledge that changes so rapidly that it never has time to become embedded within culture before it becomes outdated.

Beliefs

Close to pragmatic knowledge lies belief, which is much wider than just religious belief since it includes ideology, personal ideas and systems of meaning. Frequently, we learn ideologies and beliefs in precisely the same way as we learn knowledge, since both ideologies and beliefs are derived from information systems. Geertz (1964: 62) defines what he calls 'symbol systems' as:

> extrinsic sources of information in terms of which human life can be patterned – extrapersonal mechanisms for the perception, understanding, judgement and manipulation of the world. Culture patterns – religious, philosophic, aesthetic, scientific, ideological – are 'programs'; they provide a template or blueprint for the organization of social and psychological processes.

Belief systems are cultural information that we might learn since they seek to explain the human condition. As we have already pointed out this is disjunctive, so that we might find that a particular belief system answers some of our existential questions. But we are constantly confronted with questions – about existence, about power and social processes – to which we can find no answers. In the same way, as we pointed out earlier, the 'holy place' or the religious experience also demand answers to the questions that they implicitly pose. Then cultural ideological and belief systems may be seen as answers to human questions about existence.[3] However, once the system has been constructed, if it is successful in as much as the people adopt it, then it becomes embedded in the culture of the social group. It is these systems that Scheler (1980) classifies as the less artificial types of knowledge because they are slow to change since, unlike science and technology, belief systems are responses to unchanging existential questions. However, I feel that Scheler has confused knowledge and belief in his classification, although its emphasis on change and relativity so early in the twentieth century is quite significant.

Like rational knowledge, many of these belief systems are logically argued from certain premises – often unproven – and present themselves as very reasoned statements. It is not surprising, therefore, that they are confused with rational knowledge, since it is certainly very possible to have rational beliefs. Moreover, like pragmatic knowledge, they often appear very practical for the believer since they appear to 'work' in the believer's life. In this sense the belief system is legitimated for the believer by the believer.

Within the Christian tradition, Fowler (1981) has endeavoured to demonstrate the way in which faith develops and he outlines a six-stage model (Table 5.3) through which we can move given the level of our experience and ability to learn from it.

Table 5.3 Fowler's stages of faith development

Stage 1	Intuitive–Projective	Ego-centric, becoming aware of temporality, productive of image formation that will affect later life
Stage 2	Mythical–Literal	Awareness of the stories and beliefs of the local community which begins to provide coherence to experience
Stage 3	Synthetic–Conventional	Faith extends beyond family, provides a basis for identity and values
Stage 4	Individuative–Reflective	Self-identity and world outlook are differentiated, develops explicit system of meaning
Stage 5	Conjunctive	Faces the paradoxes of experience, begins to develop universals and becomes other-orientated.
Stage 6	Universalising	Totally altruistic and the felt sense of the environment is inclusive of all being

Fowler admits that the final stage is rarely achieved, but since he only researched these stages of faith within a Christian context, it has to be recognised that his picture of belief development is considerably limited. Nevertheless, the saint, or guru, can emerge in precisely the same way as we discussed above for the sage. But the fact that by learning from experience faith develops until it reaches a plateau is indicative of certain elements of this process. The reason why individuals reach a plateau may refer to the unwillingness to think and learn about beliefs beyond a certain stage, or that they find the beliefs they hold satisfying, or that this also reflects other limitations in the person's growth process. Clearly, more research needs to be undertaken both on the international and the multi-faith aspects as well as on ideological and other non-religious belief perspectives.

One of the most prevalent manifestations of belief in contemporary society is fundamentalism – both religious (Christian and Islamic) and political (see Jarvis and Parker 2005). These approaches to belief not only give the believer a sense of knowing the 'truth' but also, therefore, a sense of security. They are emotively extremely powerful. Consequently, there is a tendency to reject learning opportunities that would threaten such a personal or social belief system. This is what Botkin *et al.* (1979) refer to as 'maintenance', as opposed to innovative, learning, and in these cases it is initially the rejection of one form of learning opportunity for another which is merely one of reproducing and reinforcing. By so doing, individuals retain their sense of self-identity and their membership of their social group or network and build 'walls' around these groups which make them harder to penetrate and interact with.[4]

We learn these systems cognitively and they become part of our biography in precisely the same way as knowledge and because of their proximity to knowledge they become confused with it. But we are often far more committed to beliefs than we are to knowledge. Nevertheless, information does get transformed into knowledge and belief in the learning process and what I am calling belief here might well be no different from knowledge in the mind of the believer, although there is a greater sense of commitment. Nevertheless, there are major differences from the perspective of academic analysis.

Values

In the same way as we learn beliefs – both through being taught and through learning from experience – so we learn values since they are also embedded in culture.[5] As we have already pointed out, children go through the process of conceptual development, similar to the one described by Piaget. Kohlberg (1986) examined the process through which children develop in their acquisition of values. He did not find that children moved from one stage to the other based upon age, nor were the stages discrete. Nevertheless, he also had a six-stage model (Table 5.4) but his was based on three levels.

Kohlberg argued that as we mature and gain experience, so we move through these stages – from selfishness, to social concern and duty, to rules and finally to live by principles. These principles are integrated into our biography and we seek to conform to them in our everyday behaviour. However, sometimes these values which are integrated into our biographies do not guide us into behavioural patterns that conform to the expectations of society and once again we suffer disjuncture. There are at least three different responses to this disjunctural experience:

Table 5.4 Kohlberg's stages of moral development

Level 1 – Pre-conventional	
Stage 1: Heteronomous morality	Stick to the rules
Stage 2: Individualism/instrumentalism	Involved with own interests, aware of other people's interests
Level 2 – Conventional	
Stage 3: Mutual interpersonal	Lives up to others' expectations in order to be seen to be good and can have self-image as good
Stage 4: Social system and conscience	Fulfils social duties in order to keep the social system going
Level 3 – Post-conventional	
Stage 5: Social contract	Upholds relative rules in the interest of impartiality, welfare for all
Stage 6: Universal ethical principles	Follows self-chosen ethical principles even when they conflict with laws

- We can conform to what we perceive to be society's expectations, or the expectations of those whom we perceive to have power over us, even though they are contrary to our own predispositions, and then we might suffer a sense of conscience since we have acted contrary to the way in which we feel that we should behave. This might result in a greater resolve to be more consistent the next time, but we can see that moral behaviour often demands confidence or courage – in the words of one of Tillich's (1962) books, it takes 'Courage to Be'.
- We can conform to our conscience – 'Be true to thyself' – and refuse to reject the experience and the opportunity to learn something new.
- We can treat this experience as a new opportunity to learn and act differently and to develop our value system.

Once more we see how different dimensions of our being are integrated, with moral behaviour demanding courage and confidence, and so we are confronted with the idea of virtue. In addition, we can see that since people feel that they could have acted differently in such situations the argument for free will begins to emerge. When we seek 'to be true to ourselves', we choose to reject the opportunity to learn or to accept the chance to learn something new, and this is a similar position to the one we highlighted earlier when we discussed religious and political fundamentalism.

Kohlberg recognised that this is a learning process – one that stems from experience as much as does conceptual development, although as we have already seen, Piaget also regarded cognitive development as a learning process. Each of the processes that we have thus far made reference to in this chapter both affects and is affected by our attitudes.

Attitudes

Attitudes are defined as 'an individual's tendency to evaluate and respond to social objects in a consistently favourable or unfavourable way' (Fisher 1982: 46). The process of evaluating external phenomena, events or even experiences is something that is normal and everyday and we undertake it often without a great deal of thought. By so doing, however, we are learning attitudes – it may be conscious and deliberate, but often our attitudes are formed, or learned, unintentionally. While they are similar in some ways to beliefs and values, we do not develop attitudinal hierarchies since attitudes are not bound by cognitive or conceptual development in quite the same manner.

The point about 'consistency' in the definition is important, however, since attitudes do reflect our characters and our predispositions towards the world; inconsistency – a tendency to be erratic – is not one prized by people who like to live patterned existences, despite Rogers (1969) claim that fully functioning persons are free to act however they wish. Indeed, it is the consistency of attitude that enables us to live within the flow of time in relatively unchanging external circumstances. When we cannot so live, then we experience dissonance, or disjuncture. The phenomenon of cognitive dissonance is well known, which is a situation when two cognitive elements are incongruent with each other and this produces discomfort (Festinger 1957). In such situations, individuals usually seek to resolve their dissonance through learning and re-establish congruency. But this is a major point in our understanding of learning; experiencing disjuncture is the point at which we move from the flow of time and become aware of the external world, from which we can learn. It is only when we re-establish harmony with that external world that we can presume upon it and take it for granted again. Our learning is motivated by the dissonance we experience, and there is considerable similarity between disjuncture and dissonance. The internal or internal-external harmony is conducive to our daily living, but paradoxically it is not so conducive to our learning and developing.

In this sense, once attitudes are formed they contain a behavioural tendency, although attitudes are generally regarded as being cognitive, affective and behavioural. Nevertheless, I want to treat them here within the cognitive domain, in the sense of the preceding paragraph, although we will return to the subject of attitudes when we examine both the affective and the behavioural. Like knowledge, beliefs and values, as our attitudes are learned and formed they are integrated into our biographies and memorised, which is part of the process of learning.

Knowledge, beliefs, values and attitudes do not occur discretely, but they are all integrated since we rarely learn knowledge without having beliefs about it, our value system usually demands emotional commitment and so on. In this sense, each of these four sub-sections are inter-related and integrated. They all function together simultaneously, but to different degrees, in the complex processes of our learning. They all contribute to our development or to human becoming. Having examined the knowing aspect of the cognitive dimension, we now turn our minds to one way by which we respond to our experiences: thinking.

Thinking

In this section we will explore the nature of thought. Thinking is rather an ill-defined process, although Gilhooly suggests that it is 'a set of processes whereby people assemble, use and revise internal symbolic models' (1996: 1). Underlying most of our ideas about thinking is the idea of rationality, although we will meet at least two types of thought below – creative and undirected thinking – where the rules of rationality do not always apply.

Rational thought takes two forms: one looks back and seeks to explain and is in some ways similar to the next one, whilst planning looks forward. Both, however, demand that our arguments are carefully and logically constructed often from a priori knowledge, although some theorists seek to characterise it in terms of irrationality (Moser *et al.* 1998: 123). Heidegger (1968) regards this logical thinking as thinking per se. It follows the rules of logic, starting from a premise and building an argument upon it. It has come to reflect modern society – with it, beliefs and superstitions were to be eradicated and all thought should follow the rules of logic. As we have already pointed out, it is one way through which knowledge itself can be legitimated. Despite its high reputation, however, we certainly do not all abide by the rules of logic, as my own research (Jarvis 1980) into superstition demonstrated. Freud's research is, of course, the most significant when we consider the prevalence, or otherwise, of logical thought. He has shown how our unconscious mind influences a great deal of our thought and behaviour. Indeed, we certainly need to understand the unconscious a great deal better in our endeavours to understand human thought and learning. Handy (1990) also pointed us to the fact that this is an 'age of unreason'.

Nevertheless, we are frequently confronted with the ideas of instrumental rationality – we have already discussed this with reference to external history when we try to master time in order to achieve our ends by the most efficient means. Indeed, this approach to rationality is quite common, although there is another mainstream school of thought, stemming from Aristotle and Kant, which claims that rationality should be thought orientated to the well-being of humankind. In this sense, it reflects certain basic moral beliefs based upon rational argument.

Fundamentally, we live in an age where rationality is prized although it is frequently something that is not practised, but as Moser *et al.* write: 'If theories of rationality are anything, they are about making epistemically responsible inferences in the light of available evidence' (1998: 127). Consequently, we can see that not only can we examine rational thought for its logical processes, but we can also evaluate it in terms of 'sound' judgment and so on.

In addition, thinking nearly always occurs in relation to experience. Experience occurs in time and we can respond to this either by looking backwards and reflecting upon the experience or looking forwards and planning to do things as a result of the experience. These two approaches to thinking are discussed here.

Reflection

Most early studies of experience recognised that we think (reflect) about an experience after it has happened; in other words, reflection is always post-the event – a looking backwards, even though that period of time might be only microseconds, but it might be days or hours. In everyday speech, reflection has a variety of meanings – thinking, meditating, looking back, repeating past events and so on. But in education it has assumed something of a special connotation in that it implies that we are questioning, in some way, the experience that we have had, whether that be receiving information, witnessing an event, seeking to solve a problem or experiencing some other phenomenon. While we can trace the ideas underlying reflection back to Aristotle, the immediate origins of the ideas of reflective learning are to be found in the work of Dewey (1933). It is interesting, however, that in a recent study on *Thinking*, such as Gilhooly (1996), the term 'reflection' does not even appear in the index!

There is a sense that reflection can cover most of the forms of thinking discussed in the coming section except the incubation in creative thinking and non-directed thinking. Indeed, reflection is generally used in contrast to non-direction – it is a very directed form of thought. Mezirow suggests that it is 'the process of critically assessing the content, process or premises of our efforts to interpret and give meaning to an experience' (1991: 104). He therefore suggests that there are three forms of reflection based on analysis of content, process and assumption. This definition relates totally to the above discussion on the forms of learning, although in limiting it in this way he does not really focus on the self of the learner, although he does acknowledge that others do so.

Boud *et al.* (1985: 11) also use this term widely within their own understanding of learning, but they also rightly relate it to emotions since, as we pointed out earlier, human beings are rarely 'cold fishes':

> the reflective process is a complex one in which feelings and cognition are closely interrelated and interactive. Negative feelings, particularly about oneself, can form major barriers towards learning. They can distort perceptions, lead to false interpretations of events, and can undermine the will to persist. Positive feelings and emotions can greatly enhance the learning process; they can keep the learner on the task and can provide a stimulus for new learning. The affective dimension has to be taken into account when we are engaged in our own learning activities.

As more types of learner-centred teaching activities are being introduced, such as practice-based and problem-based learning, the more the idea of reflection is becoming central to teaching and learning theory. There is a tendency, however, to look backwards in our thinking about learning and underplay the idea that there is always intentionality in experience and that since time does not stand still we are always looking toward the future – something that we do when we engage in planning.

Planning

Unlike reflection, forward thinking, or planning, does not occupy a great deal of the literature on learning and yet we all learn from thinking about the future. Like reflection, however, forward thinking can assume a number of different forms: creative, rational and un-directed. Two forms of forward thinking are most common: what we anticipate/plan to happen and what we would like/desire to happen. The former can itself be sub-divided – when we plan the future dealing with inanimate objects and when we plan/anticipate the future in social situations. In the first of these, we can utilise knowledge that we have based upon empirical evidence and scientific law and be fairly certain that, barring unforeseen eventualities, we can plan the future, design a building and so on. In this way we can learn new knowledge as a result of the creative use of already known scientific information. In contrast, when we plan social situations, we do not generate new knowledge but produce hypotheses, which are most frequently based on probability. In this case, we think about future actions based upon what people usually do and the expectation that they will do it in the same way in the future. It will be recalled that in the category of non-learning, in the opening chapter, we discussed presumption – the idea that we can presume that the world will be not change from one act to another similar one. Indeed, social living is founded on this paradoxical assumption that we will always act in a habitual fashion and repeat our past successful acts; in other words, we do not learn but live in the flow of time, but we know that because events are not always unchanging – 'the best laid plans of mice and men' sometimes go astray – and we do enter new situations and have new experiences from which we do learn.

In addition, we all have wants and desires about the future. Daydreaming, as we will discuss below, comes into this category, but the idea of 'desire' is something that has occupied the minds of thinkers since the earliest of times. This can produce imaginative or visionary thinking, as well as fantasy. Levitas (1990: 191), for instance, writing about utopian thinking:

> The essential element in utopia is not hope, but desire – the desire for a better way of being. It involves the imagining of a state of being in which the problems which actually confront us are removed or resolved, often, but not necessarily, through imagining a state of the world in which the scarcity gap is closed or the 'collective problem' solved.

Basically, she is saying that utopian thinking emerges from the fact that we all have bad experiences from time to time, some far worse than others, and that we imagine a situation when these just do not happen – a future beyond reality, or a vision for which we can work. All our thinking happens in time, we cannot catch the present before it is the past – we can look backwards and reflect or forwards and plan and hope, but we perhaps think in different ways.

As we can see, there are a variety of ways to try to understand this complex topic and having briefly examined something of the nature of thinking we are now in a position to develop this. We have selected two for the purpose of this discussion; the first relates to different conceptual approaches to thinking and looks at types of thinking, and the second relates thinking to the person and examines styles of thinking.

Types of thinking

I want to suggest that in addition to Socratic thinking – questioning – which arises in the disjunctural situation, there are at least five pairs of thought processes which we will now examine: memorising and interpreting; creative and critical thinking; problem solving and decision making; directed and undirected; deductive and inductive reasoning. All are important but they do not occur in a hierarchy and they perform different functions. Many of these different types actually have their opposite, such as non-critical, irrational and non-reflective, each of which will be discussed in its relevant section. There are, in addition, a wide variety of different terms that could be used for each of these sub-sections, such as logical for rational and so on, and they will be used interchangeably throughout this discussion.

Memorising and interpreting

Memorising has a number of different meanings. It refers to unreflective learning, which is the process of committing to the mind the information that the learners have been presented. It is also simply being prepared to believe what we are told or read. We all have a tendency just to accept what we are told, and it may well reflect our primary socialisation process. In that process, we learned to believe that most of the things that people told us were true and that the individuals with whom we interacted could be trusted. This is, naturally, a conservative approach.

In contrast, hermeneutic, or interpretative, ways of thinking focus on the meaning of the communication; it is an endeavour to understand another person and the meaning of whatever is being communicated without testing it for its legitimacy, whether it is spoken or written. According to Gadamer, 'hermeneutics is the art of clarifying and mediating by our own effort of interpretation what is said by persons we encounter in tradition' (1978: 98). It is the art of trying to understand the meaning that the 'other' is seeking to communicate. Indeed, Gadamer (1978: 98) reminds us that the word is related to the word 'Hermes', the interpreter of the divine message to mankind.

Hermeneutical thought occurs in every human interaction, when we seek to understand the meaning that the person to whom we are speaking intends and, consequently, it demands the ability to listen and, in many cases, to read without trying to impose our own meaning upon what is being communicated. Consequently, hermeneutical thought transcends the situation of the thinker and bridges the gap between the thinker and the other – it is the other's meaning that the thinker is seeking which may be a new understanding; this quest demands an empathy with the other and the other's life-world. While we cannot get into the mind of the other, hermeneutical thought demands that we get as close to that mind as possible.

Throughout this study we have pointed out that facts and events have no intrinsic meaning and that in many thought processes we impose meaning upon an apparently meaningless world. Hermeneutics, by contrast, seeks to understand an external meaning and not to impose another interpretation upon it. Even if we disagree with that meaning, we have to be faithful to it in hermeneutical thought, and in this sense there is a similarity between this and the way that learners in Confucian heritage countries are expected to begin their learning process. Interesting enough, these two types of thinking find their parallel in Marton's and Säljö's (1984) surface and deep ways of reading – the surface being the memorisation and the deep being the hermeneutic. But there are other forms of thought.

Creative and critical thinking

Creative thinking is a difficult form of thought to describe because we cannot just sit down and decide that we are going to be creative – it does not happen like that! Neither can we sit and plan it – that would be rational thought, which we will discuss below. Yet there might well be stages in the creative process, as we will see shortly. However, time might play a very significant role in creative thought since the 'Eureka' experience does not often come at the end of a protracted period of deep thought, but more often it comes after a period of freedom from thinking about the topic. This is probably the experience of most of us and, indeed, I know that often when I am writing, I will prepare myself thoroughly for the task, read, think and so on – but then nothing seems to come. I may have to leave it for a day or two and then I can return to it and then I find that I can write what I wanted to write. After that, I have to reflect upon what I have written and check it all quite carefully. These third and the fourth stages might not be very clearly demarcated in quite this way, but Wallis' (1926) stages are true to my own experience. He illustrated this need to be free of the initial task and free to think and do other things in his four-stage process of the creativity: preparation, incubation, illumination/inspiration and verification.

'Creative' means to be original or imaginative and this is hard to do to order. Yet we often try to produce novel solutions in education through brainstorming, and perhaps part of the secret of this approach is that we remove the external pressures to conform, or even to make us appear different. Being free to think may mean that we have to sit at the periphery of an organisation, for instance, thus giving individuals more opportunity to think their own thoughts – but because creative thinkers sit where they do, they might not be very influential in the organisation, although some managers are able to utilise the marginal people and their ideas very successfully. Consequently, it might be space as much as time which is a constituent factor in creative thinking.

Koestler's (1964) well-known *The Act of Creation* also introduced us to another approach to creativity since he discussed the idea of bringing together two ideas from diverse sources and showing that their synthesis often produces a novel outcome. For instance, he suggested that much humour arises in precisely this way – when a normal act of behaviour is performed in the wrong setting, it can either be funny or embarrassing and so on. Gilhooly also points us to a similar approach to Koestler's, which he calls 'synetics', which involves 'joining together . . . different and apparently irrelevant elements by the use of metaphors and analogies' (1994: 229). By so doing we see things differently.

Gilhooly (1996: 218) points out that many creative thinkers disclaim the ability to tell us how they think creatively or even solve problems – it just seems to come. This may be why Ryle suggests that imagination is not 'a species of thinking' since 'it has no place in those few highly mechanized branches of thinking in which our movements are treadmill-movements, as are the steps we take in computing' (1979: 63). However, Ryle appears a little inconsistent when he also claims imagination to be in the vanguard of thinking, and we prefer to treat it as a thought form. There are, then, a number of different processes for producing creative thinking, but they require freedom from structure and expectation and also time and space. Only then, it seems, are we likely to transform experience in a creative and novel manner and integrate them into our biographies.

In contrast to creative thought comes critical thinking. This must be seen as separate from critical theory, which emerged from the Frankfurt School in the earlier part of the twentieth century. It was from this School that the idea of emancipatory thought developed, and there is a certain sense in which critical thought requires us to be emancipated from the pre-suppositions of our own thinking,[6] and even the social powers that influence our thought. Probably critical thinking has been associated with critical theory because of the common use of the word 'critical'. Nevertheless, critical thought has a much greater affinity with the philosophical school of scepticism. Moser *et al.* (1998: 13–14) tell us that there are two major forms of scepticism: knowledge scepticism and justification scepticism. The former, taken to its logical extreme, would hold that nobody knows anything, whereas the latter asserts in the extreme that no one should believe anything. While we might not want to take either of these two positions to the extreme, it is clear that critical thought demands a sceptical perspective on knowledge and belief. But scepticism is not always a popular approach to knowledge and belief and it is sometimes difficult for critical thinkers to find an accepted place in organisations that expect, even demand, conformity. Consequently, the periphery of organisations may be a more comfortable place for some critical thinkers to position themselves, but other may feel obliged to sit outside its boundaries.

'Critical' might be wrongly said to be one of those thought forms which differentiates Western thought from that of Confucian heritage countries, at least in the learning sequence – as we discussed earlier. Nevertheless, critical does not mean seeking to demonstrate that ideas and propositions are false; more significantly, it refers to the idea of testing the proposition or theory and it could be claimed that all thought should do this. But it does not! Brookfield (1987: 13) suggested that:

> Being a critical thinker involves more than cognitive activities such as logical reasoning or scrutinizing arguments for assertions unsupported by empirical evidence. Thinking critically involves or recognizing the assumptions underlying our own beliefs and behaviors. It means that we can give justifications for our ideas and actions. More important, perhaps, it means that we try to judge the rationality of our assumptions.

Basically, it means that we should take nothing for granted in our thinking, but that everything should be tested for its legitimacy. Brookfield (1987) suggests that it entails identifying and challenging assumptions, and exploring and imaging alternatives. In this sense, it is both analytical and at the same time it has an action tendency. This is the form of thought that underlies double-loop learning (Argyris and Schön 1974). Critical thinking might, but need not, be radical in its formulation. However, for the purposes of this study, I am including radical thought within this category.

Problem solving and decision making

Problem solving is a disjunctural situation and there are no simple given procedures that facilitate problems being solved, although there may be a wide variety of different possible approaches to the problem. Gilhooley (1996) suggests that experts usually concentrate on thinking about the problem itself, while novices usually focus on its solution. By focusing on the problem, through analytical thought the expert seeks to outline as many options as possible that can be examined. This is the exact opposite to decision making, which is a process of closing down different possibilities and reaching specific conclusions. As Golhooley (1996: 191) points out, making the decision also involves a lot of other factors such as risk-taking, rationality and the ability to take many different factors into consideration. Few people have the ability or time to take all factors into consideration in reaching their decisions – in chess, for instance, each player is given only a specified period of time before the move must be made. Decision making, then, is not merely a thought process but combines the cognitive with the emotive and the practical.

Directed and undirected

In a sense we have already dealt with a variety of types of directed thought above, but undirected thought is a less frequently researched phenomenon. I have used the term 'undirected' to describe the types of thought that might be called 'musing' or even 'daydreaming', which is a common phenomenon (Gilhooly 1996) and completely opposite to instrumental thought. Even so, there are times when these undirected thoughts intrude into our thought processes despite our best efforts to rid ourselves of them. There is also a sense in which we can relate this to our previous discussion on internal and external history. The more important the external factors in our lives, the less likely we are to turn inwards and muse. It is when we have 'time on our hands' that we can engage in this activity. During it, we might focus on something that has recently occurred that we wish had happened differently or think about the desired outcomes of some future action or event. Gol-hooly (1996), citing Singer (1975, 1978), suggests that there are three functions to this activity: anticipation and planning; reminding us of 'unfinished business' that we are trying to suppress; and maintaining arousal in dull environments. Singer suggests that this type of thinking occurs because there is continuous activity in the mind, which is the source of daydreaming and which, incidentally, may be the source of creative thinking during the period of incubation. We will return to this discussion in the next section when we look at forward thinking, since anticipation and planning are much more directed forms of thought and may be seen to be based on rational thought processes.

Deductive and inductive reasoning

Deduction is the process of inferring a particular instance from a general law; conversely, induction is the process of inferring a general law from a particular instance, or also it is about the production of facts to demonstrate the validity of a general statement.

Deduction is the process that is carried out in decision making, when a number of facts, which are assumed to be true, have to be considered and a conclusion reached about them which must, therefore, be true – provided the thought processes have been logical. However, we have already high-lighted how dominant discourses occupy the educational vocabulary and so we have to be prepared to question the initial facts as well as the assumptions underlying the process of reasoning. Our sub-conscious thoughts and emotions, and even our conscious ones, might well affect the process and, con-sequently, the logical progression of an argument has always to be carefully constructed and checked.

Induction, however, is the converse to this and is, in a sense, generating hypotheses and, perhaps, theorising from them. Theorising is similar in some ways to rational thought, although it may include hunches and intuitions, but it is not necessarily irrational thought. In another sense it is similar to generalisation, a box that occurs in Kolb's (1984) learning cycle but which I did not discover actually occurred in the learning processes of most of my respondents and which I, therefore, omitted. Generalisation does not occur with every learning incident, but when things appear to repeat themselves, then we seek to theorise about them. Moser *et al.* suggest that 'human knowers are primarily *theorizers* rather than simple fact gatherers. One can find evidence for this in the earliest recorded human history. We theorize about each other, in order to try to understand what makes us tick, to explain why people behave the way that they do' (1998: 183; italics in original). They go on to say that we also theorise about our environment in order to try to control it. In a sense, then, this also reflects the idea that every person is a scientist (Kelly 1955) since it starts from a disjunctural experience, but it seeks to postulate answers to the question 'why?' in a more general sense. It contains a mixture of some of the previous forms of thinking and yet, in the end, it becomes a distinct form in itself.

Having examined these different forms of thinking, we will be aware that while we probably all practise them all at one time or another, some people have a preference for being creative or critical and so on. All the forms are equally important to social living, although education has gone through phases when it has emphasised one form as opposed to the others. One significant fact that emerges from this brief discussion is that not all our thoughts are sequential and continuous. For instance, we have periods of incubation and even of daydreaming, and these seem to indicate that thinking is not a serial activity all the time but, as we will argue below, we embed the outcomes of all of our thinking in our minds. However, we can see that during the processes of learning we can and do use different types of thought and we might conclude, in passing, that individuals could be taught different types of thinking during their education.

Styles of thinking

Having examined the forms of thinking we now turn to styles of thinking and we want to differentiate thinking styles from learning styles, which we will discuss later in this study. Sternberg's (1997) work has been most significant on this topic. He (1997: 19) defined thinking style as 'a preferred way of thinking' and he is clear that individuals do not have one preferred way but a profile. He (1997: 26) suggested thirteen different styles, shown in Table 5.5.

Sternberg sees each of these styles as reflecting a type of person, which reflects the fact that human learning is not only a very complex process, it is also an individual one and so, while each person's profile is not unique, it is at least 'personalised'. While the levels, scope and leanings are comparatively clear, Sternberg's terminology of forms and functions do require a little

Table 5.5 Sternberg's thinking styles

Functions	Forms	
Legislative	Monarchic	
Executive	Hierarchic	
Judicial	Oligarchic	
	Anarchic	

Levels	Scope	Leanings
Global	Internal	Liberal
Local	External	Conservative

more explanation. They refer to the idea that people govern their own mental approaches to daily living within the social context. Sternberg actually gives examples of people and situations that he has discovered in the course of his research:

- Legislative: People who like to decide for themselves what they will do, so their disposition is conducive to creative thinking and they are forward looking.
- Executive: People who prefer to follow rules and regulations, so that their disposition is conducive to thought processes that conform to what is expected of them.
- Judicial: People who like to evaluate rules and procedures, so that their dispositions are towards analytic and reflective thinking.

- Monarchic: People who are single-minded and driven, so that their thinking tends towards narrowness and depth.
- Hierarchic: People who set goals and priorities may seek a variety of answers to the same question, so that they may set their own priorities.
- Oligarchic: People motivated by several goals of equal competing performance, so that they make their own decisions.
- Anarchic: People with wide-ranging interests and who pursue their own mixture, so that their thinking tends to be creative and challenging of the status quo.

- Global: People who tend to deal with a wide range of large and abstract concerns.
- Local: People who like concrete problems and work with detail.

- Internal: Introverts who prefer to think alone about specific tasks.
- External: Extroverts who are socially sensitive and like to work in groups.

- Liberal: People who like to go beyond existing rules and procedures to seek maximum change through their creative thinking.
- Conservative: People who work within a structured environment and think within the existing rules and procedures.

Clearly, for Sternberg different styles of thinking relate to different types of personality, which is in accord with one of the theses underlying this study: it is the person who thinks and learns. Indeed, people may have different preferred thinking and learning styles in different social situations and even for different tasks. Consequently, we must draw the conclusion that there is a relationship between the way in which individuals process their experiences and transform them into knowledge, beliefs, values and attitudes and their individual personalities. Now this raises a question to which we must return when we discuss learning styles later in this study since we will again need to ask the question as to what extent learning styles are actually personality types.

The emotion and action

Apart from the cognitive, we suggested in Figure 1.6 that there are two other ways through which we transform our experiences, and these are emotively and through action. Once again, therefore, we divide this part of the chapter into two sections, and in the first we look at emotive learning and in the second we examine action learning – but in both we cannot escape the cognitive.

Emotion

In our concern to understand learning we have traditionally focused upon cognitive and behaviour so that a great deal of discussion on emotion is comparatively recent, although it would be true to say that artists and novelists have long recognised that the human being is far more complex than this. *Collins Dictionary* (1979) provides a bland and rather meaningless definition of emotion as 'any strong feeling' reflecting the lack of consideration given to emotions. It is only recently that there has been more emphasis on them, which Goleman defines as 'any agitation or disturbance of mind, feeling or passion; any excited or mental state' (1996: 289). Despite the popularity of his work (1996, 1998), his framework for analysis appears to limit the brain to the functionality of the computer as he (1998) describes the structure of the brain and locates the emotions within it in terms of neuronal activity. For him, emotions are feelings and action tendencies. However, we have already shown in the second chapter that this model of the brain without reference to the mind is unconvincing – Goleman's (1996: 8–9) only reference to mind is the dichotomy between the rational and emotional mind, which, I feel, is a trap of over-simplification. Even so, it could be argued that Goleman's studies are popular and make sense within the world of work that he discusses. This we would not dispute, but what he has shown also reflects the pragmatism of contemporary society since his suggestions are practical – they work. Whether they are totally correct in every detail is not the point at issue. We will return to this point in the latter half of this book.

Perhaps Cell (1984) offers us a little more convincing explanation that also helps us understand human learning a little better, and he argues that emotions cannot be identical to the sensations that we experience because, for instance, there are many more emotions than possible bodily sensations. He refers to Dewey's argument that emotions are always about something, that is, we look at an object in a certain manner. Hence, we make judgments about it, that is, we reflect upon experience. It is at this point that we differ in our approach from those definitions that limit emotion to feeling. Emotions are part of our learning process and have three components: a judgment, a feeling and an action tendency. Cell correctly, to my mind, argues that judgment is basic.

Since it is the person whose emotions transform the experience, it is necessary to explore the types of experience that generate an emotional response. Basically, there seem to be three and they are all existential in nature; following Cell, we call these the functional, the dysfunctional and the profound.

Functional

Underlying these emotions are judgments that we may make about an event or phenomenon that affects our sense of self in a positive manner. Cell suggests that our 'emotional scenarios provide us with ways of being a significant self in situations that are important to us' (1986: 101); he goes on to illustrate this:

> Typically, we learn anger or fear where our physical existence is threatened, love or jealousy where our need for bonding is concerned, pride or resentment where our personal worth is at issue, a sense of beauty or of discord in our search for wholeness in ourselves and our world, a feeling of the infinite in our quest for ultimate meaning and courage.

We can extend Cell's existential discussion to emotions that may seem to be less overtly existential, such as being committed to an intellectual position – but there is a sense that once we have accepted an argument we do invest a little of our self in that position, so that we become committed to it. In this sense, even commitment must be seen as existential.

Our interpretations focus upon our sense of self and it is these that give rise to sensations and action tendencies. In this sense, our learning is hermeneutical in the first instance; we try to make sense of our experience and we do so as a result of our previous learning.

Dysfunctional

Dysfunctional emotions also revolve around our sense of self, and in this case self-esteem. We see in others abilities, skills and so on that we wished we possessed. We envy the possessor of the skills, or even we become a fan and begin to idolise that person because we wished that we possessed those skills and the person who does so must be exceptional in some way. These emotions are negative to our sense of self-worth, and through them we may lose self-confidence as well as self-esteem.

Profound

Profound emotions emerge from situations that often lead to contemplative thought. They occur when the situation or event that we experience is beyond our immediate understanding or beyond words to explain – it may just be mysterious or beautiful (Gadamer 1986) and so on. Clearly, these situations are personal, defy our immediate rationality and somehow take us beyond ourselves, and they are often defined as religious experiences. The emotions of wonder, awe, mystery and so on are to be found in this category. Here we can see the three dimensions of the emotion: the judgment that the experience is profound, maybe beyond knowing; the feeling of wonder, awe, etc.; the action tendency to wish to contemplate, to offer worship and so on.

Thus we can see that we transform some of our experiences through a mixture of the cognitive, the sense of feeling and the action tendencies that accompany them; that is, we store our emotional learning as these memories – elements in our biographies – and they influence our future understanding of similar events in our lives. We can trace emotional learning back to our primary socialisation process, and it is because some of these feelings and tendencies just seem to appear when we have specific experiences that we often claim that we 'cannot help feeling the way that we do'. But Goleman (1998) demonstrates that it is possible both to control them and to change them.

Action

Teachers will frequently say that the best way to learn a subject is to teach it; doing a thing it is certainly a good way to learn it. Consequently, this section is not about skills learning, although learning skills is naturally included within it. But neither is it about what is called 'action learning'; that will be discussed in the second part of the book. It is about 'doing'. It is about living and doing in everyday life as well as practising skills in specialist occupations and pursuits.

We do need, therefore, to have an understanding of the concept of action. Actions are rarely mindless, although Heidegger once suggested that, 'it could be that prevailing man has for centuries ... acted too much and thought too little' (1968: 4). But, as we have argued throughout this book, action must also involve thought. But not all actions actually involve thought since accidents can happen – maybe due to the lack of thought. For instance, I do not often fall over intentionally, but falling over is an action. Consequently, we must limit our discussion here to intended action; nevertheless we opened this study with the assertion that 'I act, therefore I am'. This we still hold to since even unintended actions show that we still are living beings.

Limiting ourselves to conscious action, according to Schutz (1967: 129), 'we have a picture in our mind of what we are going to do' – in other words, we have the intention to act, although we may want to refine this further now. For instance, Merton (1968: 185–246) developed a theory of individual adaptation to situations, in which he included conformity, innovation, ritualism, retreatism and rebellion. I developed and amended this theory of conscious action (Jarvis 1992: 58), but now I have changed it even more. Planning is a matter of looking forward, monitoring is a present cognitive activity, while reflecting is a matter of looking backwards (see Table 5.6).

Each of these ten potential learning experiences are:

Table 5.6 A theoretical analysis of conscious action

Category of response to potential learning experiences	Level of consciousness		
	Planning	Monitoring	Reflecting
Non-action			
Anomic	None	None	High
Preventive	Low–high	None	None–high
Non-response	None–high	None	None–high
Action			
Experimental/creative	High	High	High
Repetitive	High–none	High–low	High–none
Presumptive	None–low	None–low	None
Ritualistic	None–high	High–low	None–high
Alienating	None	None–low	None–high
Reaction			
Retreating	None	High–low	High–low
Rebellion	High	High	High

- *Anomic*: normless and meaningless because the disjuncture between people's biographies and their socio-cultural situation is too large to be bridged.
- *Preventive*: individuals are prevented from acting despite experiencing disjuncture because of the power/authorities in their situation prevents action.
- *Non-response*: disjuncture is experienced but, for whatever reason, no action is taken.

- *Experimental/creative*: disjuncture is experienced and innovative action undertaken to re-establish harmony through learning.
- *Repetitive*: disjuncture lessens as individuals carry out procedures that begin to re-establish harmony – but this is a key stage, for it can either lead to a re-establishment of harmony or else it can lead to new understandings of the action, a deepening of the skills and so towards expertise.
- *Presumptive*: individuals experience no disjuncture.
- *Ritualistic*: no disjuncture – just going through the motions – sometimes extremely thoughtfully.
- *Alienating*: no real disjuncture – just not involved in the situation, even though still performing actions, but powerless to change them.

- *Retreating*: either disjuncture or not, but removing oneself from the situation.
- *Rebellion*: disjuncture, but acts to change the situation rather than to change oneself initially.

Now is not the time or place to discuss these in detail, but we can immediately see that the motives underlying any action could begin with creative and innovative ideas, but over time it may move towards ritualistic and even alienating action. At the same time, the repetitive stage is seen as crucial and does demand more discussion (Simpson 1995). It will be noted that this is one of the only stages in which all three of planning, monitoring and reflecting can vary from high to non-existent. Where there is little of any of them, then the natural progression is towards presumption – that the actors merely presume upon their situation and repeat past acts. However, if there is considerable thought – planning, monitoring and reflection – this 'natural' stage can be averted and even reversed, so that it can lead to further experimentation and creativity. The other stage in which this occurs is ritualism. Ritualism might merely be 'going through the motions' and lead to alienation, but when ritual is practised in its highest cultural forms, it does stem from considerable planning and leads to monitoring and reflection which, in turn, might lead to further experimentation and creativity. It should not be forgotten that Confucius was a teacher of ritual (Liu 1955). Hence, in both stages thought and action are combined and this can lead to skills being refined and new meaning being seen in traditional actions; both might lead to more wisdom and expertise developing in the actors.

Consequently, the experience of the action changes, and with it the learning that follows differs from action to action. In addition, we can see that there is a relationship between the types of learning discussed in the opening chapter and these types of action. We can also see, therefore, that the relationship between theory and practice is much more complex than the crude idea that we learn the theory in the classroom and go and put it into practice. This theory is one that de-humanises the actor, since action is not mindless. Indeed, it would be more true to claim that we have the experience in a practical situation and then reflect upon it and generate our own theory (Jarvis 1999), so that we reverse the traditional relationship and talk about theory following practice rather than practice emerging from theory – as we saw earlier, human beings are theorisers. What is taught in the classroom might well be a theory of action that is learned and espoused by the actor. But if the type of action changes over time, so might the apparent theory in action change, so that we are presented with a situation in which the espoused theory and the apparent theory for the same action differ. This is precisely what Arygris discovered and in a number of books, with co-authors, he discussed espoused theory and theories in use. 'Espoused theories are those that an individual claims to follow. Theories-in-use are those that can be inferred from action' (Argyris et al. 1985: 81–2). Argyris et al. regard theories-in-use as tacit knowledge.

Doing is also about having the skills to perform the action, and different people have different preferences about how they do things. Cell (1984: 208–16) has produced a learning skills profile in which he lists 180 different ways to learn through doing, and the following actions are an ad hoc selection of what is included within it:

- I learn well from books.
- I can communicate well by writing a letter.
- When listening to someone:
- I am good at understanding some one else's point of view.
- I am good at making myself understood orally.
- I'm good at role playing.
- I make outlines of what I have learned.
- I can learn new dance steps quickly.
- I am good at applying what I learn to my life.
- I find touching is a good way of communicating.
- I can easily learn things like riding a bike.
- I can get my ideas down on paper.
- I can easily pick up thinks like roller skating.
- It often saves time to learn from some one who is an authority.
- Putting my thoughts on paper is often helpful to me.

- Listening to things like music, . . .
- I have a good memory for complicate procedures.
- I find working in a group a good way to learn.

Reading, writing, listening, speaking, acting, summarising skills, touching, appreciating and sharing are but a few of the activities included in this profile through which we learn. Indeed, we could add travelling, experimenting, playing, practising and rehearsing and so on. From the outset of this study we have maintained that 'I am, therefore I do' and in doing we learn. We transform experiences not just by thinking about them but by doing something about them, for this is fundamental to our understanding of the person as being both mind and body. At the same time, it accounts for the fact that people find it hard to isolate and discuss their own processes of learning – these occur naturally in the process of everyday living. But it does not mean to say that we immediately become skilful in the practice of any of these skills.

Dreyfus and Dreyfus (1980, cited in Benner 1984: 13) developed a skill acquisition model in which they argued that we pass through five stages of proficiency:

- novice;
- advanced beginner;
- competent;
- proficient;
- expert.

Dreyfus and Dreyfus developed this model in their study of airline pilots, while Benner used it with nurses. For novices, experiences are new and so they have to find ways of responding to them, whereas advanced beginners can 'demonstrate marginally acceptable performance' (Benner 1984: 22). For Benner, competence comes after two or three years of practice – although this might actually be too long a timescale, proficiency arises when practitioners perceive whole situations immediately based upon their past experiences, and expertise comes when nurses act almost intuitively. It is both the body and the mind that have to master the situation – pianists' fingers seem to acquire a sense of automatic movement through constant practice, as the pianists learn to understand, appreciate and perform a piece of music; the body and mind act in harmony. Eventually, they master it and can perform it. Benner (1984: 32) writes:

> Capturing the descriptions of expert performance is difficult, because the expert operates from a deep understanding of the whole situation; the chess master, for instance, is asked why he or she made a particularly masterful move will just say: 'Because it felt right' . . . Or when expert business decision makers are asked . . . 'It all depends'.

Experts assess the whole situation and are able to respond accordingly. Becoming an expert takes many years, and while we all become experts in our daily living, we can take things for granted and presume upon situations (non-learning) because of our expertise. Even so, the time taken to develop this type of expertise is usually too long for those who want to master time, for career-orientated individuals who are moved by their employers or seek new positions quickly – at even advanced beginner or competency stages! As we pointed out earlier in this study, expertise comes with living and doing.

Not everyone moves from novice to expert, some retreat and move on, or are moved, to another role so that they are no longer exposed to the same types of experience, but others do tend to presume on the situation and then move into ritualism and maybe to alienation, whereby they 'go through the motions of the action' but do not learn anything from it. These are the ones who work at the same thing for twenty-five years, but only have one year's experience twenty-five times rather than twenty-five year's experience once! In one sense their life has been impoverished since, as we argued earlier, learning is living.

In a similar manner, Confucius argued that we learn by ritual action. As Kyung (2004: 119) writes:

> Ritual practice . . . has a creative dimension. Even though rituals inform the participants of what proper actions are, it is the participants who actually appropriate the rituals through performing them. When performing rituals, participants reformulate rituals to accommodate uniqueness and quality of the participants; the participants personalize the rituals. Rituals, on the one hand, inform the participants of the shared set of values. On the other hand, rituals offer persons the opportunity to contribute novel meaning to the community and thereby to be integrated in a way enriching the community.

Each person is unique but lives in the community and through the performance of ritual the individual reinforces the community while continuing to learn from the community's practices, but re-interpreting them from the individual's own uniqueness. In ritual we see two different ways of looking at repetition in learning: in the West we tend to regard repetition as rote learning, whereas in Confucian heritage countries repetitive learning is regarded as a way of learning more deeply and gaining more understanding and meaning. In this sense, it is seen rather like meditation. Significantly, in Confucian heritage countries more emphasis is placed on the effort underlying the learning than in the West, where achievement is emphasised. However, the Western ideal of effortless achievement is something of a pervasive myth that might be better discarded, or at least recognised for the myth that it actually is. The emphasis placed on effort is important, since it suggests that everyone can engage in the learning process throughout their lives and achieve desired outcomes.

Consequently, this process is not free of emotion: we experience frustration when we do not succeed, boredom if we have to practice the same skill innumerable times, satisfaction when we succeed and pride when we do sometime really well and so on. Of the three processes of transforming experience, depicted in Figure 1.6, it would be rare for anyone to act totally independently of at least one of the others, and impossible for the action pathway not to occur in combination with both of the others. It is the whole person who learns, and the outcomes of what are learned are memorised and become part of our biography.

Conclusion

All that we process through thought, action and emotion, we memorise, and in this brief concluding section I want to focus on the process of memorising, although in the chapter on the changed person we will return to the subject of memory once again.

Marton *et al.* (1996) suggest that there are two forms of immediate memory – they call these, 'mechanical memory' and 'understanding memory'. This can be seen to reflect Marton's earlier work on deep and surface learning. Mechanical memory means that things are memorised through mechanical processes without a great deal of understanding, whereas understanding memory means that a clear relationship between the things being remembered is worked out before the memorisation occurs. They then trace this process so that they reach the point where they can talk about understanding through memorisation. However, the significant thing about this research is that they show that each time the learners repeat what they are trying to learn and remember, they develop a greater understanding of what they are learning. In this sense, repetition (which need not be rote learning) aids and abets understanding. Marton *et al.* think that this is important in seeking to understand the achievement of Chinese learners.

In the process of conscious living we all have short-term, or working, memories, which stores the sensory inputs – meanings, emotions, actions, senses – for a brief time, which might be no more than just a few seconds. It is almost like the 'now' of the perceived experience or the outcome of the process of transforming that experience. The content of the working memory has to be maintained by repetition or else we could lose it before it gets stored in a more permanent manner, as Marton *et al.* have demonstrated above. The extent to which we lose it permanently remains an open question since we have shown that we can recall to mind some experiences which we have had that are of a pre-conscious nature.

However, it is the long-term memory that is functionally important to our everyday living, to the sense of self-identity and to future learning. We store the constructions of our experiences and the outcomes of our thinking and acting upon them. The storage process takes a number of different forms. Ormrod (1995: 237–43) suggests at least four: verbal codes, imagery, meanings and propositions, and procedural knowledge. These relate to our previous discussion since they cover the cognitive, emotive and practical dimensions. The way in which we store these memories is more complex and, as Gardner (1993) has shown, they are stored in different parts of the brain. Even so, we appear to store memories in at least two ways simultaneously:

- *Hierarchically*: within categories and sub-categories, i.e. as families of phenomena. In order to illustrate this from the bottom upwards, a Scottish terrier is a dog (and there are many other types of dog) and a dog is an animal (and there are many more types of animal) and so on.
- *As a network*: we connect ideas and events so that one idea leads to another and so on.

However, we do not store these memories in such a way as we will recall them in precisely the same way as we perceived them in the first instance. Bartlett (1932), for instance, showed that while we retain the core of the phenomenon being memorised, we are likely to change words and parts of the memorised phenomenon tends to be distorted and we tend to add explanations or meanings.

Moreover, it will be recalled that from the outset of this book we have claimed that 'I am' means that I-am-in-the-world, which means that the memories we store are not merely of the event or phenomenon as we have perceived and experienced it, it is the perception and experience in the world. We remember in context much better, so that memory without context may actually not reflect total memory at all. Many of us will be aware of how we recall much more about an event or phenomenon when we are actually in the place where it occurred, and yet we often examine children's memory out of context by trying to get them to remember isolated facts and trivia – preparing them for quiz games rather that the actual world in which we use our memories contextually.

This discussion can be taken one stage further since we can see that as we gain new knowledge and new skills, so we are more able to cope with the situations of daily living – as I have put it in the diagram, the person is more experienced. This means that our crystallised intelligence is continuing to develop. But the person is body and mind and there is another form of intelligence which is biologically based, fluid intelligence, and this begins to decline as the body ages (Cattell 1963). The extent to which individuals do involve themselves in the external world and continue to learn throughout their lives means that the combination of these intelligences results in the possibility of a developing intelligence until later in our lives.

In addition, the Freudian approach to psychoanalysis suggests that we are likely to suppress unpleasant things into the unconscious mind, so that while they are not apparently present they do affect the way that we behave. Crane (2001: 70) maintains that psychoanalysis demonstrates how the conscious mind has accommodated unconscious thought, desire and mentality in general.

In this chapter, then, we have examined some of the complex ways in which our experiences are transformed, memorised and then integrated into our biographies. In all of our learning we are continually being changed and continue to become who we are. Consequently, we now turn our minds to the changed and changing person.

Chapter 6

The person

Changing and becoming more experienced

Human beings are always in the process of becoming – we are always incorporating into our own biographies the outcomes of our new learning and thus creating a changed, but also paradoxically re-creating the same, person. Being is transitory, it is always a manifestation of the 'now' in the process of becoming; we are always developing beyond what we already are and this continues for as long as we live, although if we opt out of a great deal of social interaction in our life-world we slow down the processes of becoming and perhaps speed up the decline in our human faculties.

In as much as we are in control of our learning, we are the authors of our own biographies, but it would be a mistake to assume that we are its sole authors. We are not islands but we live in socio-cultural surrounds and interact with a wide variety of people, all of whom impinge upon our freedom to act and learn. The outcomes of our learning are stored in our memories and so memory is crucial to our self-understanding, sense of identity and even to the autonomy and freedom that we can exercise. In a real sense our memories are 'the treasure within' us (Delors 1996) that contribute a great deal to making us who we are. Loss of memory, or the inability to access our memory, prevents us from being ourselves and eventually from manifesting our humanity. For so long as we can tell our stories, we are identifying ourselves. Being able to narrate our life history is telling the story which links together the outcomes of our various learning episodes and this has, consequently, become part of our research into adult learning and also into studies of the third and fourth ages. We are conscious of many of the outcomes of our learning and we will examine some of these in the first part of this chapter, but there are also hidden outcomes and these will constitute the second section.

The outcomes of learning: being and becoming a person

During the processes of learning we store the outcomes in our minds – we regard this as a process of memorising – as we discussed in the previous chapter. But when we perceive an external object our perception is affected by the memories stored in our minds – in this sense we are seeking to release and utilise what has been stored – but there is a problem here. When we learn scientific facts, we memorise them and we remember the original outcomes of our learning, since they are facts. That learning cannot be repeated, although it can be reinforced. Bergson (2004 [1912]: 94–5) refers to this as 'spontaneous memory' and it is interesting that schooling and society in general has placed significance on this form of memory and has tended to test intelligence by it. No doubt this is because it is the correct remembrance of facts that can be tested, and this tends to be the basis of scientific knowledge. At the same time, when we remember significant moments that induce changes in our lives – creative, transformative, rebellious, momentous and so on – we often remember the complete context which also tends to be integrated into our biographies. But we keep returning to these and perhaps embellishing or re-adjusting them to fit our current experiences in some way. Likewise, during the process of everyday living we keep adding the outcomes of all of our other learning, even re-interpreting them, and integrating this into our memories so that we have a learned memory that is in the continuous process of development. However, this learned memory might not always be accurate and we might not recall specific events of learning or we might even make mistakes as we try to recall things. In addition, certain aspects might have been repressed into our unconscious. Psychological tests show that we do make mistakes in our recall, but it is still this interplay between the past and the present that enables us to live normal lives, even though they might not be quite as rational as we often assume. There is a sense, then, in which we have two types of memory:[1] the one that is about storing the facts that we learn, and the other which is the outcome of learning from our everyday life, which is always changing and that we use, as it were, to interpret new experiences. The former, then, is about recollection and the other about utilisation. Both are integrated into our biographies and both are personal, although Bergson suggests that the latter passes out of time and becomes more impersonal. But the idea of an impersonal memory seems problematic since I am always becoming and learning, and learning is about my personhood, so that the memory must also be personal and must always be a major constituent in the way that we give meaning to actions and to experiences. Memory, then, lies at the basis of what we called hermeneutic thinking in the previous chapter, and the meaning that we give to experiences underlies our narratives about ourselves.

In this section it is the outcomes of these processes that we are going to discuss: perception, self-identity, self-esteem, authenticity, self-efficacy, autonomy, social identity. These are all outcomes of our learning, all part of the process of becoming a changed and more experienced individual.

Perception

Both philosophers and psychologists have been interested in perception, the former because of its epistemological significance and the latter in order to understand its mechanisms. If we are to understand the construction of experience, we certainly need to understand the processes of perceiving the external world and transforming our perception into knowledge.

Thus far we have assumed that underlying perceptual experiences is a real object in the external world, but it would be possible to suggest that in some instances that that real object is actually an hallucination, so that we actually reflect on something that we mistakenly think exists. If we are having an hallucination, we still have data that are transformed in the brain and so on. Hence, it is necessary to have a clear understanding of any distinction between hallucination and perceived reality. In social situations it is easier to demonstrate this if we perceive that there is a real object in the external world; because others have similar experiences, then there is a good chance that we are not all having an hallucination but perceiving an external object. But if we are the only person perceiving and external object, we cannot use the same argument. Perhaps we can develop a similar one, however, since we experience the world through all our senses and if there is a congruency between the various senses about the object being perceived, then there is a good likelihood that the perception is of a real object. Perception, however, is a mental state that has occurred as a result of the transformation of the sense data that we have received and after the transformation has occurred the mental state is no longer physical, although it was sparked off by physical sensations, and this we discussed in the second chapter. Perceptions are mental states and Crane (2001, *inter alia*) argue that all mental states are phenomenal and that they are all intentional. An intentional state is one to which the mind is directed, and the direction of this will occur to a considerable extent because our minds contain our memories which recognise objects that are already known. Significantly, however, such mental states are not reducible to physical phenomena. Our minds are not synonymous with our brains. Neither is what we perceive a photograph of the external world, but it is a mental state that has occurred as a result of the transformation of sense data received about the external world. The actual object of our perception is seen in the way that it is partly because our memories of previous learning experiences frame the object of which we have become aware. This process results in us being able to have meaningful lived experiences, which we can transform through thought, action and emotion and add to the store of memories which then help guide our continuing perception of the world. Consequently, the sense of continuity is enhanced as a result of perception, which means that paradigmatic shifts in our understanding of the world do not happen very frequently, and neither is our understanding of ourselves likely to undergo too many major shifts, although we would not rule out that these do happen occasionally in such occurrences as religious conversion.

Self-identity

Throughout the history of thought about self-identity, the place of memory has been important. Locke (1993 [1690]) first appeals to it and Noonan (2003: 9) refers to this as experience-memory in order to separate it from the process of memorising. It does seem clear that memory is important to self-identity and loss of memory is clearly related to loss of self-identity. Nevertheless, there are still problems with the idea of memory as being the criterion for personal identity since we cannot recall all our experiences, although it can be argued that we can remember a sufficient number of experiences to provide a sense of continuity and, therefore, personal identity. Whilst recognising that there are other criteria for personal identity, such as body as well as mind (Noonan 2003), it is argued here that we can see in the way that we learn who we are during the process of everyday living and learning, and this sense of self-identity relates very strongly to memory.

While we do have a sense of continuity, we also retain the sense of who we are – this does not change and it will be recalled from our earlier discussion that this is what Harré (1998) called self 1. Each person (body and mind) is unique in time and space and the trajectory through time and space that we carve out through our learning is uniquely our own. We are conscious, however, that we are the same person even though we are living through time and in space and that we are learning, and therefore our mind is changing, and our body ageing, so that while we are conscious of being the same person, both our body and minds are undergoing change. Naturally this leads to certain philosophical questions about the nature of self-identity, but we conclude that identity does not demand indenticality, so that the same identity does not demand identical body or mind over time.

Although our learning is our own, it does not happen in isolation. Our sense of self stems in part from our reflection of how we perceive that others perceive us through our actions in the external world – this is a dialectic relationship. Hence our learning enhances both our own singularity and individuality (Harré 1998: 8). However, through this process of becoming we continue to develop our personal attributes, so that we recognise ourselves and the actions that follow from them. This is what Harré called self 2. That others recognise us by our actions is what he called self 3, and we will return to this when we examine social identity at the end of this section. But, as we have already pointed out, cognition rarely occurs in isolation from the emotions, so that we also have feelings and beliefs about ourselves.

Recently, however, a new term has appeared with reference to identity – identity capital. Reflecting the way both humanity and our language have been colonised by economic globalisation, this term joins human and social capital (Schuller 2004) as the three 'Cs', although had he wanted to, Schuller could also have included the idea of cultural capital within his theoretical framework. Identity capital refers to the person's assets and has two meanings, according to Côté and Levene (2002: 14):

- tangible assets, which are socially visible, such as qualifications and networks; and
- intangible assets, such as ego-strengths, self-esteem, sense of purpose.

(cited from Schuller 2004: 20)

Schuller prefers to use the term with reference to the intangible assets of the person only, and while this concept has a certain attraction in referring to personal assets, it also bows to the hegemony of the language of economic capitalism. It not only seems superfluous to add the idea of 'capital' to the concept of identity, it is also unconvincing because the assets of a person include identity as well as esteem and efficacy. But esteem and efficacy are assets of the person and not of the identity. It is not the identity that is esteemed, neither is it the identity that is efficacious, so that the term is both imprecise and misleading.

Self-esteem

As a result of what we do and how we are received, we evaluate ourselves. For instance, we may feel good about ourselves and believe that we have something useful to contribute to society, or we may not like ourselves and the way that we behave and so on. In reflecting upon ourselves and our actions and the way in which other people respond to us, we may develop a low or a high self-esteem, and this is a part of our personal identity. Self-esteem is not a property and we may not have a drive to achieve a positive sense of self-esteem, as Maslow (1968) suggested, but we may actually learn to esteem ourselves because of what we do or because of the way in which we are received by others and so on. Having a sense of self-esteem is a major factor in our human being, but it may best be understood as something that we acquire as a result of our learning experiences. In precisely the same way some acquire a low sense of self-esteem, as Belenky *et al.* (1986) demonstrated for some of the women whom they interviewed. In this sense, the women did not have the confidence even to listen to themselves and they placed little or no value upon their own views – this was also a condition that they had learned.

Authenticity

Amongst the most common forms of learning is the uncritical acceptance of what we are told, the imitation of skills that we are expected to learn and so on. It is non-reflective learning, but for Nietzsche it is passive nihilism. This is an outcome of his thinking about the death of God. When we are confronted with the disjunctural question 'Why?', if we merely accept what we are told we are admitting that we ourselves have no answers to the question and neither is there a god to provide them for us. Hence, it is a failure to grapple with the challenge of our human nature, 'of the uniquely human capacity for self conscious concern with beliefs, values and purposes' (Cooper 1983: 2). In a sense, for Nietzsche, non-reflectivity – almost our normal condition and understanding of learning – is about inauthenticity. Without mentioning inauthenticity, we touched upon this type of belief when we discussed the social situation in which we have our experiences and noted that social forces direct us towards conformity and acceptance. Indeed, this is also something that greatly influenced the Frankfurt School of Critical Theory. Schroyer (1973: viii) suggested that Adorno attempted 'to transcend and include in the perspective of critical reason the truth of the existentialist concern for the fundamentalness of human subjectivity' in his own formulation of critical theory. What Adorno was also claiming was that we cannot just blame the socio-economic conditions for our human inauthenticity, even though they may contribute towards it. For Nietzsche, authenticity is about the 'true' self being realised in action. This is similar to how Heidegger describes it, according to Cooper's summary: 'the authentic person will live in full awareness of the possibilities of action, belief, and purpose that are open to him, and which anyone concerned with his existence as an "issue" must consider' (1983: 19).

The point of disjuncture is, therefore, also the starting point for authentic existence. It is here that we, as human beings, can respond to disjuncture and write our own biography, and this is about being authentic. In a sense, authenticity overlaps with autonomy, the concept that British philosophers of education, such as Peters (1973), appear to favour, although they do discuss both. I am including both here since the two overlap without being the same: authenticity is about the self – which is central to my argument here – whereas autonomy has generally been discussed in a more abstract forum and is seen as an attribute of the person and of liberal society. Cooper (1983) suggests that the term 'authenticity' has two basic meanings: correspondence and genesis. Our actions reflect our own humanity and sense of being. They correspond to our ideals of humanity but we are responsible for them. Copper (1983: 9–19) discusses two approaches to this, which he calls the Polonian and the Dadaist models. The former is summed up in what Polonius said to his son, 'To thine own self be true', and the latter that 'the authenticity of a person's actions and commitments is that these issue from his spontaneous choices, unconstrained by convention, opinion, or his own past' (Cooper 1983: 10). Both of these interpretations point to the individuality of the person, free from the constraints of the social situation. The former suggests that individuals are guided by their past learning and by the memories that constitute their self-identity. Consequently, people will tend to reject many situations from which they might learn new things because they have to be true to their past. Naturally, this rejection of learning opportunities may also be seen in a positive light since it means that they will not be swayed 'by every wind of doctrine' and that if they have embraced high moral standards, for instance, they will always keep to them whatever the situation.[2] In contrast, the latter position implies that since every situation is a new one, the potential learning opportunities that each situation presents will be embraced with open arms. Open-mindedness can also be seen to be a good thing, but inconsistency might not be. Both forms of authenticity have their weaknesses, and we could extend this argument much further here, as Cooper (1983) has done.

However, a different moral position is that adopted by Buber (1959) and Marcel (1976), who were both concerned with the I↔Thou relationship, and this is one which actually combines the Polonion and Dadaist models. Elsewhere, I (Jarvis 1997) argued that the one universal good is the principle of being concerned for the Other, even though when we put that principle into practice we might not succeed in fulfilling our high moral principles. It is in the application of this that we have to learn when we are in potential learning situations and, at the same time, we have to be true to ourselves as we reach out to the other. Authenticity in the context of human relationships, then, is about being true to the high moral principles that we have adopted so that our actions might correspond to the high ideals of humanity itself. Through such responses to disjunctive situations, we both learn new things and learn to live in accord with our beliefs. This demands reflective learning – both critical and creative – and a sense of responsibility. It is individualistic without being self-centred since a great deal of our growth and development is unintended because our actions should be guided by our beliefs about meeting the needs of the other, and thereby by being true to ourselves.

Self-efficacy

At the same time, we rarely act unless we believe that we have the ability to perform successfully, and this belief is something that we have learned as a result of both past successful acts and by watching other people behave. This sense of self-confidence has been called 'self-efficacy' by Bandura (1977, 1989), which may be defined as 'our belief in our behavioural competence in a particular situation' (McAdams 2001: 207). We gain this belief, according to McAdams, from four different sources:

- past experience of success and failure;
- witnessing other people's performances;
- being told by others that we can do it; and
- our own emotional arousal.

Clearly, this belief is the outcome of learning. It is a sense of self-confidence, although it is normative and relative, but if we are over-confident we may run the risk of little learning. The idea of self-efficacy is quite central to Bandura's theory of social learning, and we shall return to it in the second part of this study.

Autonomy

Inauthentic existence is one in which we are situated in such a way that we are forced to accept and respond to all the outside social pressures, whereas authentic existence indicates that we have learned to be sufficiently free to be true to ourselves irrespective of those outside pressures. Since none of us are islands, we need to ask ourselves whether we actually do have free will. Belief in autonomy and free will are quite fundamental to our understanding of liberal society and perhaps in more contemporary, open, society the freedom of the individual is increasingly assumed. But the defence in many a criminal court – especially in war crimes courts – has been 'I have only done what I was ordered to' as if free will is a myth. There have been many philosophical treatises about free will and this is not the place to explore it, but from the preceding sentences we can see that a philosophical argument that ignores the social and the psychological will be deficient. This also points to a fundamental difference in being autonomous and in having the opportunity to exercise that autonomy. Agency, then, presupposes a degree of autonomy and freedom so that 'I am, therefore I act' is a statement of belief that the human being is an autonomous person, or that underlying our humanity lies a belief that human beings have free will. But this does not always mean that individuals will be able to exercise that autonomy since we live in rule-governed society.

At the same time, we have always assumed that by virtue of our humanity we have a freedom of choice, even though we recognise that by living in social organisations that freedom is constrained. Peters (1973: 121) suggests that human beings are choosers. That is given situations where decisions are made – disjunctural situations – individuals are free to choose what to do. But this does not mean that we are totally free. We have already argued that our memories help guide our perception and that our actions are guided to a great extent by successful past experiences. Consequently, it is possible to argue that we are imprisoned by our own previous learning. Since we are all imprisoned behind the bars of our own minds we may not have the total freedom that we might think we have. Acting automatically, as a result of our previous learning, both may have made us more able to live in society, but less free as a result of our previous learning. Nevertheless, on reflecting upon something that we have done, we sometimes assume that we could have done it differently, suggesting that we feel that we actually do have more freedom than we have exercised.

However, Peters (1973: 127) suggests that:

> It is, surely, the learning of forms of understanding such as these (e.g. seeing something as a 'means to an end') rather than the assimilation of any particular content of experience that is crucial to the development of free men.

Peters' concern is the development of practical reason and his emphasis is on reason referring to developmental psychology in the form of Piaget and Kohlberg in support of his position. The ability to reason is fundamental to freedom, and Peters sees learning as gaining different forms of understanding. Nevertheless, Peters does not rule out the content of experience, and he shows how having experience of not being free curtails individuals' ability to act autonomously. While Peters' understanding of learning tends to be a little restricted since he appears to separate learning from experience, he does maintain that autonomy is something we learn. But Fromm (1942: 2), writing at the time of the Second World War, suggested that millions of Germans were quite as willing to surrender their freedom at that time as were their fathers willing to fight for it in a previous generation. He suggested that people fear freedom – that there is a sense in which we do not want to be free, but without pursuing his arguments further here we can conclude that both the desire for freedom and the fear of it are learned conditions, and that even the exercise of freedom itself is a learned condition. We are, therefore, dealing with a complex outcome of learning.

Indeed, we feel that there might be degrees of autonomy in practice which may relate to the pressures exerted on the individual in the social situation, and/or to the strength of will or beliefs or desires of the individual in pursuing a specific action. Lindley (1986) provides a nice illustration of this: we call somebody bald, even though they might still have a considerable amount of hair around the back and sides of their head – modern fashion would remove all the hair! Mostly, only in modern fashion are we likely to find complete baldness and only on a desert island are we likely to find a high degree of freedom, but this does not mean that we can only realise our humanity to the full on a desert island because we have argued that it is only in relationship that we can become the persons that we are, and so we would argue that in the realisation of our humanity in social living only degrees of autonomy are possible.

As an outcome of learning we acquire personal knowledge, beliefs, values, attitudes and skills that enable us to achieve levels of autonomy depending upon what we learn from previous experiences, store in our memories and are able to exercise in specific disjunctural situations. But it might be argued that we feel free when we take for granted our world and presume upon it – we feel no pressures to do anything other than we have done in the past. This is precisely the point; we have learned to conform and so we do not have to exercise our free will since we are lost in the flow of time. Only when time 'stops' and we become aware and have to do something different from what we have normally done, do we have the opportunity to exercise our will. Taken-for-granted action (presumption, we called it in the first chapter), whilst fundamental to social living, is also like being imprisoned behind the bars of our own minds. In order to live in society, we have to accept that for some of the time we are not free and neither do we always want to be so but, as we pointed out in the opening chapter, we are frequently confronted with disjunctural situations and learning opportunities where we are forced to exercise some degree of freedom.

This brings us to an important point about the relationship of learning and will. The decision to learn is an act of will; it is an exercise of our own humanity, as is the decision not to learn. Our motive, or intention, to learn specific things reflects the beliefs, values and interests and so on that we have already learned. Many forms of education and teaching deny that autonomy to the learner, especially children's education, which brings us to a central idea in the education of adults: self-directed learning. This refers to those forms of learning which occur outside of formal education and are directed by the learner. Here the learners make a conscious decision to embark upon their own learning projects (Tough 1979, *inter alia*). Candy (1991) distinguished between self-directed learning and autodidaxy, and he did this to make the point that in many educational institutions there is a claim that self-directed learning is practised, but he rightly claims that within educational institutions the influence of the teacher cannot be discounted even though educational institutions may claim to offer learners self-direction. Autodidaxy occurs outside of the educational institution. Here the learners' autonomy is retained and Candy (1991: 108–9) claims that autodidacts have a number of the characteristics of autonomy in that they:

- conceive of goals and policies independently of pressure from others;
- exercise freedom of choice and action;
- reflect rationally;
- are prepared to act fearlessly;
- have self-mastery; and
- perceive themselves to be autonomous.

However, as we have already pointed out, if we are guided by interests, values, beliefs and so on learned from the past, there is a sense in which we do not think or act in a completely autonomous manner. We have already learned knowledge, belief, attitudes and so on and these have made us who we are. The extent to which we can free ourselves of our past is a much more debateable point. Indeed, it can be doubted whether we ever can since it is our prior learning that has made us what we are. But the fact that when we reflect upon an action and think to ourselves that we could have done it differently, it demonstrates that we all believe that we can stand out against our previous learning and still be ourselves. This indicates that we think that we have a level of autonomy that enables us to be free, provided we have the will-power, strength, beliefs and confidence so to do. It is here that autonomy and authenticity meet and the paradox of the pressures of our past learning exercised through our memories might inhibit opportunities for future learning, even though we have the potential freedom to learn new things. However, if we embark upon too many new things the consistency of our selfhood is in some way threatened and our social identity put at risk, unless we are known as individuals who are always learning new things and whose behaviour is unpredictable. However, even our unpredictableness is then, paradoxically, predictable and we are being true to our character.

Social identity

From our earliest childhood we have a social identity and the way that our significant others perceive us and then act towards us helps to determine our personal identity. Thereafter, the social identity (identities) and the personal one interact and influence each other, even though we do generally remain true to our character. But one of the themes that has run through this study is that we are actors – I am, therefore I act – so that through our doing we present our own understanding of ourselves to the exterior world, and as a result of the ensuing interaction we get feedback about the way that people perceive us. It was, above all, Goffman (1971 [1959], 1961, 1968, *inter alia*) who studied this process of presenting ourselves in public through everyday behaviour. Goffman's work has been nicely summarised by Jenkins (2004: 69–70) under four headings:

- *The embodiment and spatiality of social interaction*: our physical presence in the world.
- *Performance/drama*: the manner through which we present ourselves.
- *Framing*: each social situation provides a frame within which we act consistently within that frame in relation to the other actors who play roles within it.
- *The interaction order*: the patterned domain of daily living.

Two other themes run through his work – both of which are important to our understanding it:

- *Impression management*: we present ourselves in the way that we want others to see us, so that we take the initiative in the dialectical relationship with externality.
- *Stigma*: the way by which individuals in the external world respond to disfigured bodies or abnormal behaviour.

Through these social processes, we learn more about ourselves and others also learn about us, and we will learn about them and their perception of us. Through what we do and say in the external world, others gain an impression of us and identify us. This social identity is what Harré (1998) called self 3 and this, in turn, reinforces the self-identity. Harré is clear, however, that while he suggests three selves, we are actually a singular self – a person

What we have shown in this section is the way in which we learn to be the persons we are and how we change and develop through the processes of learning. The human being is always in the process of becoming and learning is an essential element in our humanity. Even so, these processes are rarely intended and often tacit. Consequently, they are hidden outcomes of learning, but as we have argued from the first chapter, it is the person who learns.

Other outcomes of learning

The person is both mind and body, and consequently we have to explore their inter-relationship when we look at the outcomes of learning. Additionally, the person is in the world and so we also have to look at the ways that being in the world brings benefits to our learning and, therefore, to our humanity. It is at this point that we are confronted with a problem: it is easy to equate our learning with our education since this has been traditionally where a great deal of our learning has occurred and then we might suggest that the outcomes of our learning are the outcomes of education, but this is a false equation although we do have to recognise that our learning occurs in a wide variety of social contexts, education being but one of them.

In addition, there is another conceptual problem that requires brief consideration at this point since the person is both mind and body. There may be benefits that are to be acquired from physical activity, which also incorporate a mental dimension, such as the ability and desire to learn, so that learning must be included as an outcome in this discussion, as well as a causal phenomenon. The process is more cyclic than linear. But there is a great deal of research that demonstrates this, some of which I (Jarvis 2001: 119–26) discussed elsewhere and which I wish to revisit briefly here. Because the body and the brain are both physical, the condition of the body impinges on the way that the brain functions, as James and Coyle (1998: 3) show:

> since the brain accounts for some 25 percent of blood circulatory activity (despite representing a far smaller percentage of body weight and tissue) maintenance of cardiovascular fitness, through aerobic exercise, may entertain particular benefits for the brain and hence cognitive processes, including memory. Ivy et al. (1992) review literature that points to reduced blood circulation and deterioration of the blood-brain barrier

with age, both of which may be associated with tissue loss and impaired cognitive functioning.

In a similar manner Gardner makes the point that malnutrition is also associated with 'deleterious consequence for both emotional and cognitive functioning' (1983: 48). Cusack and Thompson (1998) report from a project that they initiated in Vancouver, in which older people were engaged in workshops and games and there was an increase in creativity, optimism, openness to new ideas, willingness to take risks, mental flexibility, willingness to speak their minds, ability to learn new things, memory and confidence that they can remember. There is a considerable amount of research that all points in the same direction. Indeed, Cusack and Thompson conclude that a 'mental fitness course is not a self-indulgent luxury for seniors – it is a critical component for healthy ageing and it is foundational to meaningful intergenerational dialogue and exchange' (1998: 315). Much of this research of the relationship of the body with the brain and the mind is being conducted with older adults, since developments in third age activities provide the opportunity for a great deal of research in this area.[3]

As a result of the project in the United Kingdom on the benefits of learning, Hammond (2004: 37) reports:

> Analyses of the fieldwork data suggest that learning can develop psychosocial qualities – namely self-esteem and self-efficacy, a sense of identity, purpose and future, communication and other competences, and social integration – which promoted well-being, mental health and the ability to cope effectively with change and adversity, including ill-health. Respondents' accounts also indicate which aspects of the learning experience may be important in relation to the promotion of positive health outcomes.

Apart from Hammond's two chapters, Schuller et al. (2004) also point to other social benefits of learning within family and social life,[4] which I will not pursue here since their work is beyond the purview of this chapter.

While there is a great deal of evidence that shows that learning has very positive results on the development of the person, we have to remember that Shakespeare observed that 'Much learning has made you mad', and another common expression is that 'A little learning is a dangerous thing' – producing self-confidence where it should not rightfully occur. Both of these expressions still illustrate that it has been generally recognised that learning has tremendous effects on the person and, occasionally, they might not all be positive. This is just the point that Fromm (1942) was making, which we discussed above, when he pointed to the fear of learning. Even in these instances, however, we must conclude that the outcomes of learning affect a far greater part of human existence than just the cognitive domain, and the cognitive domain is itself affect by other elements of our body. The person is both mind and body.

Conclusion

The changed and more experienced person is the major outcome of learning. We do not teach mathematics or philosophy, but we do teach persons these subjects. We are people who have learned, but more than this, we are the outcomes of our own learning. Our theory of learning must always incorporate the learners since learning is itself an existential phenomenon. We learn throughout the whole of our lives, and so it is to lifelong learning that we turn to for the final chapter in this first section of the book.

Chapter 7

Lifelong learning

We have now reached the point where we can begin to formulate a theory of lifelong learning which will reflect the discussion of the previous six chapters, and the first part of this chapter embarks upon this exercise. The second part examines how the term 'lifelong learning' is being used in contemporary society and highlights its major characteristics. Finally, the two approaches are compared and the reasons for the differences highlighted. In a sense, this prepares the way for the second volume of this work, but before that can be started, we will examine all the other major theories of learning to compare them with this approach to the theory of learning and that will comprise the second section of this book.

Towards a theory of lifelong learning

As we move towards a theory of lifelong learning, we need to examine issues surrounding: the definition, the outcomes, the lifelong journey, the changing person and the way that we interact with our world.

Definitional issues

In order to understand the concept of 'lifelong learning', we need to understand life, lifelong and lifelong learning. Dealing first with 'life': for instance, the desk upon which my computer is placed has existence, but it has no life. Human beings exist in the world – in space – but they have life, they are beings-in-the-world, and our existence is about being-for-itself. That is, we exist of ourselves, we have a sense of self, self-concern and we can reflect upon ourselves. In this sense, we are intelligent beings and our life vibrates with the intention and the capacity to respond to the world in which we are, to adapt to it and also to seek to change it. Life, then, is intelligent existence, about our being, covering the breadth of our being, and so it is almost tautologous to talk about life-wide learning. Life is about being: human being is about learning.

'Lifelong' implies duration – we live in the flow of time and our physical body ages as we journey through time, although our mental capacities may expand for as long as we live. Throughout our lives we have the capacity to learn and without learning it is hard to conceptualise human life as we understand it. Lifelong is about being in time.

Learning, then, is intrinsic to living; it is about the mechanisms whereby the personal dimension of human life changes and as such it is essential to human life itself. It is about the changing person – it is about becoming. 'Lifelong learning' is about being and becoming. We offered a definition of learning in the first chapter and we can now adapt that slightly to define lifelong learning as:

The combination of processes throughout a lifetime whereby the whole person – body (genetic, physical and biological) and mind (knowledge, skills, attitudes, values, emotions, beliefs and senses) – experiences social situations, the perceived content of which is then transformed cognitively, emotively or practically (or through any combination) and integrated into the individual person's biography resulting in a continually changing (or more experienced) person.

At the heart of our being is existence and this precedes our becoming, when our human essence emerges and develops through the processes of learning.

Outcomes of learning

Thus far we have restricted our discussion on outcomes of learning to the way that the individual grows and develops and becomes a person in relationship with others. The interpersonal relationship is crucial to our discussion of this process since we are all participants in mini-social systems of ourselves and our significant others (I↔Thou). If, for a moment, we think of an individual entering an organisation, we know that some people are so malleable that they will just adapt the whole lifestyle, ways of thinking and acting and so on, and become organisation people. They are lost in the totality of the system and it is a similar process in our mini-social systems. Some people are lost within the system, as it were: they appear to lose their freedom as they respond to and identify totally with the demands of the wider entity. It is this that Levinas (1991) calls 'totalised'. There is a sense in which we have to learn to transcend these demands to become ourselves, and Levinas (1991: 36) writes:

> To be I is, over and beyond any individuation that can be derived from a system of references, to have identity as one's content. The I is not a being that always remains the same, but is the being whose existing consists in identifying itself, in recovering its identity throughout all that happens to it.

In a sense, in order to be ourselves we have to learn to exercise our will and transcend the system without destroying it. Levinas (1991: 35) says that we are only free when we know that our freedom is in peril, and that we have to transcend those demands without denying the relationships that make us who we are and which continue to sustain us. Indeed, this is the paradox of relationship – we have to sustain it and yet transcend it at the same time.[1] It is the power of language that helps to sustain this relationship. Within it we can be empowered to reach beyond ourselves and even beyond our own capacity, and this is to reach towards infinity:

> It is therefore to *receive* from the Other beyond the capacity of the I, which means exactly: to have the idea of infinity. But this also means: to be taught. The relationship with the Other, or Conversation, is a non-allergic relation, an ethical relation; but inasmuch as it is welcomes this conversation is a teaching [ensignement]. Teaching is not reducible to maieutics;[2] it comes from the exterior and brings me more than I contain. In its non-violent transivity the very epiphany of the face is produced.
>
> (Levinas 1991: 51; italics in original)

Only in such a relationship we can be free to reach toward infinity – infinity is the absolutely other (Levinas 1991: 49), it is perfection (1991: 41) when there are no boundaries and no limits – it is the realisation of the authentic person. Only in relationship, through learning, can we reach towards the fullness of our humanity. Only in death do we terminate all of these relationships that sustain us in our quest towards infinity. The outcome of all our learning is to continue to reach towards infinity – to the extraordinary in our humanity to which each of the psychological processes of maturation that we detailed in the previous chapters pointed but were never in a position to specify. Even more than this, the infinity beyond our experience lies beyond the finitude of humanity itself, so that the incomplete nature of lifelong learning points us to developments in humanity that still lie beyond our experience, and maybe beyond our imagination.

Hsun Tse (1928: 36, cited in Watkins and Biggs 1996: 32) echoes these sentiments from a Confucian perspective:

> Sincerely put forth your efforts, and finally you will progress. Study until death, and do not stop before. For the art of study occupies the whole of life; to arrive at its purpose, you cannot stop for an instant. To do that is to be a man, to stop is to be a bird or a beast.

All people can achieve sage-hood provided that they do not spare the effort and continue to learn throughout their whole lifespan.

The lifelong journey

Life is a journey and, as we pointed out earlier, our experiences are episodic and we impose meaning on them as we join them together in telling our story. Not every one of those episodes are of equal value to our story, however, since there are some moments that are life-changing. Aslanian and Brickell (1980), having interviewed 744 adult learners, discovered that 83 per cent of them identified life transition as a reason that they returned to learning. Other major events may also have the same effect. Life transition is like a major disjunctural experience which causes learning. Consequently, we need to recognise that some experiences are much more significant in our life stories than others.

But it is no accident that many images of life are of a journey, a journey through time. In order to describe a journey we need landmarks, and perhaps this is what Erikson (1962: 239–66) has tried to give us in his eight ages, shown in Table 7.1.

In these alternatives Erikson is demonstrating to us that the pathway toward to infinite is not without its pitfalls. Indeed, the problems start with the I↔Thou relationship itself – we have to learn trust. Through our experience of others we learn trust or experience mistrust and so on through each of these stages of learning, until towards the end of our lives we have learned to be confident in the paths that we have journeyed through life so that we can reach that stage which Erikson calls 'ego integrity', or despair, which 'expresses the feeling that the time is now short, too short for the attempt to start another life and to try out alternative roads to integrity' (1963: 260).

But many years before Erikson, Confucius depicted lifespan development as a learning process. Learning is not only important for personal development but, like Plato's philosopher-kings, society requires learned people to become officials. All people can learn, everybody is educable irrespective of whatever talents with which they are born; it is the attitude to learning that enables some individuals to grow and develop more than others – more attitude than intelligence, and in this sense Confucius was more prone to argue for nurture than for nature as a basis of achievement (see Lee 1996: 25–41).

Table 7.1 Erikson's eight ages of man

- Basic trust v basic mistrust
- Autonomy v shame and doubt
- Initiative v guilt
- Industry v inferiority
- Identity v role confusion
- Intimacy v isolation
- Generativity v stagnation
- Ego integrity v despair

Others have depicted life's journey in a similar but not, I think so profound a way as either Confucius or Erikson. Sheehy (1995), for instance, depicts the life cycle by ten year shifts and in a very interesting journalistic manner depicts the generations. Levinson *et al.* (1978, Levinson and Levinson 1996) has studied both men and women over specific life periods.

However, as Erikson started with some of the problems of creating relationships, it is Birren (1963) who looked at old age and saw that for some it is a period of disengagement from a rapidly changing social world; it becomes a period when we seek harmony with our environment (Jarvis 1992), when we no longer welcome disjuncture in order to keep on growing and developing. There may be many reasons why those who disengage do so – it may relate to physical incapacity or to mental tiredness or even because few opportunities exist for those who get older, although more opportunities are now emerging for older people to keep on learning, to keep on doing and so on. We came into the world in a physical relationship with our mother and had to learn relationship and trust beyond the physical in our early years, but we leave the world alone when the final I↔Thou is severed when living and learning come to an end.[3]

Interaction with our world

Crucial, then, to our understanding of lifelong learning is the way in which we interact with the world. Much of this lies beyond the scope of this study since it will have become obvious over the foregoing pages that we can never totally understand the processes of human learning and that even to begin to understand it, as I hope we have begun to here, we need to grasp all the sciences and social sciences and it lies beyond anything that we can imagine. In a sense, we cannot totalise our knowledge of learning!

Clearly, the way in which we interact with our world may reflect our genetic constitution or our personality. We have certainly seen how Confucius recognised the significance of will power to keep on learning. Nevertheless, it may be that our approach to our world is more than personality, but method, strategy or style. The strategies or techniques that we use to enhance our learning is something that we want briefly to look at here and some studies of this have been conducted as learning styles – an idea that has become more debateable in recent years. Nevertheless, we will briefly look at learning styles here.

A great deal of work has been undertaken in recent years on learning styles, or strategies of learning, and amongst the leading researchers has been Entwistle (1981) who has both undertaken research himself and has co-operated with Marton, whose work on students making meaning of texts was discussed earlier. Elsewhere (Jarvis 2004) I have summarised some of the styles of learning that have been reported and, for the sake of convenience, I will reproduce and expand that summary here and in Table 7.2.

Table 7.2 Learning styles

Learning style	Comment
Active v passive	Some learners actively initiate the experiences from which they learn – self-directed and autonomous – whilst others are more passive recipients of the social events
Assimilators v accommodators	Those whose dominant learning preference is abstract conceptualisation and reflective observation (assimilators), whilst others prefer to experiment based on concrete experience (Kolb 1984)
Concrete v abstract	Similar to the preceding – some prefer actual situations whereas others abstract, theoretical thought
Converger v diverger	The former is best at abstract conceptualisation, whereas the diverger prefers reflective observation
Field dependence v field independence	The former's perception is dominated by the way that the field is organised, whereas the latter's perception is discrete from the organised background (Wilkin 1971)
Focusing v scanning	The former examine the issue as a whole and then generate hypotheses which can be modified in the light of new information, whereas the later jump to one solution to a problem and assume it to be correct until subsequent information disproves it and then they have to recommence the whole process
Holistic v serialistic	Some learners see the phenomenon as a whole, whereas others string together the parts
Reflection v impulsivity	One who thinks about the whole phenomenon, whereas others jump to a response – the first idea that occurs to them and act upon it (Kagan 1971)
Rigidity v flexibility	Some use the same approach all the time, whereas others are more adaptable

First, research into learning styles has been conducted within formal educational settings when learners undertake prescribed learning tasks. This constitutes a major weakness if the researchers are actually trying to understand strategies that learners adopt in learning projects since they are not isolating them from the power relations of their life-world. Second, we have already limited our discussion of learning styles in another direction – to conscious projects that the learners have themselves undertaken and so, like the research from which the above table emerged, this statement restricts discussion to these active projects. Third, the relationship between style and the way that the researchers viewed learning is itself problematic. If, for instance, Kolb's theory of learning styles is based on his learning cycle –

which it is – and his learning cycle has been shown to be questionable, then his work on learning styles is even more suspect. In addition, little of the research is conducted into learning per se and nor is it conducted with people of all age ranges and experiences. Finally, there are other variables that need analysis if we are ever to reach a position where we can claim to understand styles of learning. Therefore, we can conclude that all of these dichotomous alternatives only relate to certain forms of learning rather than learning per se.

But we have seen that learning is fundamentally about living-in-the-world and interacting with the world.[4] Often we are not the initiators of our learning but others are, and we are recipients of experiences. If we are seeking authenticity and autonomy we are perhaps more likely to initiate our own learning in the world, but if we are inauthentic we may be passive recipients. We may have strategies of action in our planning and then strategies of thinking in our reflection (as we might have strategies of thinking when we respond to others who have initiated interaction with us and it appears that some of the above nine dichotomies confuse action strategy and thinking style) such as reflection versus impulsivity, while others describe personality types, such as active versus passive and still others describe preference in the way the learners think – converger versus diverger.

It would appear, therefore, that these styles of learning have been formulated without having a comprehensive theory of learning, and this has led to an over-simplification of the views about the way that people live in their relation to the world. However, we have already shown that there are a variety of different ways of thinking and we are aware that some people respond to their world differently from others. Consequently, we are coming to the conclusion that the idea of learning styles as formulated by the research reported here does not add a great deal to our understanding of lifelong learning because of the limitations of the thinking of learning in relationship to being-in-the-world. We do recognise that people respond to their world in a patterned manner and that some are more impulsive and others more reflective, but this is more about our living in our world and about our relationship to it in which potential learning experiences occur.

Having reached this conclusion, we also recognise that other scholars have described lifelong learning differently from that which have been discussed here, and so in the next section of this chapter we will examine a selection of writers on the subject and review how they understand lifelong learning.

Lifelong learning: a selection from recent scholarship

The first book on lifelong education was published in 1929 (Yeaxlee), but it was a lot later before adult education and lifelong education actually became significant in social policy terms. Perhaps the first major thrust in this direction occurred in the United States with the ill-fated Mondale Act on lifelong learning. Lifelong learning was being defined at that time as 'a conceptual framework for conceiving, planning, implementing and co-ordinating activities designed to facilitate learning by all Americans throughout their lifetimes' (Peterson *et al.* 1979: 5). While the Act was passed the individual states did not take up their allocated funding in order to implement the policy.

By the mid-1990s, however, policy-makers had brought this concept to the fore and so the European Commission published its White Paper on the learning society in 1995 and initiated the European Year of Lifelong Learning in 1996. By the start of the new century, the European Commission offered the following definition of lifelong learning as 'all learning activity undertaken throughout life, with the aim of improving knowledge, skills and competences within a personal, civic, social and/or employment related perspective' (EC 2001: 9). Strangely enough, this functional European Commission definition was for a form of education that excluded education and training, and higher education, from its policy considerations! Some of the emphases of the EC document, however, reflect those that came form the Organisation for Economic Cooperation and Development which offered the following definition: 'the continuation of conscious learning throughout the lifespan' (OECD 1996: 89). The OECD document recognised the selective nature of any definition given to lifelong learning, and this is clear when we compare the definition offered in the previous part of this chapter to those being offered here. As lifelong learning policy came more to the fore, a great deal of hype surrounded the debates about it (Field 2000: 38) and campaigns to interest more people in lifelong learning were launched by a number of organisations, including the Royal Society of Arts. Another group which was formed to promote lifelong learning was the portentously named World Initiative on Lifelong Learning. Another definition of lifelong learning to appear at this time and associated with the above initiative was that offered by Longworth and Davies (1996: 22):

> Lifelong learning is the development of human potential through a continuously supportive process which stimulates and empowers individuals to acquire all the knowledge, values, skills and understanding they will require throughout their lifetimes and apply them with confidence, creativity and enjoyment in all roles, circumstances and environments.

Here we see the values of the writers being including their understanding of the aims and functions of learning inserted into the definition of learning, which is logically invalid. Other writers on the subject, such as Field, offer no formal definition but Claxton (1999: 6–7) approaches the position adopted in this study when he writes that 'To be alive is to learn', and he points out that learning is not primarily intellectual although we learn many different things. He goes on to discuss all forms of thought and situation in which he illustrates how people can learn in different contexts and in different ways.

Without pursuing the volume of literature and the multitude of definitions that have been offered in the past decade or so about lifelong learning in the final part of this chapter, we will look at the differences in approach that have occurred.

Towards a comparative perspective

From the outset it can be seen that my work has specifically focused on learning, where the word is used as the present participle of the verb 'to learn', which is the most common way of using the term. Many of the other definitions apparently confuse education, as institutionalised learning, with private and personalised learning, but it is technically a different use of the verb. When lifelong learning is used as institutionalised learning, the word 'learning' is used as a gerund or even a gerundive. Gerunds are nouns formed from verbs denoting an action or a state, such as 'the learning', so that lifelong learning can correctly be interpreted as the learning provided throughout the lifespan. Gerundives are adjectives formed from the verbs qualifying the nouns indicating the desirability of the state denoted by the verb, so that lifelong learning, as a term, can here be expressing a desirable state for life – one of learning. In this case, however, it would be rather tautologous, since we have argued in this text that living entails learning. However, the gerundive might be a more appropriate way for us to understand concepts such as the learning society, learning organisation and so on. We will return to this in the next volume. But both of these approaches would be correct usages of the term 'learning', although it is to be doubted whether the sophistication of the latter was deliberately intended when the term was introduced. The question remains, however, what are the reasons why it was introduced in the first place?

There might be many reasons for this: perhaps the first and most obvious is that the term 'education' is restrictive – it has barriers around it and it recognises that learning can still take place beyond it. The use of the word 'learning', however, has no bounds and can refer to any time and any place. In addition, the use of 'learning' overcomes the problematic distinction between education and training that was rather forced and artificial as the knowledge economy emerged. But there is another major reason: since education is institutionalised, it is the responsibility of the State and, perhaps, the employers to provide education, but once the focus is upon learning, then the responsibility rests with the learners. Consequently, the term 'learning' seeks to perform many different functions, although it must be said that it is perhaps not the most ideal word to cover its many functions and there is a tendency through its use to mislead.

In the latter definitions, the breadth of human learning is rarely discussed, perhaps Cell and Claxton being exceptions, so that the types of learning focused upon tend to be very selective. Since the term emerged out of specific socio-economic conditions, it is not surprising that vocational learning tends to predominate in many of the discussions. Indeed, the economic imperative to be competitive underlies the growth in popularity of the term, so that the campaigns to generate more learning should be set within the focus of the need to produce more and flexible workers rather than to produce learned persons. Since lifelong learning is a natural process, the illogicality of having campaigns to produce lifelong learning becomes self-evident, but the logic underlying the campaign is not to produce lifelong learning at all but to produce more interest in learning specific topics or in specified fields – even to produce more involvement in institutionalised learning. Lifelong learning, as a concept, almost tends to be restricted to work-life learning, and this was one of the major criticisms levelled at some of the early thinking within both the EC and the OECD. More recently both organisations have begun to broaden their focus.

It could also be claimed that the focus of my discussion here is philosophical and psychological, but many of the ideas contained in these latter definitions have a greater sociological and moral basis. This is natural since it was the social conditions that gave the impetus for the rise of interest and concern in lifelong learning.

These fundamental differences imply that the social use of the term refers not to learning in the theoretical sense but much more to it in the policy sense. The term 'lifelong learning' has, therefore, assumed a dual meaning – the one relating to the learning that occurs in the social context for vocational and other specified purposes, whereas when it is used more broadly it refers to learning and, ultimately, to the lives of people. It is this latter meaning that is the aim of this volume, although in the next volume we will turn to the sociological and economic trends and the policy and moral issues that stem from it.

Conclusion

In precisely the same way as we have begun to contrast the uses of the term 'lifelong learning', so it is also necessary to examine the different theories of learning and to see how they relate to the theoretical perspective generated here. Consequently, the second, shorter, section of this book examines the different theories of learning in the light of the discussion in the first section. It starts with an examination of the behaviourist theories.

Part II

Towards a comprehensive theory

Chapter 8

Learning and action

If learning is existential, as I maintain, then these processes of learning should be common to all humankind and the different theories and research projects should all fit into a comprehensive theory. The aim of this section is to analyse each of the major theories of learning, highlight some of the strengths and weaknesses of both the research and subsequent analysis and examine the extent to which they can be seen as part of a comprehensive whole.

Broadly there have been four approaches to analysing human learning: behaviourist, cognitive, emotive and experiential. However, it must be stressed that few of the approaches are entirely devoted to a single domain and some, like later Gestalt thinking, were important springboards in the development of learning theory crossing the boundaries from one area to another. For instance, Lewin's approach bridges the Gestalt and the experiential. In the West, the earliest theories of learning were the philosophical analyses of Locke and Hume, while Confucius and his followers were much earlier in the East. Thereafter came the behaviourist, psychological, the emotive and experiential. Each of these contains elements that were discussed in Figures 1.5 and 1.6. However, the experiential model described by me in 1987 and criticised in the opening chapter of this book was a comprehensive model about which Merriam and Caffarella (1991: 257–9) wrote:

> Jarvis' model does deal with learning per se. The thoroughness of his discussion, which concentrates on explaining the responses one can have to experience, is a strength of the model. These responses encompass multiple types of learning and their different outcomes – a refreshingly comprehensive view of learning.

Even so, the model that I have now presented is, I think, much more comprehensive than the one that they discussed. But it is important to discuss the other theories within this framework if we are to test the comprehensiveness of the model presented earlier. This is the intention of the following four chapters, starting with those that emphasise the action component of learning. It is not, however, the aim merely to criticise the theories in a negative manner but to offer an analysis of their strengths and weaknesses from the perspective thus far developed.

We have started this study with the recognition that we do, therefore we are, and it is to doing that we first turn our minds. Learning by doing is something that we have always recognised as a basic way of learning and so this chapter focuses upon different theoretical perspectives that have arisen from learning by doing. Amongst these are behaviourism, the social action theories of Bandura and action learning theories that owe their origin to the work of Revans. Consequently, this chapter has three parts: behaviourism, social learning and action learning.

Behaviourism

Behaviourism is a psychological school that studies the external workings of the human being and of animals, rather than the internal processes. The phenomenon being studied is observable and measurable and, in this positivist age, this might be considered to be one of its strengths. At the same time, it is also a fundamental weakness since not all phenomena that are experienced can be observed or measured and so we must start by pointing out that while behaviourist theories of learning may accurately describe what can be seen and measured, they can in no way measure what actually goes on in the mind. They cannot, therefore, be complete theories of learning. Indeed, they may actually have distorted our understanding of learning by defining it as any more or less permanent change in behaviour as a result of experience. We will return to this definition below.

There have been many behavioural theorists of learning including Pavlov, Thorndike (who was the first researcher to study adult learning and he thought that the adult's ability to learn reaches a plateau at about twenty years of age and later declines: Thorndike 1928), Hull, Watson and Skinner. Between them they produced a number of stimulus and response theories, laws about learning and two widely used major theories: classical and operant conditioning.

Watson (1925) actually introduced the term 'behaviourism' to the vocabulary and was an ardent advocate for it. Thorndike (1913) both worked with the ideas of trial and error and stimulus-response (S-R) learning, and he was an early connectionist. These theories of learning are what psychologists describe as S-R theories and they all argue that scientific research must ultimately be translatable into something that can be observed – and usually measured. They are positivist and quantitative. According to Borger and Seaborne (1966: 68), Clarke Hull (1943, 1952) was the most influential psychologist of S-R theorists. He endeavoured to combine a particular stimulus with one's past experiences and he also recognised that there were other intervening variables in the stimulus, such as habit. He was seeking a broader perspective than the simple S-R model, but he had by no means reached the conclusion that it is the whole person who experiences and learns.

Pavlov (1927) and Skinner (1938, 1953), however, are the best known of the behaviourist scholars. From their work arose two types of theory: classical and operant conditioning. Classical conditioning involves a neutral stimulus – in Pavlov's dog's case it was the sound of the bell – and an unconditioned stimulus, that was the food on which the dog was fed. The dog salivated in response to the food (response) and, at the same time, a bell was sounded (neutral stimulus) just before the food was given (conditioned stimulus). If this procedure is repeated a number of times and thereafter the bell is sounded without the food being given, the dog still salivates (a conditioned response). In other words, the dog has been conditioned to associate the sound of the bell with the food. Considerable research has been conducted on classical conditioning since Pavlov's initial work and it has been replicated with other animals and with human beings, so that we can see that during this process some form of behavioural learning occurs.

Operant conditioning is slightly different. In this case, Skinner was concerned about producing desired behaviour and his work consisted of rewarding the correct response, immediately after its occurrence. Unlike in Pavlov's research, the response is voluntarily emitted by the subject, but only when it is the desired response is it the one rewarded. The reward must follow immediately after the desired response, and it has been found that the subject learns to repeat the desired response voluntarily for as long as it is appropriately rewarded. Significantly in this case, the reward can be other-administered or self-administered: if the former, then it is a technique of control; if it is the latter then it might be either a matter of pleasure or even superstition. In a sense, however, the response precedes the reward, which becomes the stimulus for subsequent behaviour. In this case, the reward (stimulus) is generally referred to as a re-inforcer.

In both forms of conditioning there is an element of control – in the former the experimenter controls the provision of the stimulus and in the latter the experimenter may control the rewards (stimuli for subsequent behaviour). But Skinner (1971) not only recognised it as such, he regarded his work as a 'technology of behaviour'. However, conditioning occurs in all forms of socialisation (Figure 1.5) since the reward for correct social behaviour is for the new member (child, initiate) to be accepted into the group, which produces a feel-good factor, a sense of harmony or belonging.

Borger and Seaborne suggest that from this perspective, learning is 'any more or less permanent change in behaviour which is the result of experience' (1966: 14). That both forms of conditioning achieve the desired results is not disputed here, but what it commonly agreed now is that all learning cannot be reduced to behaviour. Indeed, it is recognised that operant conditioning especially is a common phenomenon and sometimes a useful therapy in contemporary society. Consequently, our problem is not one of validity, it is one of explanation and analysis, and there are at least four areas that demand further discussion: the nature of stimulus, of reward, of method and of definition. Each of these is now discussed.

Stimulus and reinforcement

In Pavlov's experiments we cannot prove that there was only one stimulus for the behaviour since the food was not given to the dog in total isolation. The experimenter was also present. Even if there had been total isolation, that isolation is itself a social situation providing a stimulus other than the food. In addition, the dog did not have all its past memories removed from its mind, so that there was an input, however small, from the dog's mind, which also relates to Hull's point discussed above. While these may not be very pertinent to dogs, they are much more so when human beings are the subjects in which both their social situations and their life histories provide additional stimuli, and so we can conclude that in classical conditioning more than one stimulus might play a role in the learning. This has been recognised by psychologies and is called sensory pre-conditioning (Ormrod 1995: 37–8) in which another neutral stimulus might also be affecting the outcome. This may also account for phobias and so on, since other stimuli might have been learned without being recognised – these are what I have called 'pre-conscious learning' in my own work. Consequently, the subjects' life history and the social situation in which the stimuli occur may also provide additional stimuli by which the intended stimulus is construed and the experience from which the learning occurs transformed.

In operant conditioning, the subjects are freer but they are still people having life histories and they live in social situations. Both of these factors might impinge upon their reasons for acting in the manner that they choose and so it might be over-simple to argue that one form of behaviour, even if it the desired one, has no other cause than that for which the reward is given. It might be argued that even if there are other factors in the life history that are affecting the outcome, this is still a form of operant conditioning since the reinforcer is still operating and has become part of the life history. Unless those other conditions are isolated, however, it is impossible to theorise adequately about the nature of reinforcement. Additionally, it might be argued that individuals sometimes act in the way desired by the provider of the reinforcement because of the power or influence being exercised by the giver of the reinforcement. This would not worry Skinner since he recognised that conditioning is a technique of control.

There is a sense in which we can see that the stimulus is, in fact, an element in creating disjuncture, although it is a limited one and while it can account for the fact that learners move from the flow of time and create an experience, it is insufficiently contextualised to provide some explanation as to why some stimuli might be effective with some learners but not with others, e.g. in non-learning situations. In addition, we have seen that the stimulant provided by the experimenter is only one of a number of contributory factors to the process whereby individuals construct their experiences, even if it is a major one.

Response

Naturally the response has traditionally been seen in behavioural terms, so that the whole of the mind–body problems are assumed and the mind is a redundant concept. But we have shown that it is problematic to try to separate behaviour from the accompanying cognitive dimension, since this demands either that we reject the concept of mind or else we accept a crude dualistic approach to the mind–body problem. Thought always accompanies action, so that the response to every stimulus contains a cognitive outcome as well as the observed response. In addition to the cognitive response, there might well have been attitudinal, values and emotional change and so on, and these cannot always be seen or measured. Indeed, early Greek thinkers placed contemplation, pure thought, amongst the highest forms of learning, but behaviourism cannot account for contemplation. Fundamentally, it is the whole person that changes as the outcome of the learning and this affects future learning experiences, although for the behaviourist the only change that matters is in behaviour. At the same time, in certain therapies it is the behavioural response which is most important and so this might also be regarded as a therapeutic technique, one that it a relevant and actually 'works', but it remains an incomplete theory of learning.

Methodological

Skinner's approach has been described as the 'psychology of the empty organism' (Borger and Seaborne 1996: 77) which incorporates a methodological problem since the emphasis of the approach is based on the behavioural dimension, so that the thought processes are neither considered nor examined. But we are all aware that we think (I am, therefore I think) and so an important variable is omitted from the process. It might be argued that thought is not always an important variable because we usually conform to what is expected of us in social situations – Nietzsche's inauthenticity – but while this may occur in the majority of situations it is certainly not true that it occurs in all of them. Neither was Skinner able to examine situations where the stimulus did not produce the desired outcome, or where the stimulus was itself rejected, since his subjects were mostly animals. However, we do have a sense that we are free to reject a stimulus, to make another choice and so on – but free will is not really taken into consideration in Skinner's research.

Even if the organism is empty, the observed behaviour still needs explanation so that we cannot agree with Skinner (Borger and Seaborne 1966: 78) that his approach is only technique. Data always need interpretation since facts have no intrinsic meaning. Underlying Skinner's work is a philosophy, one that led him to interpret his data in the way that he did. Consequently, we can see that the methods employed in his research are suspect and so we can also doubt the validity of the stated explanations for what he did. But this is not to doubt the data, only his explanation of them.

Definition

The behavioural definition of learning is 'a relatively permanent change in behaviour as a result of experience'. However, this definition is open to a number of criticisms. In the first instance we can see that learning is not the change in behaviour since learning is a process whereas the change in behaviour is the product of a previous process and the process cannot be the same as the product. This is not logically possible.

At the same time, if there is a change in behaviour as a result of an experience, then the whole person has been changed and learning has occurred. Failure to include the whole person in the discussion about learning has meant that behaviourism has always provided an inadequate understanding of the learning process. On at least two counts, therefore, the behaviourist definition of learning is illogical and so it should be rejected, although behavioural learning is not rejected as we pointed out above.

From the foregoing discussion we can see that behaviourism has a number of flaws, which means that the original explanations need further qualification. The behaviourist explanation is valid in some instances within the context of human behaviour, but its weaknesses make it an unacceptable theory of human learning as a whole. Amongst its strengths, paradoxically, are the theories of reinforcement, which help explain why individuals act in the way that they do, but this also takes behaviourist theory into the emotive domain! Nevertheless, in a society that has traditionally demanded measurement it is not surprising that the emphasis on measurable behaviour has meant that it has retained its popularity. Even so, to limit learning in this manner is both to do a disservice to our understanding of human learning and, in my opinion, a disservice to the nature of the human being.

Nevertheless, every element in the behaviourist approach to human learning can be incorporated within the existential model discussed at the outset of this study. For example, the person is in a social situation and receives a stimulus – something that creates a disjunctural situation, which results in an experience. That is transformed, although the only outcomes of the transformation that can be measured are behavioural and, perhaps, the acquisition and reproduction of certain facts. That other outcomes happen has just not been given sufficient consideration in behavioural approaches to learning.

A number of behaviourists studying learning worked with pigeons in pigeon boxes and rats in mazes. Bauman (2002) makes a pertinent observation in which he likens the maze to a miniature replica of the 'big world' in which humans live, although he does not liken the rats to human beings! Indeed, Bauman (2002: 29–30) suggests that:

> Constructors of the maze were 'within reason', or at least not wide of the mark, when they insisted that whatever goes on in the rat's head cannot be established with any degree of certainty, but this is only a minor irritant, since the mysterious things called thoughts and emotions can be left out of account without damage to the precision with which the learning process can be measured and the course of streamlining, regularizing and routinizing the learning creatures' behaviour can be modelled. Taking the shortcut from stimulus to response might be dictated by technical necessity, but no harm is done once the shortcut is taken to be the sole thing which counts as the quantifiable relation between 'input' and 'output'.

This perhaps helps explain why such an incomplete theory of learning still has such currency in contemporary society.

Social learning

The behaviourists who first contextualised their understanding of learning were Miller and Dollard (1941), who claimed that all behaviour is learned in a specific cultural, historical and social context. They claimed that learning involves four factors: drives, cues, response and reinforcement. As we have already seen, the behaviourists fail to see that it is the whole person who learns, but we can see that drives relate to a mixture of motivation and bodily needs that point us towards later developments in learning theory; cues are stimuli in the social context and are in some ways similar to disjuncture, although not as fully formulated; response is what leads to the experience; and reinforcement are the rewards for achieving what is desired. The emphasis in this theory is more on the learner and less on the one who provides the stimulus, so that it can be regarded as a development in learning theory. But this was almost inevitable since the subjects were human beings rather than rats and pigeons, etc.

Perhaps the most common form of social learning is imitation – a behaviourist approach to learning, although one which needs much more than a simple explanation of merely copying behaviour. Another term for imitation is 'modelling', and in sociology the concept of role model has been well developed but without any emphasis being placed on the processes of human learning since the concern is basically fitting into the social institution and successfully performing one's roles. Bandura (1977) has, above all, been the theorist who has produced a conceptual scheme for imitation, or observational learning. Imitation, to be successful, has four stages: attention, retention, motor reproduction and motivation. Once the learner has successfully imitated the other's behaviour, the processes of reinforcement arise so that the more that the learner wants to exhibit that behaviour and the more there is positive reinforcement, the more easily the behaviour is performed. It is within this context that Bandura developed the idea of self-efficacy, which was discussed earlier in this study since it relates to the learners' confidence that they can perform the behaviours that are expected of them or that they expect of themselves. However, if the original desire to behave in a specific manner is lost, or if there is no self-confidence that the behaviour can be performed, then learning may occur without behavioural change and social learning theorists do indeed recognise that learning can occur without a change in behaviour (see Ormrod 1995: 132). Cognition, consequently, plays an important role in learning, although we will discuss cognitive theories in the next chapter. Nevertheless, successful performance of the behaviour increases the learners' sense of self-efficacy so that such behaviour is more likely to be successfully repeated on subsequent occasions. Social learning, as developed by Bandura, is socially and culturally reproductive and the ideas of reflection upon experience, cognition and emotion are not as fully developed since the place of the person was downplayed in this early research.

The theory was developed using observation as a research technique, and Bandura went on to describe the process of memorising in terms of symbolic coding, cognitive organisation and so on, which are not the way that learners would describe their processes of memorisation to a researcher in qualitative research. Consequently, the richness of the human experience is lost, even though these theories of learning are about human learning and about the I↔Thou, although imitation of another's behaviour need not always imply social interaction. Reinforcement of successful behaviour, however, is frequently given by others.

Even so, it can be seen how this theory approaches the model of learning discussed in Figure 1.5 in the first chapter – the learner is in a social situation and receives a stimulus – which might cause a form of disjuncture. The stimulus causes a cognitive and a behavioural response.

Social learning has, as a concept, in more recent years not been widely employed, although it was recognised in the use of informal and non-formal learning and in unintended learning. Even so, the social context played an important role in my initial thinking about learning (Jarvis 1987) when I deliberately set out to undertake a sociological study of adult learning. This approach was, of course, subsequently popularised by Lave and Wenger (1991). Since the early social learning theorists were psychologists, the sociology of learning remained undeveloped until the 1980s, although socialisation and role theory – as sociological concepts – have always included learning within them but have never emphasised it. Hence, we can see once again the need for integrated studies of human learning and how the development of learning theory has been inhibited by the separation of academic disciplines and by the exclusive claims of some psychologists.

It might also be claimed that when we discuss the learning organisation and the learning society we are actually talking about social learning. In one sense this is true, but in another it is manifestly false and misleading. No organisation learns since it does not have a brain, but organisations change. It is possible, however, to adapt the behaviourist definition of learning – a relatively permanent change as a result of experience – to organisational contexts, so that it might be possible to claim that organisational learning is a relatively permanent change in organisational procedures as a result of previous events (experience). Nevertheless, the organisation does not have a conscious experience, but its members do. It is the members' awareness of the inability of the organisation to respond efficiently to contemporary events that provides them with the awareness that the organisation needs to change. If those members are in a position to effect change in the organisation, i.e. they have the power to do so, then they can introduce new procedures and thereby generate the 'relatively permanent change, in behaviour'. If they do not have that organisational power, then the organisational members have to work to persuade others who do that the organisation needs to change, or they fail to generate the necessary changes in procedures that their learning calls for. But in both cases it is the people who are learning and then they are effecting the change.

Organisations, and societies, tend to generate procedures that members follow and when they have learned the procedures they can act in a taken-for-granted manner, what I called 'presumption' in the first chapter. Both organisations and societies, by virtue of the fact that they do tend to introduce procedures actually means that their smooth functioning has been based on the assumptions that their members do not continue to learn once they have learned the established rules, norms and mores. Organisations are, therefore, premised on non-learning. Learning societies and organisations have, however, loosened their procedures and control mechanisms in such a way as to enable their members to act more upon their own learning and become more flexible performers. It is also recognised that this need to change introduces elements of risk that led Beck (1992) to write about the risk society, and management theory to recognise that unsuccessful innovations are natural but innovation itself is essential if organisations are to survive in contemporary society. In this sense, learning organisations are more open and flexible and this leads to greater job satisfaction for their members.[1] People working within these contexts are learning in their work place, something which has become a major focus for learning theory and practice in recent years, and we will return to this theme in the second volume of this study, but we can see that their learning is situated with their actions or behaviour.

However, openness and flexibility, or even changed organisational procedures, are not actually learning.

Action learning

'Learning by doing' has always been a common sense maxim and the apprenticeship model of training was based on this basic assumption about learning. In addition, it is hardly surprising in a society which emphasises practical knowledge, such as late modern society, that action learning has become a major focus in writing about learning. Despite its title, action learning is not the same as learning by doing. Action learning is more than learning by doing, it is about learning by doing and learning from doing within a specified social context with a support group, or set, which helps members engage in reflection upon their actions.

According to McGill and Brockbank, action learning may be described as 'a continuous process of learning and reflection that happens with the support of a group or "set" of colleagues, working on real issues, with the intention of getting things done' (2004: 11). This is a tautologous description of a process that owes its origins to a number of different sources. In the first instance, in the United Kingdom, Revans (1980, 1982) developed some of these ideas in his management training programmes in which he developed his famous formula $L = P + Q$ (where L = learning, P = programmed knowledge gained and Q = questioning insights). However, his work was subsequently enhanced by Schön's (1983) work on reflective practice and Kolb's (1984) work on experiential learning. However, this is a theory that reflects the emphasis placed on small groups in industry and commerce during this period.

The distinguishing feature of action learning is the provision of time that members of a group make to engage in a supportive set reflecting upon their own learning. In the early days of action learning, I had a student working with me who was both facilitating and researching a small law practice. The practice partners decided that they had to expand their expertise as a group and each of the participating partners opted for a new area of law that they would each learn, and then they would regularly meet to report on their learning process and enable each to reflect on their learning. The idea was that by the end of the period they would have expanded the areas of law that their practice could offer and it would have been done through mutual support and encouragement, helping each other to reflect on the way that their studies were developing and suggest further developments that were necessary. From the outset, the group of partners decided that they would meet regularly to report and support each other over a calendar year. Unfortunately, because it was a small practice, the intentions of this action learning set were never fulfilled because the demands of the practice prevented them giving the time either to engage fully in their studies or in meeting regularly throughout the year. While this was unfortunate, it was a way in which a small action learning set could function within a legal practice to enhance the work of the practice, but it also points to the fact that as a technique it is time consuming.

In this sense, action learning is simply a process of learning and, as such, it fits easily into the model of learning discussed at the outset, although the person is clearly not the focus of attention but the new behaviour learned is, even though this behaviour might be skills or cognitions or both. The point of the process is that the life-world – the support set – plays a more significant role than in some other theories in helping the learners to reflect upon their learning. We will explore the dimensions of reflection a little more in the following chapter, but we can see that as learning theory has developed, so it has combined the three dimensions of behaviour, cognition and emotion. The 'action' in action learning is not quite the same as in behaviourism, but it refers to the outcomes of the learning – the problems solved, the skills gained, or the actions undertaken and so on, that are developed as a result of the learning. It is still instrumental learning in the same way as is behaviourism, but it is much broader because involving the members of the set – usually a group of individuals who are working together, respecting each other as whole people and supporting each other in their endeavours. Different theorists of action see the learning component of action learning differently, depending on their own understanding of learning. Marsick and O'Neil (1999) suggest that action learning falls into three schools:

- *Scientific method*, which reflects Revans' own background as a physicist and this had three stages: understanding the system within which the problem resides, negotiating and implementing a solution against a background of scientific method (hypothesis, experiment, solution), and then the learners check reality against their way of seeing the world.
- *Experiential*, being based on Kolb's learning cycle; see the opening chapter of this book.
- *Critical reflection*, based on the work of Argyris and Schön, Habermas and others who have understood learning from within the critical reflection paradigm, which we discussed earlier.

In fact, any approach to learning could fit within the framework of action learning and the handbooks about its practice (McGill and Beaty 2001; McGill and Brockbank 2004) are, to a considerable extent, handbooks about successful facilitation of the support group and the advantages of using small groups in this way. Certainly, McGill's works reflect the experiential learning approach, which is to be expected since his and his co-authors' concerns are about the development of the whole person through the group involvement and reflect Figure 1.6.

Action learning is pragmatic and instrumental in its formulation, although in the experiential approach espoused by McGill and his co-authors it is possible to see broader aspects of human learning than those that would fit easily into a traditional management training programme. While this approach provides a wide framework within which learning theories will fit, it actually adds nothing to the theory of learning per se since it is much more a method of learning effectively than it is about the learning process. Its strength, however, lies in the group support which provides assistance with the processes of reflection (in the same ways as other small group teaching might do) and a powerful motivating factor in a sustained learning project.

Conclusion

This chapter has incorporated the idea that learning is about a relatively permanent change in behaviour as a result of experience, even though the final set of theories that we have discussed are not necessarily behaviouristic. At the same time, the intention is 'to get things done' (McGill and Brockbank 2004: 11) so that it is a behavioural change. But learning might also be described as a relatively permanent change in knowledge as a result of experience, and so in the next chapter we will explore the cognitive basis of some of the theories of learning in which learning might be described as a relatively permanent change in cognition as a result of experience.

Chapter 9

Cognitive theories

Cognitivism is not only a set of theories about how people learn, it is also about how they think (Winch 1998: 63). Hence, we discussed how people think quite extensively in Chapter 5. This is a major part of the learning process and we now return to cognitive theories of learning. But in resticting learning to the cognitive domain as some psychologists did, they unintentionally did a disservice to the wider understanding of human learning. Cognitivism is:

> a solitary and a social theory of learning *par excellence*. Modern cognitivism holds that individual brains, acting as solitary units from birth, possessed of representational structures and transformation rules, and receiving 'input' from the exterior, can account for the way in which we learn.
>
> (Winch 1998: 46)

In this description we can see a number of reasons why we should reject the crude cognitive approach to learning: first, it isolates the individual from the social; second, it identifies the body/brain with the mind – which we rejected in Chapter 2; it assumes an innate structure within the brain which allows it to receive direct information in representational form, which is contrary to our argument depicted in Figure 1.5. Such an approach enables cognitivists to restrict their definition of learning to the process whereby the internal representations more clearly reflect the reality of the external world that they depict. There are many other types of learning as we have seen.

Nevertheless, it is perhaps natural that the early philosophers of learning, Confucius in the East and Locke, Hume and Rousseau in the West, should have restricted their thinking about learning to the cognitive. But as they wrote in pre-modern times, some of their emphases have been downplayed and so the nature of the person and the place of the body in learning has not played such a significant part, and a major purpose of this study is to locate learning within the wider framework of the person-in-the-world.

Clearly, then, the classical cognitivists', such as Chomsky and Fodor, approach to learning is not in accord with the understanding of the human being espoused here and, following Winch's (1998) argument, once we have rejected their philosophy of the person the remainder of their discussion about learning is difficult to accept. We are not restricting the use of the term 'cognitive' to the way that the cognitivists use it, but rather we are employing it to refer to the whole domain where thought plays a significant, but not exclusive, role in the processes of learning. We will examine a number of theories which are more concerned with the process – from boxes 1 → 2 through box 3 and on to box 6 (Figure 1.6). Amongst the cognitivists that we are going to look at include: Confucian philosophy, gestalt psychology, the cognitive developmental theorists, Vygotsky, Engeström, Marton and his colleagues, Robert Gagné, Argyris and Schön, Mezirow and a very brief look at the work of Wildermeersch. Our concern is to examine their strengths and weaknesses and to relate their work to the model that I have suggested.

Confucian philosophy

In different parts of this book we have made the occasional reference to Confucian philosophy and the Chinese learner, and if we were to take the impression Western educationalists seem to have of learners from Confucian heritage countries (CHC), it would be of them seeking to memorise the learning material with which they have been presented – a form on non-reflective learning – and reproducing it. But a paradox then arises because, while Westerners seem to be critical of the approaches of students from CHC countries, they actually score better on many tests of learning than Western learners.

A great deal of recent work on Chinese learning points to the fact that it is true that Chinese learners seek to memorise what the teacher has taught, but the process is much more profound than this. Zhu (Chu 1990: 135, cited by Lee 1996: 35–6) wrote:

> Generally speaking, in reading we must first become intimately familiar with the text so that its words seem to come from our own mouths. We should then continue to reflect on it so that its ideas come from our own minds. Only then can there be real understanding. Since, once our intimate reading of it and careful reflection on it have led to a clear understanding of it, we must continue to question. Then there might be additional progress. If we cease questioning, in the end there will be no additional progress.

Memorising, understanding, reflecting and questioning are, according to the above quotation, the four components of learning. Elsewhere, Lee (1996: 36) cites Wang Yangming (cited by Chiang 1924: 87):

If you simply want to memorize, you will not be able to understand; if you simply want to understand, you will not be able to know the sources [of truth] in yourself.

For Wang, then, we can see that memorising, understanding and incorporation into one's own biography are the three significant components of learning. Drawing these two formulations together we see that within Confucian thinking memory, understanding, reflecting, questioning and incorporating into the person are some of the constituent elements of learning. However, learning is not totally cognitive for, as Kyung points out, 'For Confucius, learning is a lifelong effort . . . for forging a morally excellent life and . . . becoming a virtuous person' (2004: 117), but learning cannot be limited to book learning.

It will be noted, however, that learning is never separated from the social situation and in both of the above quotations learning occurs in the context of teaching, and this in a society where the teacher had a high status and the dominant teaching method was didactic. Consequently, all of these formulations include – whether implicitly or explicitly – the social situation and with it a dimension of power. Hence, being able to recall and understand the teaching of the master was the 'correct' approach to learning, and only after having understood what the master taught was the learner in a position to reflect and question.

It could be argued, however, that the act of memorisation itself actually deepens understanding and this is precisely what Marton and his colleagues (1996: 69–83) discovered. As they recognised, deepening understanding through repetition is not new. But deepening understanding is still learning at a deeper level about what others have selected as the content of the learning programme. In addition, repetition does not always lead to deeper understanding – there are occasions when the main outcome is merely remembering the same words better. Nevertheless, Simpson (1995: 58) points out, the repetition also brings about self-development, which is a major element in Confucian thinking about education. Repetition might bring about self-development, but it can also lead to the ritualised process of just repeating the words in a meaningless way – as Merton suggested and we discussed elsewhere (see also Jarvis 1992).

I want to suggest that the references to reflecting and questioning in the above quotations are exhortations to think in different ways, as we discussed in Chapter 5. Questioning before memorising was perhaps not socially or politically correct and in a sense, therefore reflecting and questioning before memorising might be something that students from CHC countries need a license to do. But we should also recognise that memorisation does not imply agreement with what is written, and Zhu states quite categorically that we should not take for granted that what we read is correct.

Confucius recognised difference in ability between people, claiming that there are four different types of people: those born with knowledge; those who attain it through study; those who turn to study as a result of being vexed with difficulties; and those who make no effort to study (Lee 1996: 28, from *The Analects*[1]). In this sense Confucius is not discounting intelligence, but Lee says that Confucius disclaimed membership of the first group for himself. However, it does not matter how they learn, the knowledge is still the same[2] and all can learn if they are willing to exert the effort to do so – all people are educable and 'anyone can become a sage' (Mencius, cited in Lee 1996: 29). In this sense, Confucius may be seen as falling on the nurture side of the nature/nurture debate.

The motivation for learning is not included in either of the above statements, but Confucian philosophy is replete with references to this. In *The Analects* we read: 'Is it not pleasant to learn with a constant perseverence and application?' (Lee 1996: 27). Or, as we read in *The Great Learning (IV)*,[3] a person should 'cultivate himself, then regulate the family, then govern the state, and finally lead the world into peace' (cited in Lee 1996: 37). Elsewhere in *The Analects*, we also find that individuals are instructed to learn 'for the sake of the self, [so] that a person has good grounding upon which to become a noble or superior person' (Kyung 2004: 120). Here we see that the outcomes of the learning are incorporated into the learners' own biographies and the person is developed. It is significant that Confucian philosophy recognises that learning is an individual act and, despite the emphasis on community and family in Eastern thought, the significance of the individual self and its development is clearly recognised.

These descriptions of learning from the Confucian tradition combine a social philosophy with basic psychological truisms about learning, but they recognise that the learners are changed and developed as they go through the cognitive learning process and in this sense they locate learning in the person.

It appears that the approach to learning stemming from the CHC falls comfortably within the cognitive framework, but the difference between my model and the Confucian thinking lies at the start of the learning process. But I think that that can be reconciled when we recall that Confucian thinking, like Engeström's located learning within an institutionalised social framework – this time learning from the teacher. The teacher must be respected and his teaching properly understood. But that teaching might, in itself, be disjunctural and lead to questioning. Clearly, in Confucian thought there are some fundamental points about the human person, although these are much more social than metaphysical and the concept of experience is not discussed. Nevertheless, there are no major disagreements between this approach and the geneal model in the opening chapter that cannot be accounted for.

Gestalt theories

Gestalt psychology bridges research with animals to other forms of learning. Amongst the most famous researchers were Wertheimer, Köhler and Koffka. Ormrod (1995: 165–8) suggests six basix tenets to gestalt:

- the perception may be different from the reality;
- the whole is more than the sum of the parts;
- the organism structures and organises experience;
- the organism is predisposed to organise and structure experiences in particular ways;
- learning follows the law of Prägnanz;
- problem solving involves restructuring and insight.

Gestalt is very important to our understanding of many approaches to learning, and we can fit it neatly into Figure 1.6 inasmuch as we have seen how we do not perceive the external world like a camera but that we construct our experiences according to previous learning and in accord with our memories of previous events. Underlying Werthheimer's (1912) early work was insight into the relationship between perception and reality, and also the realisation that many people perceive the whole even if they do not actually examine each aspect. Consequently, we see patterns and relate elements of the whole so that we impose some form of 'meaning' upon a reality. Hence, the law of proximity suggests that we relate elements of the whole according to the distance they are from each other, and the law of closure suggests that we complete incomplete wholes, so that if we are given a picture which has three drawings, each of three lines that could be three sides of a square, we will 'see' the picture as forming three squares. It is from these basic premises that we have experiences which we then transform and store in our memories, so that the basis of the law of Prägnanz is that we organise our experiences in the simplest and yet most complete way that we can and that we continue this process during memorisation. Consequently, we remember 'wholes' and even over-simplify what we remember, so that there is a tendency to remember the regular and transform the irregular into more regular forms.

However, it was Köhler's (1925) famous research projects with an ape, Sultan, that are perhaps the most well known pieces of research from the gestalt schoool. The ape was able to use his memory to construct primitive instruments (from sticks) that enabled him to solve problems, such as getting fruit from beyond his reach that lay just outside of his cage.

These early gestalt theories actually help us to understand aspects of experiential learning and fit them into the model of learning that we have produced in the first part of this book.

Cognitive developmental theorists

As we saw in Chapter 5, cognitive development has formed a major focus for psychological study (Selman 1980; Piaget 1929; Fowler 1981; Kohlberg 1986) and we now briefly return to these stage theories. Each of the theories mentioned here are about how we think rather than how we learn, even though we have claimed that the cognitive development that occurs does so as a result of previous learning and experience rather than being age related. However, Piaget and other developmental theorists place considerable emphasis on biological age because there is a tendency to confuse the natural biological process of development with the cognitive one. Moreover, since they have not taken the wider world into their reckoning, they are not in a position to discuss the place of experience in learning, nor are they able to recognise the effect of the wider world on the development of the individual. Vygotsky's own criticism of Piaget is:

> If we were to summarize the central flaws in Piaget's theory, we would have to point out that it is reality and the relations between the child and reality that are missed in his theory. The process of socialization appears as direct communication of souls, which is divorced from the practical activity of the child. The acquistition of knowledge and logical forms are considered as products of the adjustment of one set of thoughts to another. The practical confrontation with reality plays no role in this process. If left to himself, a child would develop only dilirious thinking. Reality would never teach him any logic.
>
> (Vygotsky 1988: 51–2)

If cognitive development is a natural process, then the relationship between persons and their life-world is insignificant so that, while we can have some sympathy with the stages in cognitive development per se, we can see that this approach to learning is incomplete compared to my model in which the person is located within the life-world. Moreover, this omission removes a major reason for learning – to understand the world and when there is disharmony between the biography and the life-world to re-establish that harmony.

One developmental theorist who is aware of the significance of feedback to move people between their levels of learning is Bateson (1972), initially a physical scientist who became increasing involved in philosophical and interdisciplinary research. His work is discussed quite fully by Illeris (2002). Basically, Bateson postulates five levels of development, which he calls 'zero learning and levels 1 to 4':

- *Zero learning*: broadening our range of habitual responses.
- *Level I*: we learn about our habitual responses but nothing else changes.

- *Level II*: we learn about contexts, so that we change the process of learning, so that we are either involved in context or process reflection.
- *Level III*: major perspective transformations.
- *Level IV*: are changes that Illeris (2002) suggests probably do not occur in any human organism and so we need not consider this level further.

The middle three stages are the most significant for human learning. In order to move from one level to the next it is necessary to use feedback to transcend the conditions of the current level (Illeris 2002: 53). Feedback is used in this study (see Chapter 1) as the mechanism in human interaction whereby the learners are able to assess the extent to which their learning enables them to be 're-integrated'; from the state of disjuncture into society having learned the correct or an acceptable answer to the disjunctural problem.

It will also be recalled that Piaget's research samples were very small; too small to allow for generalisation. Indeed, they were also culture-specific, so that the type of developmental theory posed by Western researchers needs to be tested in non-Western cultures. Nevertheless, there has been a tendency in Western education, having accepted the Piageian approach, to assume that there is a correct time to teach children certain subjects – indeed, my own Masters degree dissertation was based on such an assumption – but this has subsequently proved to be an incorrect assumption.

Thus we can see that the omission of the social in these developmental stage theories demonstrates the flaws in them as learning theories. The models suggested in Chapter 1 enable us to see the weaknesses in these these theories, and now we turn to Vygotsky who, as we have seen, was well aware of Piaget's work.

Lev Vygotsky

In contrast to the above theorists, Vygotsky was 'the first modern psychologist to suggest the mechanisms by which culture becomes a part of each person's nature' (Cole and Scribner 1978: 6). Basically, then, Vygotsky would accept the first part of the model, that individual selves are always located in their life-world and that in early childhood it is the interaction between the child's own internal thought (egocentric language) and practical activities that help to shape the mind. In other words, in contrast to Piaget, 'things do shape the mind' (Vygotsky 1988: 39).

Vygotsky's own research was with learning in early childhood, and there is a sense in which his concerns were with the way that children developed in relation to their capacities to learn. In *Thought and Language* (1988), for instance, we see the careful studies that he conducted to examine the development of both thought and language and the relationship between them. He highlights the processes that we alluded to in Figure 1.5. However, this process can be enhanced though interactions with more advanced individuals (I↔Thou), and this is important to his understanding of learning.

Even so, Vygotsky started with reference to an S-R model of learning and maintained that there was not a direct relationship between the stimulus and the response but that there is mediation between them. This mediation occurs through two instruments: tools and signs. Tools are the means of mastering nature, e.g. he (1978: 53) suggests that 'the tongue is the tool of thought', whereas signs are the instruments of psychological activity, i.e. they are the auxiliary means of solving given psychological problems – remembering, choosing and so on (1978: 52). These may be subsumed under the concept of mediating activities, and it is here that Vygotsky incorporates culture into his understanding of the learning process. This is precisely the same type of approach as we have suggested in Figure 1.5 when we suggested that children's learning involves the transformation of sensations.

Vygotsky (1978) then asked a fundamental question about the relationship between learning and development. He suggested that at the time when he was writing there were three suggested answers to that question:

- Child development is independent of learning since the latter is an external process not actually involved in development but it utilises its achievements.
- Learning is development.
- The third response simply combines the other two but, ultimately, the two do not coincide.

Vygotsky rejects all three approaches and concludes that the developmental process lags behind the learning process and the fact that it does results in the zone of proximal development. Learning and development are related from the first day of life and as chldren grow they may reach actual developmental levels, but it is only when they are at school that their potential level of development becomes apparent. Vygotsky (1978: 85) observes that:

> Over a decade even the profoundest thinkers never questioned the assumption (that given assistence from teachers children can solve even more problems); they never entertained the notion that what children can do with assistence of others might be in some cases more indicative of their mental development than what they can do alone.
>
> (my italics)

It is this difference that Vygotsky described as 'the zone of proximal development'. The zone is an area where the children meet with the more advanced and more logical adult and in so doing they can reach beyond the limits of their own capacities. In this sense, Vygotsky was more concerned with the future than the past, with potential than with achievement, which can be achieved by tutoring or mentoring and so on. One of the problems with this formulation, however, is that it allows for a teacher-centred and teacher-controlled education which is contrary to a great deal of Western thought, although it would find some sympathy with Confucian thinkers who emphasised memorising the master's teaching as the first stage of learning.

He recognised that in order to gain a full understanding of this zone it is necessary to re-evaluate the role of imitation in learning theory. He suggested that by imitation children can achieve beyond the limits of their own capabilities. Finally, he argued that support mechanisms should be provided for children to grow and develop within their zone of proximal development – these he called 'scaffolding'. As children achieve this additional growth, then the scaffolding can be gradually removed.

Basically, we can see that the strengths of Vygotsky's innovative work lies in his recognition that the individual person always functions within a wider social context and that learning is also future-orientated, both of which are in accord with our models of learning in the opening chapters. While Vygotsky clearly studied the cognitive processes, he never neglected the practical, although emotion plays a less significant role. He also concluded, for instance, that 'play provides a much wider background for changes in needs and consciousness' (1978: 102) in the process of development.

Clearly, Vygotsky was influenced by the context within which he worked and so it is not surprising that his concern was with the way that the individual was shaped by the wider world, reflecting Marx's own thinking about the structures of society and the place of the individual within them. Having adopted such a social psychological orientation, it is not surprising that his work was well received in USSR. In addition, the interdisciplinary nature of his thinking is in accord with the models of learning developed here. While Vygotsky was able to expand our understanding of childhood learning, and indeed expand psychological thinking itself, through the perspective he adopted his work on learning would have been enriched had he been able to examine the development of the person in the process of learning. Nevertheless, it is unfortunate that for many years few scholars who in the West were sufficiently knowledgeable in Russian to be able to read his work, but there is one Finnish scholar who has been greatly influenced by his work, and so we will briefly examine the work of Engeström now.

Yrjö Engeström

Engeström (1987, 1990) has taken, not uncritically, the work of Bateson and Vygotsky and combined aspects of both and fitted these into his own theory of activity – which in itself relates back to Vygotsky's ideas on mediated learning. For Engeström, however, activity has three major elements – instruments, rules and division of labour – which are always socially located.

His model of society has a Marxist basis and it is of a consumer society controlled by production, distribution and exchange, which he has always depicted as four equilateral triangles within one large equilateral triangle (see Figure 9.1).

Consumption forms in middle triangle and production, distribution and exchange the corner ones. The three elements of human activity he locates at the corners of the large triangle, so that the instrument and production go together, the distribution and the division of labour, as do the exchange and the rules. Engeström's own Marxist background is clearly evident within this framework. One of the strengths of the model is that he never discusses human activity outside of the social context within which it occurs – a weakness being that his is a rigid and perhaps over-simplified Marxist perspective. I would not, however, dispute the theoretical orientation, although I feel that the formulation needs more justification than Engeström has been prepared to give it here, although his triangular model is now widely recognised and accepted. We will return to it in the second volume of this work.

Engeström recognises that the relationship between individual and societal development is a major problem, as is the one between learning and development itself – a point discussed above by Vygotsky. Contrary to Vygotsky, however, Engeström concludes that 'Learning is not only a necessary precondition of development – development is also a necessary and always present ingredient of learning' (1987: 157). He suggests that there are two types of development: transitions between the levels of learning (building on Bateson) and from operations, to actions and to their activity.

However, it is necessary to understand that for Engeström (1987: 124ff.), learning activity has three elements:

- Human learning necessarily begins in the form of learning operations and learning actions.
- Learning activity has an object and systematic structure of its own and it mediates between social institutions.

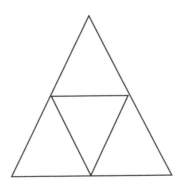

Figure 9.1 The four equilateral triangles.

- The essence of learning activity is production of objectively, societally new activity structures.

For him, learning activity is mastery of expansion from actions to new activity. Engeström says 'learning activity is an *activity-producing activity*' (1987: 125).

From this discussion it is clear that Engeström restricts his discussion of learning to institutional frameworks: school, work and art and science. It is within these institutions where the three elements of consumer society – production, distribution and exchange – operate, and where individuals are exposed to the skills (he talks of handicrafts), power and ceremonies of social living. From this exposure, three learning actions are generated: imitation, memorising and trial-and-error learning. However, his claim that learning necessarily generates learning activities is too deterministic. In addition, while individuals function within social contexts, there is still the possibility of pure thought and, therefore, contemplative or meditative learning – but Engeström does not discuss this. From these basic approaches to learning, through activities learners are necessarily driven into double-bind situations, which I have called 'disjunctural', and in attempting to solve these the learners are driven to higher levels of learning and, therefore, to expansion through new activities.

Finally, in adopting the idea of the zone of proximal development, Engeström necessarily limits learning to the institutional sites that he has suggested which, to my mind, is too narrow. Nevertheless, it is within these institutional structures that the zone of proximal development is apparent. The zone of proximal development is the zone through which learners may develop, given the necessary institutional support, so that they can acquire new skills through interaction and teaching until they have achieved conscious mastery of the topic. Engeström (1987: 174) finally defines zone of proximal development as:

> The distance between the present everyday actions of the individuals and the historically new form of social activity that can be collectively generated as a solution to the double bind potentially embedded in everyday actions.

There is considerable similarity here between his idea of a social location in which individuals' zone of proximal development may be experienced and the idea of the learning organisation or even the learning community.

Like Vygotsky, Engeström's understanding of learning omits the person and he limits his discussion of the wider life-world within which the person lives. Learning is an impersonal process, almosy like a sophisticated cog in a very complex machine. In this sense, I find the formulation too narrow although very insightful. He overcomes the problems of Piaget and other biologically orientated stage theorists, and he combines the cognitive and the behavioural. Like many theorists of learning, the emotions do not play a large role in his thinking. Overall, his approach does nothing to contradict the overall model of human learning with which we began this study – indeed, it can be assessed from within that theoretical framework.

Ference Marton and colleagues

Like the previous theorists discussed, Marton and his colleagues have under-taken their work within the education institution and have, therefore, con-fused it in some ways with teaching. Hence, we can see that they are open to some of the same problems that we discussed when we looked at Confucian philosophy.

Marton and his colleagues are clearly not interested in the transformation of sensations into conceptions (Figure 1.5), but they are interested in what happens thereafter. In fact, Dahlgren defines learning thus: 'To learn is to strive for meaning, and to have learned something is to grasp its meaning' (1984: 23–4). Immediately we see that learning is regarded as a cognitive process and that the other senses are not central to their thinking. Säljö discovered that his subjects had five different conceptions of learning:

- a qualitative increase in knowledge;
- memorising;
- the acquisition of facts, methods, etc. which can be retained and used as necessary;
- the abstraction of meaning;
- the interpretative process aimed at understanding reality.

(Marton and Säljö 1984: 52)

In a sense, this relates to the different routes through the learning process that I discovered in my original work (Jarvis 1987) since I think that for everybody learning is a multifaceted process. Through further analysis Marton and Säljö suggested that the first two of these approximated to what they called 'the surface approach, while the latter two were 'the deep approach'. They merely say that the third one is the dividing line between the two, rather than that it is a fundamentally different approach to learning.

Indeed, in their early work Marton and Säljö (1984) studied the way that students learned from reading a text. Through quite rigorous empirical analysis of interview data following the reading, they showed that students used either the surface approach or the deep approach to seeking to understand what they were reading. They wrote (1984: 40):

The first way of setting about the learning task was characterized by a blind, spasmodic effort to memorize the text; these learners seemed, metaphorically speaking, to see themselves as empty vessels, more or less to be filled with the words on the pages. In the second case, the students try to understand the message by looking at the relations within the text, or by looking for relations between the text and its underlying structure.

Methodologically, like my research, they relied on data being presented to them by the learners and thus far in their work we see a rather limited cognitive approach to understanding learning, conducted with considerable rigour, but without reference to the personhood of the learners or to their experience. But later, Marton and Booth see learning 'in terms of the experience of learning, or learning as coming to experience the world in one way or another' (1997: 33). This is a major shift in Maron's thinking, for now the emphasis is on the experience as well as the cognition. It also reflects the emphasis on experience in learning which had grown quite considerably during the previous decade, and their approach is very much in accord with the work that I (Jarvis 1987) produced. Since they were coming from a cognitivist background, however, it is now important to see how they deal with the issue of experience. By this time, also, they had extended their typology of learning: increasing one's knowledge, memorizing and reproducing, applying, understanding, seeing something in a different way, changing as a person. The first three refer to surface learning or reproduction and the latter three to deep learning or meaning-seeking, which is similar to my six types of learning categorised as non-reflective and reflective (discussed fully in Chapter 1). Despite including the person in their types of learning and discussing the experience of learning, there is still no reference to the selfhood of the learners.

Marton and his colleagues have been consistent in their focus on the cognitive route and in their study of *Memorizing and Understanding* (Marton *et al.* 1996) they looked at the effects of Chinese learners seeking to memorise what they had been taught. They discovered that repetition was not only a matter of repeating the same words over again, but that during the process the learners actually discovered new meanings. They (1996: 81) acknowledge that discovering new meaning through repetition is not new and go on to cite their own and other research reaching back to 1976. However, for meditation and contemplation, analytical thought and so on, this has been a truism for centuries (see also Simpson 1995). Indeed, it has often been said that you can have 50 years of experience or one year of experience 50 times! However, what they have done here is to demonstrate empirically with the learners that they studied how their new knowledge was discovered. Whether this constant repetition is an effective and efficient use of the time, however, is another question (see Simpson 1995; Jarvis 2005).

Marton and Booth (1997) do focus on the social context within which the learning occurs; they write that we both experience the whole context and those elements of it upon which we focus in relation to the whole. For them, awareness is the world as experienced by the person (1997: 108). But this is to confuse two concepts awareness and experience – awareness is much more psychological, while experience is both phenomenological and psychological – and this we discussed quite fully in Chapter 4. Marton and Booth recognise the attractiveness of the phenomenological approach but then introduce us to the idea of phenomenography – this is the study of the way in which we experience something, and so they avoid actually seeking to understand the effects of the learning experience itself on the person of the learner.

Having critically examined the work of Marton and his colleagues, we can see that while it is empirically very thorough, it is constrained by cognitivism. While it tries to reach out to the wider world though their recognition of awareness and experience, they really have still failed to examine the person who is the learner and therefore their understanding of learning is still quite narrow. We can trace their route through our diagram, but it does not tell us the whole story of human learning.

Robert Gagné

Like many psychologists, Gagné's (1977) approach to learning comes through teaching, or in his case instruction, which is his major concern. But also like Marton and his colleagues, Gagné is not concerned with the person of the learner, although he is concerned with attitudes and skills, as well as knowledge. He also is a stage theorist, holding that there are seven levels in the hierarchy and an eighth form of learning that can occur anywhere along it. These levels are:

- Signal learning – (which can occur anywhere)
- Stimulus-response (S-R)
- Motor chaining
- Verbal chaining
- Multiple discrimination
- Concept learning
- Rule learning
- Problem solving.

Signal learning is the one which Gagné claims can occur at any level of the hierachy and this reflects Figure 1.5, which I called 'the transformation of sensations', which are basically into knowledge and attitudes – signals that affect the way that the person responds to experiences. Experience, however, is a concept not discussed by Gagné, although he and his colleagues are concerned about the situational factors that affect learning (Gagné et al. 1992).

S-R is the same as operant conditioning, while he places motor and verbal chaining on the same level and they are the same as the two non-reflective learning courses that I discussed in my earliest work on learning (Jarvis 1987). Thereafter, we see Gagné examing intellectual skills in discussing two abilities: those of making choice and classification, discrimination and concept learning. These are about reflective learning but stangely we find nothing about sophisticated skills learning. Rule learning is basically learning the procedures, or being able to generalise from the specific, and finally problem solving is his highest level. Gagné's work has certainly been influential in instructional design, especially in relation to problem solving. However, confronting problems, as I suggest in my elaboration of disjuncture, is also the beginning of the learning process in some ways and it may, therefore, be doubtful that it is the highest level of the hierarchy. Indeed, this approach is open to the same criticism that all stage theories are susceptible to, and recognition that one or more of his types of learning does not fit into the hierarchy is an indication of this.

While Gagné does not extend his theory of learning into personhood, he is concerned with the nature of the learner and he examines, attitudes, skills and the nature of memory. These are aspects of personhood that are relevant to instructional design, so that this is unsurprising. In precisely the same way, Gagné mentions the situation within which the learning occurs, but he is not concerned with the learners' life-world. Since instructional design is the central purpose of Gagné's work, it is not surprising either that his theory of learning is not really systematically researched or constructed, nor is it a complete theory. Nevertheless, it was a major step forward from the basic S-R models that have been prevalent in education and training.

C. Argyris and D. Schön

Since Argyris and Schön are both organisational theorists who were very influential in intoducing us to the idea of the learning region (Schön 1971) and the learning organisation, we shall return to their work again in the next volume of this study. For now, however, we are to concentrate on their contribution to learning theory, which was profoundly influenced by the insights from this first book. For instance, once professional practice had moved 'beyond the stable state' so that practice was no longer the process of applying learned rules and procedures to practice, it meant that professionals had to think in practice. Consequently, this meant that the ideas of technical rationality and learning theory to apply in practice were outdated (see also Jarvis 1999), so that practitioners had to think in practice. This led to *The Reflective Practitioner* (Schön 1983), a book that has had a profound influence on professional practice and together, with its follow-up (Schön 1987), an influence on professional education and training.

Schön maintained that professionals have knowledge, and so he talked about 'knowing in action' and he recognised that sometimes professionals do reflect on the knowledge that they have. However, he highlights disjunctural situations – although he does not use the word – in which practitioners are forced to think and therefore learn afresh. He (Schön 1983: 62–3) wrote:

> When the phenomenon at hand eludes the ordinary categories of knowledge-in-practice, presenting itself as unique or unstable, the practitioner must surface and criticize his intial understanding of the phenomenon, construct a new description of it, and test the new description by an on-the-spot experiment. Sometimes he arrives at a new theory of the phenomenon by articulating a feeling he has about it.

In this quotation we have, basically, a simple theory of learning which goes from disjunction→reflection→experiment. This is an individualistic theory since he does not even suggest other ways in which the practitioner can learn, such as imitation. The strength of his work, however, lies in its common sense recogntion that the situation within which the practice is conducted is no longer stable and unchanging. His understanding of reflection stems from the work that he did with Argyris, although the theory of learning is not a great deal more sophisticated than the model above.

Argyris and Schön (1974) started their work with the intention to investigate the relationship between theory and practice, and they concluded that there is a fundamental difference between practitioners's espoused theories and the theories that they actually practise, or theory-in-use. Conformity to the theory-in-use is Model I behaviour. They then analysed behaviour that re-inforced the theory in use, which they called single-loop learning. In other words, 'we learn to maintain the field of constancy by learning to design actions that satsfy exisiting governing variables' (Argyris and Schön 1974: 18). Fundamentally, this is a theory that begins and ends with behaviour ('disjunction and experiment' in the above three-stage model) and learning is the process of devising new behavioural forms that fit the prevailing theories in use. In this formulation, theories-in-use tend to be individualistic and ask little about the prevailing sub-culture, or even the life-world of the practitioners. Fundamentally, it is non-reflective learning.

Double-loop learning starts by questioning the theory-in-use, and in this sense it is reflective learning. 'Model II behaviour is an attempt to make operational some governing variables that are broadly espoused, although infrequently realized, in our society' (Argyris and Schön 1974: 85). In this sense, this demands a new approach to action, incorporating values and beliefs that are acknowledged but not practised in organisational terms. Individuals will move to this position if they have a 'disconfirming experience', in other words, if they suffer disjuncture. Consequently, they are open to these other values and so on, which they incorporate into their actions, which means that they are going beyond the stable state, and this is double-loop learning. Yet again, it contains the same three stages that we have discussed above, with the only major difference being that the process of reflecting on the theories-in-use is seen to be one in which the actor is more open to consider the suggestions of others in the work situation. However, in their discussion of Model II behaviour, Argyris and Schön are clear that the nature of the self-image of the actor has to be protected and the final stage of action needs to be tested for its effectiveness.

This, then, is a simple non-reflective/reflective model of learning located, like the work of Engeström, within the world of work. In this sense, it is also a theory of pragmatic action in which disjuncture is the trigger that starts the learning process. The work is carefully researched and has been effective in work-based learning research, but it adds little to our understanding of learning per se since it is an incomplete theory of learning.

Jack Mezirow

Mezirow got involved in studying human learning through an adult basic education research project in which he was involved at the end of the 1960s and the beginning of the 1970s (Mezirow et al. no date). In this work he studied perspectives. The components of a perspective include: definition of a situation; activities which are proper, reasonable and appropriate to the situation; and criteria of judging the situation (Mezirow et al. no date: viii). However, it was perspective transformation which became the focus of a great deal Mezirow's work thereafter. Perspective transformation is 'a developmental process of movement through the adult years towards meaning perspectives that are progressively more inclusive, discriminating and more integrative of experience' (Mezirow 1977: 159). During this time he was influenced by studies in life crisis, which he had noted in his original research and by the writing of Habermas. This led him to discuss the idea of different levels of reflectivity. He proposed seven levels: reflectivity itself, affective, discriminant, judgmental, conceptual, psychic and theoretical (Mezirow 1981: 12–13). The last three he regarded as the types of reflection that only occurred in adulthood, so that he was able to proclaim that 'the formative learning of childhood becomes transformative learning in adulthood' (Mezirow 1991: 3). However, like many adult educators who distinguish between childhood and adult thought processes, he did not conduct research amongst children and so this simple division never had an empirical foundation. Basically, I think that he also omitted from his analysis the transformation of sensations, which we discussed in the opening chapter.

However, Mezirow's next step was to claim that:

> reflective learning becomes transformative whenever assumptions or premises are found to be distorting, inauthentic or otherwise invalid.

Transformative learning results in new or transformed meaning schemes or, when reflection focuses on premises, transformed meaning perspectives.

(1991: 6)

At this stage, learning is 'the process of using a prior interpretation to construe a new or revised interpretation of the meaning of one's experience in order to guide future action' (Mezirow 1991: 12). Significantly, here meaning is about the interpretation of experience and 'perspectives provide *principles* for interpreting' (Mezirow 1990: 3) those experiences. In addition, Mezirow is quite consistent about this definition of learning, citing it again nearly ten years later (Mezirow 2000: 5). Meaning perspectives are 'for the most part, uncritically acquired in childhood through the process of socialization, often in the context of an emotionally charged relationship with parents, teachers and other mentors' (Mezirow 1990: 3). These are taken for granted in the process of daily living and they enable us to act in a presumptive manner. Clearly, he is discussing a similar process to the one discussed in Figure 1.5, although he does not trace this process back to sensations and the body, for the body is noticeably absent from his discussions. These perspectives are built into schemes of meaning which he regards as being 'made up of specific knowledge, beliefs, value judgements, and feelings that constitute intepretations of experience (and they) become more differentiated and integrated or transformed by reflection on the content or process of problem solving in progressively wider contexts' (Mezirow 1991: 5–6).

It is these experiences that form the basis of the movement through the adult years triggered by life crises, although these may be no more than disorientating dilemmas rather than full-blown crises. In other words, they are disjunctural. These dilemmas may also be facilitated by critical reflection on experience and criticality is the ability to challenge the assumptions of prior learning. We can clearly see that Mezirow is locating learning almost entirely in the cognitive domain, even though he is also trying to situate it within the life-world of the learners and their life experiences. But from the early 1990s, he was discussing perspective transformation as a form of learning. This was soon to be transformed into the concept 'transformative learning'.

Transformation, for Mezirow, connotes a sense of breaking away from what had gone before and, in this sense, it incorporates Habermas's emphasis on emancipation, although Mezirow is not quite as radical in his use of transformation as Habermas was with emancipation. In order to pursue this idea further would demand that Mezirow examined some of the ideas of inauthenticity and authencity of the person.

In his later writings, Mezirow also endeavours to focus on the emotions and he (2000: 22) suggests that while there is not an invariate route for the process of transformation, it does approximate to the following:

- A disorintating dilemma.
- Self-examination with feelings of fear, anger, guilt or shame.
- A critical assessment of assumptions.
- Recognition that one's discontent and the process of transformation are shared.
- Explorations for new roles, relationships and actions.
- Planning a course of action.
- Acquiring knowledge and skills for implementing one's plans.
- Provisional trying of new roles.
- Building competence and self-confidence in new roles and relationships.
- A re-integration into one's life on the basis of conditions dictated by one's new perspective.

I think that Mezirow has over-emphasised the emotional feelings in the second stage because there are other emotions that are not so threatening that also play a part, such as determination, inquisitiveness, excitement, enjoyment and so on. The third and fourth stages also call for comment since learning might not always entail a critical assessment of assumptions so much as a building upon incomplete ones, and the idea of shared discontent might omit the idea of self-directed learning. Whilst the theory is a cognitive one, there appears to be no place in this sequence for meditation or contemplation since it is action orientated. Consequently, this sequence seems to pose many problems for our understanding of learning to be totally acceptable.

In his later work, as we have seen, Mezirow has been influenced by Goleman's work on emotions – to which we will return in the next chapter – when he suggests that since transformation requires reframing of our meaning systems it might be an emotionally threatening experience. Clearly, this is one of the emotional paradoxes of learning: that in order to be emancipated we must be willing to break away from many of the attitudes, values and beliefs that both support and constrain our thinking.

In many ways, Mezirow's is amongst the most sophisticated cognitive theories of learning, but with its emphasis on transformation and adulthood it really does not constitute a complete theory of learning per se. It has: omitted the place of the body; no analysis of the nature of the person; omitted the centrality of the place of experience; omitted the complexity of the social context of learning and so on. Consequently, we can see that it neglects some of the most crucial elements in the learning process.

Danny Wildermeersch

Wildermeersch (Stroobants *et al.* 2001) also introduces us to transformative learning; his concern is how individual learners relate to their world – especially the world of work – and he suggests a simple model of learning but one in which the learners, whom he regards as interpretative professionals, are affected by and interact with their world. For him and his colleagues 'transformative learning arises when individuals are faced with unpredictable changes in the dynamics between their life ·course and the transforming context' (Stroobants *et al.* 2001: 117). Basically, what they are suggesting is that in a rapidly changing world, there will frequently be disjuncture between individuals, personal demands and the demands made upon them by their changing world; these demands are needs, values, norms and aspirations. In addition, people have perceptions of this situation which relate to the social expectations that surround them. They have to come to terms with this complex situation and they have four basic strategies: adaptation (to social demands), growth (of the person), distinction (developing alternative approaches) and resistance (leading to transforming the demands of society). It is within this framework, which is basically offering four possible ways of restoring harmony between the persons and their life-world, that Wildermeersch constructs his model of learning.

Basically, his concern is with the way that people try to find a balance between their own authenticity and the changing demands of the life-world in which people are continually seeking to be 'meaningfully connected'. This, then, is both a cognitive and an action process which arises from the individuals' experience of this complex situation. The theory, therefore, offers an analysis of the interaction between the learners and their life-world but little about the actual processes of learning itself, nor about emotions of the learners.

Conclusion

We have examined some of the major theorists in the cognitive approaches to learning here and we note that none of them really examine the nature of the body nor the nature of the person in their discussions. Most of the researchers have looked at learning from within an institutional context – usually an educational or work setting – with Mezirow being a noteable exception since he is more concerned with the lifespan. Each theorist adds to our understanding of the learning process and emphasises one or more of the elements mentioned in Figures 1.5 and 1.6. None, however, has produced a theoretical perspective that would call into question the approach advocated here. More recently, there has been a greater emphasis placed upon emotion in learning than ever before, although no theorist, with the exception of Goleman (1996, 1998) has made emotion their primary focus, although we did look at the work of Cell (1984) earlier in this study. We shall, therefore, briefly examine Goleman's work in the next chapter and relate it to some wider theories of learning.

Chapter 10

Emotions and learning

Emotions play a major role in behaviour and in human learning since they are at the heart of our personhood. However, no learning theorist, to my knowledge, had actually researched emotional learning, although Cell's (1984) study was one of the most significant and many years before Bergson (2001 [1913]: 1–74) examined how the body is affected by the emotions with different experiences. Goleman's (1996, 1998) studies of emotional intelligence do indicate some of the ways in which the emotions relate to human learning. Emotion, Goleman suggests, refers to 'a feeling and its distinctive thoughts, psychological and biological states, and range of propensities to act' (1996: 289). But feelings are not synonymous with emotions. Cell (1984: 95), for instance, argues that feelings are not emotions since the same feelings can occur in different emotional states and emotions are about something specific and are arrived at through reflection, whereas feelings are not. Bergson also points to the relations of emotions and feelings to bodily states. Emotions revolve around our own sense of self-worth or self-esteem (Cell 1984: 77) and they are, therefore, functional in giving us this sense of worth, or dysfunctional if they do not. They are, therefore, intimately related to our sense of self-identity.

Goleman suggests that there are eight basic families of emotions, with each having a number of different forms of that emotion: anger, sadness, fear, enjoyment, love, surprise, disgust and shame (Goleman 1996: 289–90). In contrast, Cell (1984: 93) has suggested that someone has listed 550 types, but not categories!

Basically, emotions are a combination of the physical and the cognitive, which affect both our behaviour and our learning, but they are not behavioural since they cannot always be identified by our behaviour. However, Cell suggests that they have three components: a judgment, a feeling and an action. Basically, they are evaluative judgments which we learn both in the situation and as a response to it. Emotions, then, are learned and having learned them, they influence our lives to a considerable extent in both positive and negative ways. There is a great deal of evidence that shows the power of emotions, and Goleman (1996: 78) suggests that the emotional brain can overpower, even paralyse, the thinking brain. We probably all know of situations, for instance, where anxiety gets in the way of concentration and prolonged thought. In precisely the same way it can prevent learning. Since emotions occur at all stages of the learning process, my intention in this chapter is to rely heavily on Goleman's[1] work and relate his discussion to each of the stages of learning discussed in the first chapters. I want to show that not only does emotion relate to each of the stages of learning, but that it also adds to our understanding of non-learning. Consequently, there are eight brief sections to this chapter: emotions and the brain/mind; developing the person in relationship; time; motivation and disjuncture; experience; thought and action; the outcomes of learning; and, finally, non-learning.

The brain and the mind

Neuroscience has come to the fore in recent years (see, for instance, the chapters by Stein on neuroscience and Hall on emotional intelligence in Jarvis and Parker 2005). The emotions can be located in the amygdala, which is above the brain stem and near the bottom of the limbic ring; the limbic structures do most of the brain's learning and remembering. Research has shown that the neocortex is where thinking occurs and the amygdala is 'the storehouse of emotional memory and thus of significance itself; life without the amygdala is a life stripped of personal meanings'[2] (Goleman 1996: 15). We know that the circuits in the brain are completed during early childhood as a result of our experiences, and this is also true of those that affect our emotions also.

LeDoux (cited in Goleman 1996) has shown that the amygdala has a key role in the emotional brain since physical sensations, which go to the thalamas to be translated into the language of the brain, are then transmitted directly to the amygdala and to the neocortex. However, the former acts more rapidly than the latter and can, therefore, affect the thought processes. Indeed, it can take control of the thinking brain, but the thinking part of the brain often balances the emotive response when it acts moments later. The emotions, then, are in some ways more powerful than the thinking part of the brain. Goleman gives a clear example of the way that memory and emotion work together: following LeDoux he writes, 'The hippocampus is crucial in recognizing a face as that of your cousin. But it is the amygdala that adds you don't really like her' (1996: 20).

The emotions then can be located in a specific part of the brain and it is possible to see both how the brain acts emotionally and also how it combines with the thinking brain in more thoughtful action. While the physical brain is fully discussed here, Goleman also raises the possibility that we might have two minds – one a thinking mind and the other an emotional one – but, as we have seen, both have their physical locations in the brain. Goleman appears to accept a mind–body identity since in his discussion of self-awareness he never moves to a metaphysical position, although in his discussion of life without meaning he does hint at this possibility. What is clear, however, is that he thinks that neuroscience has demonstrated the fact that since the functions of the amygdala have been better understood, the brain cannot be like a super-computer (Goleman 1996: 50–4), thus ruling out another of the possible mind–brain relationships. He gives an example to confirm this: when the amygdala is isolated through surgery, the brain becomes computer-like but the person is unable to feel or to be decisive. As we pointed out in Chapter 2 of this book, the mind is not like a super-computer and this invalidates information processing as an adequate theory of learning.

Developing the person in relationship

The child is born into a social world and we have seen how Mead (Strauss 1964) placed emphasis on the significant other for the acquisition of language and also how one form of early learning was socialisation. Elsewhere, I (Jarvis 1997) have suggested that values are learned pre-consciously through interaction with the significant other, and this is precisely how emotions are learned. Goleman (1996: 195) writes:

> Such emotional learning begins in life's earliest moments, and continues throughout childhood. All the small exchanges between parent and child have an emotional sub-text, and in the repetition of those messages over the years children form the core of their emotional outlook and capabilities.

In this process of primary socialisation, those early sensations and experiences of interaction generate the growth and development of more and complex emotions as we grow older. There are many studies that support this conclusion, all of which point to the significance of pre-conscious learning in early childhood. The significance of the I↔Thou relationship is immense, for the better the relationships in early childhood the more a person will be capable of relating to others later in life.

Elsewhere in this study we have pointed out that being committed to a solution to a problem is itself an emotional phenomenon, and we might also claim that the more we are integrated into our cultural group, or life-world, the more we are committed to it. Consequently, the emotional commitment is going to influence the way that we see and respond to situations and, therefore, the way that we learn from them. Clearly, we see this in being committed to our family, our religion, our local region and also by being committed to the company for whom we work. We do not learn in isolation and we are influenced emotionally by those with whom we live and work. Goleman (1998: 120) makes the point about the significance of the relationship to the groups to whom we are committed – we must be self-aware so that we know that what we feel fits into the purposes of the groups of which we are members.

Time

It will be recalled that living in the flow of time, *durée*, is significant and it is only when we have a novel experience with which we cannot cope – disjuncture – that we suddenly start to question and in this sense appear to step outside the flow of time. But the idea of living within the flow of time is tremendously important in the study of the emotions. Living in the flow represents 'harnessing the emotions in the service of performance and learning' (Goleman 1996: 90). This is a state where everything we do seems to fit into place easily, rapidly, and almost without effort we seem to be aware and able to do things. He (Goleman 1998: 106) suggests that it is like being 'out of time' – it is a state of being when we are not self-conscious, indeed we are not conscious of ourselves. Csikszentmihalyi (1990) suggested to Goleman that 'People seem to concentrate best when the demands on them are a bit greater than usual, and they are able to give more than usual. If there is too little demand on them, people are bored. If there is too much for them to handle, they get anxious. Flow occurs in that delicate zone between boredom and anxiety' (cited in Goleman 1996: 91–2). This is a state of inner joy in precisely the same way as Confucius in *The Analects* asked 'Is it not a joy to learn?' Being in the state of flow is one of the highlights of both learning and doing; it is a sense of literally being relaxed, aware and doing things without being aware of time.

Motivation and disjuncture

Disjuncture occurs when the flow of time is interrupted and we are not able to do what we would do in an unthinking manner – the external world has changed or we have changed internally. Nevertheless, immediately we feel unease, we are no longer in harmony. The first emotion, then, is one of being in disharmony, dissonance, unease with ourselves and our environment. This sense might vary from just a trifle uneasy to experiencing a major upset, but there is always a desire to establish harmony once again. Other emotions also set in at this time: optimism that we can do it and pessimism that we cannot. Both of these affect our learning in many ways.

There are a number of research studies that show how anxiety hinders thinking and undermines learning itself. Being able to master that anxiety is an important stage in motivation. On the positive side, Goleman (1996: 86) records how Snyder studied the academic achievement of new students to the University of Kansas and compared their grade with their previous examination scores and their levels of hope: he found that hope was a better predictor than previous examination scores of their examination grades. Unfortunately, students with low levels of hope tend to give up.

Optimism, then, is something of a self-fulfilling prophecy – believe that you can do it and you will. This reflects Bandura's work on social learning that we have already examined. Bandura (1977, 1989) was interested in self-efficacy, a sense of self-confidence, and he found that people having this confidence not only achieved but they also bounced back from failures. This sense of optimism, Goleman (1998: 129) claims, is expressed and interpreted differently in Asia, the United States and Europe. The Asian might say, 'This is a very difficult challenge, and I'm trying, even though I might not be able to do it.' The American might express it, 'I know that I can do it, I know I'm good' – but to the European this is just arrogance! Optimism or arrogance, it is more likely to achieve. The Asian is also likely to achieve since the challenge is to become a better person. It is emotions like hope and optimism that lead to self-confidence, which in turn might lead to risk-taking and entrepreneurship. It is also beliefs like these that foster the will-power to keep going when things get difficult – something many commentators comment upon, including Confucius. He claimed that everybody is educable, reflecting a widely held belief amongst adult educators. Consequently, the significance of emotions, attitudes and beliefs in the learning process are considerable; it is the whole person who learns.

Experience

Anxiety hinders learning, but if more positive emotions are masters during the experience of learning there will most likely be more positive outcomes. The advice often given to people before an examination or an interview is to relax – to take a few deep breaths, etc. It is sound advice, since anxiety detracts from the resources devoted to thinking. We have already seen how the emotive brain can control the thinking one and so it is necessary to take control of the emotive brain in order to allow the thinking one to operate. Indeed, for some people involved in creative undertakings a mild sense of anxiety (hypomania) is necessary to stimulate them. Consequently, experience is not just a matter of perception, it is an emotive response to the situation and one which we can, in part, control provided we are aware of the types of exercise necessary to lessen the factors that inhibit thought and learning.

Thought and action

Goleman (1996: 85–6) writes:

> Even mild mood changes can sway thinking. In making plans or
> decisions people in good moods have a perceptual basis that leads them

to be more expansive and positive in their thinking. This is party because memory is state specific, so that while in a good mood we remember more positive events; . . . By the same token, being in a foul mood biases memory in a negative direction, making us more likely to contract into a fearful, overly cautious decision.

It is, therefore, not just relaxation but being in a good mood that enhances thinking, especially creative and flexible thought. Maybe it is because we are more likely to take risks when we are in a good mood but, in any case, we are more likely to see the positive side of things and this will affect both our thinking and our learning.

The outcomes of learning – the more experienced person

From all that has been written in this brief chapter, we can see that the way that we respond to our emotions has the same effects as the way that we respond to the cognitive aspects of our experiences. The more we learn to control and manage our emotions, the more that we can learn from our experiences and, moreover, the more that we will be able to use our memories in future learning. We have known for many years about the way that the development of our brain in early childhood has affected out speech and thinking capacities and, therefore, our learning. There is ample evidence that the ability to control our emotions in early life has long-term consequences on the way that we behave in the future (Goleman 1996: 81), and so now we have to give the same consideration to our emotions and the way that our brain is developed by our emotional experiences in early life, as we have done to the development of thought and language.

Non-learning

Throughout my work I have been keen to emphasise the need to understand the phenomenon of non-learning as well as that of learning. I have suggested that we do not learn for a number of reasons, such as living in the flow of time and not being stopped by disjunctural experiences may prevent us from responding to potential learning experiences but, also, when we are aware of such experiences we may refuse to consider them or we may be too busy to undertake the exercise of learning. We have already seen, for instance, that if we are in a bad mood we may be cautious and this might result in us feeling too busy or because we do not want to take the risk to learn something new. Goleman (1996: 27) writes:

> The prefrontal cortex is the brain region responsible for the working memory. But circuits from the limbic brain to the prefrontal lobes mean

that the signals of strong emotion – anxiety, anger, and the like – can create neural static, sabotaging the ability of the prefrontal lobe to maintain working memory. That is why when we are emotionally upset we say that we 'just cannot think straight' – and why continual emotional distress can create deficits in a child's intellectual abilities, crippling the capacity to learn.

In precisely the way that our early experiences affect our ability to learn throughout our lives, negative experiences curtail the opportunities to learn later in life. But more than this, it appears that if these circuits are not completed in a satisfactory manner in early childhood, then it is difficult for the emotional brain to be involved in rational thinking later in life, which leads to certain inabilities to learn.

Conclusion

Goleman's wide-ranging studies on emotions has enabled us to understand the relationship between emotion and learning much better, although it is clear that we need a great deal more research into the relationship between the emotions and learning. What I have tried to show here, however, that is that emotion cannot be separated from any stage in our understanding of learning and that it is as important to learning as thinking. Perhaps we can do no better that to close this chapter with a final quotation from Goleman (1996: 80):

> To the degree that our emotions get in the way of or enhance our ability to think and plan, to pursue training for a distant goal, to solve problems and the like, they define our capacity to use our innate mental abilities, and so determine how we do in life. And to the degree to which we are motivated by feelings of enthusiasm and pleasure in what we do – or even by an optimal degree of anxiety – they propel us to accomplishment. It is in this sense that emotional intelligence is a master aptitude, a capacity that profoundly affects all other abilities, either facilitating or interfering with them.

Chapter 11

Experiential learning

It is clear that almost all learning is experiential, the only exception being pre-conscious learning. However, we have seen how most research into learning has tried to separate it from the human experiences of the learners and to study it 'objectively' and 'scientifically'. Only when qualitative research began to gain a place in social science did more humanistic and subjective research projects into learning gain ground. Consequently, some of the approaches to learning which emphasised the experience of the learners gained ground and they became known as experiential theories. There is a sense that these theories could only gain credibility when the age of rationalism and scientific objectivity was over, or at least coming to an end, so that experientialism might be considered to be an indication of the emergence of a late modern society. These approaches to learning, my own included, reflect the times in which the research was conducted, so that most of the approaches to learning at which we shall look in this chapter do fit into the framework of Figures 1.5 and 1.6. However, there are a number of writers whose work we do need to look at briefly here who have contributed to our understanding of experiential learning, including Dewey, Rogers, Knowles, Kolb, Boud, Cell and Weil and McGill.

John Dewey

Dewey, like most early thinkers about learning, located his thoughts within the context of education and he actually argued that 'education in order to accomplish its ends both for the individual learner and for society must be based upon experience – that is always the actual life experience of the individual' (1938: 89). Indeed, he wrote that 'learning here means acquisition of what already is incorporated in books and in the heads of elders' (1938: 19). This is an extremely narrow definition of learning, one that we would now find it difficult to accept and, indeed, one which he used within the framework of this one book on progressive education, since elsewhere (1916: 51) he suggested that we all learn in the process of living for as long as we live.

Educative experiences should always occur in continuity with previous experiences in the process of human growth and development and the direction of these experiences needs to be controlled, to some extent, for children: 'It is the business of the educator to see in what direction the experience is heading' (Dewey 1938: 38). Experiences also always involve interaction between the internal and the external – both are changed through experience. But there is a slight confusion in this passage in Dewey's work. For the most part, the emphasis is on how the internal is changed by experience. It is through experiences that learning occurs and it is the learning that changes the learner whose behaviour can then change the external conditions for future experiences. Dewey (1938: 39) did not distinguish clearly between education and learning in his assertion that experience changes the objective conditions under which the experiences are had, so that he confuses internal experience and its effects on the person in learning. Indeed, Dewey actually uses the word 'experience' in this passage as if he were writing about learning. It is the outcomes of learning that actually change the objective conditions under which future experiences are had rather than the experience itself that change them.

Continuity and interaction are the two principles that form the framework for the social situation within which experiences occur. Dewey (1938: 43) indicates that we live in a series of situations, i.e. episodic experiences, as we suggested earlier in this study. He (1938: 47) draws his thinking about the nature of experience together thus:

> In a certain sense, every experience should do something to prepare a person for later experiences of a deeper and more expansive quality. That is the very meaning of growth, continuity, reconstruction of experience.

Dewey's thinking was clearly very influential in changing the nature of education, and his thinking about the nature of experience has also influenced adult educators, from Knowles to Kolb and, apart from the conceptual disagreement we raised above, it is clear that his thinking also underlies the model of learning that we have discussed in this study.

Freedom to learn – Carl Rogers

Carl Rogers has had a considerable influence on our understanding of human learning, although he wrote from within the context of teaching and therapy, since he regarded himself foremost as a therapist concerned with developing the whole person. Underlying Rogers' (1983; Rogers and Freiberg 1994) writing is a humanistic existentialist philosophy that is similar to the approach adopted in this book, except in respect to his discussion on authenticity and autonomy since he seems to regard authentic persons as ones who are free to act totally freely, whereas we want to argue here that authenticity must always be worked out in relationship. Nevertheless, it is the whole person who learns and that the learners have to be allowed to be themselves – to be authentic human beings. The normal educational process, however, deprives them of their authenticity as they slot into the educational system. Learning is the process of becoming a 'real' person and by this Rogers is reflecting the ideas of authenticity and authenticity in learning. He (1969: 157–64) claims that experiential learning is typified by the following principles:

- Human beings have a natural potentiality to learn.
- Significant learning occurs when the learner perceives the relevance of the subject matter.
- Learning involves a change in self-organisation and self-perception.
- Learning that threatens self-perception is more easily perceived and assimilated when the external threats are at a minimum.
- Learning occurs when the self is not threatened.
- Much significant learning is acquired by doing.
- Learning is facilitated when the learner participates responsibly in the learning process.
- Self-initiated learning involves the whole person.
- Independence, creativity and self-reliance are all facilitated when self-criticism and self-evaluation are basic.
- Much socially useful learning is learning the process of learning and retaining an openness to experience, so that the process of change may be incorporated into the self.

In these principles we can see that it is the whole person who is involved in learning, but we can also see that they are enunciated within the context of being taught. Significantly, many of his ideas evolved in his work as a psycho-therapist and this is an important overlap between two fields of professional practice that has enhanced our understanding of learning and, significantly, of teaching.

Andragogy as experiential learning – Malcolm Knowles

Knowles' theory of andragogy was a student-centred theory of teaching and learning which he defined as 'the art and science of helping adults learn' (1980: 43). He did not define learning as such but rather assumed that it related to the outcomes of the teaching and learning process, but his approach did have something of a behaviourist orientation since he suggested that 'learning experiences should be organized around competency-development categories' (1980: 44). Consequently, he added little to our understanding of learning per se, although he helped us to re-focus on the role of experience in learning. Nevertheless, there is an explicit theory of learning elaborated throughout his writing.

Since Knowles always wrote about learning within the context of teaching, we have to recognise that his starting point in the learning process had to be the needs of the learners rather than the demands of the curriculum or the learners' biography in relation to their life-world. But as the learners mature it is their self that is changing. Learners move from dependency to independency, he claimed, but maybe this is an over-generalisation about adulthood that needs a great deal more research. However, as they grow they acquire an increasing reservoir of experience from which their self-identity develops. Experience, then, for Knowles, is the store of memories in the mind which, as we have seen, is one major aspect in our understanding of the nature of experience. In his idea of teaching, Knowles was also keen to emphasise the experiential, and in this we can see how he has influenced experiential teaching theory. Knowles claimed that when the learner's reservoir of experience is insufficient to cope with their daily living, they develop a need to learn, but only so that they can then put the outcomes of their learning into practice – in other words, adult education had to be relevant to the learner's situation.

Knowles wrote about andragogy for many years and in the process he kept modifying his understanding of the concept, which is to be expected as he continually reconsidered his formulations. By 1989 he wrote:

> Adults come into an educational activity with both a greater volume and a different quality of experience than youths. This difference . . . has several consequences for adult education.
>
> It assures that in any group of adults there will be a greater range of individual differences of background, learning styles, motivation, needs, interests and goals.
>
> It means that for many kinds of learning the richest resources for learning are within the learners themselves. Hence, the greater emphasis being given in adult education on experiential techniques . . . Hence, too, the greater emphasis on peer-helping activities.
>
> (Knowles 1989: 83–4)

He also recognised that great experience also had negative effects on learning because that experience potentially closed people's minds, instilled biases and presuppositions and so on.

While Knowles' emphasis was on adults learning, his own understanding of learning was never explicitly worked out or researched. He described his own orientation to teaching and learning, which was a straightforward student-centred approach. This he called 'andragogy' as a result of learning about the term from the Serbian adult educator, Dusan Savicavic. His writings have had a considerable effect on education for the twenty-year period from about 1970, but he added nothing to our understanding of human learning as such.

David Kolb

Kolb (1984) acknowledges fully Dewey's influence on his thinking about experiential learning, which has been deeply influential in the development of experiential learning. His learning cycle, depicted in the opening chapter, is probably as well known a diagram in educational writing as Maslow's triangular hierarchy of needs. Nevertheless, as we argued in that opening chapter, his cycle is over-simple in part and wrong in another. But his stages of experience, reflection/observation, abstract conceptualisation/generalisation and active experimentation do appear to be attractive, almost common sense, in the first instance. Indeed, experience and observation/reflection are to be found from the earliest writings about learning, such as Locke. It is the third stage where the problems lie because in my research into adult learning hardly any of the respondents saw generalisation/abstract thinking as a stage in their learning. Indeed, few actually included it at all, although many did include active experimentation as the stage following reflection. Paradoxically, it is these stages that describe my own research process into learning – since I put my respondents in pairs and then in fours to discuss their own learning experiences. They were, in fact, participating in the process of generalisation. Thereafter I used their findings as part of my thinking for the next time I undertook the same research workshop. My model is one that emerged initially after nine learning workshops, and one which I have continued to work on thereafter.

As Kolb actually built his understanding of learning styles and personal growth and development upon his basic cycle, and since I could not replicate his cycle in my own research into learning, I have been forced to abandon the specifics of his thinking about both of these, even though discussion about both learning style and human development are important to our understanding of learning and personhood.

Since I was not able to replicate his cycle, we might ask why it has been so popular in recent years. Perhaps there are a number of reasons for this:

- experientialism has been a feature of contemporary society and so his book captured the spirit of the age;
- the focus on experience is actually central to our understanding of learning itself;
- his cycle is simple and appears to be common sense to the reader; or
- his research has been accepted uncritically by those who have read it.

Whilst his work has been tremendously influential, I have now conducted this workshop on more occasions than I have counted and I have never been able to replicate the cycle from any single group of adults, although I have sometimes had a few in those groups who, when asked to analyse their own learning, did so by following the cycle to which they had already been introduced rather than using their learning to assess the validity of the cycle. Even then these have always been in the minority. But as I pointed out in the opening chapter, it could be claimed that a flaw in my research was actually giving the respondents the learning cycle and asking them to redraw it to depict their own learning experiences, and in this case we might have expected far more to have accepted Kolb's cycle had it actually represented the respondents' learning process.

David Boud

About the same time as Kolb wrote, Boud was developing his understanding of reflective learning, having been influenced by John Heron.[1] Boud (1985), together with Rosemary Keogh and David Walker, produced an edited book in which their focus was reflection, but they understood that learning is the process of transforming experience through reflection. Like many experiential learning theorists, they were more interested in the reflective process than they were in the experience, and for them experience could be contrasted to classroom-based teaching and learning (Boud et al. 1985: 18). Here we see how experiential learning was to develop throughout the 1980s – in contrast to formal educational processes of teaching and learning.

Nevertheless, Boud and his colleagues defined experience as 'the total response of a person to a situation or event: what he or she thinks, feels, does and concludes at the time and immediately thereafter' (Boud et al. 1985: 18). They recognised that the experience could occur in many different situations, both formal and informal and so on, although they continued to think about experiential learning as something to be contrasted to classroom learning. While this was a necessary comparison to make in the development of their work, failure to pursue their own understanding of experience resulted in the experiential nature of learning per se not really being fully developed. However, in common with many experiential learning theorists at that time, they were more concerned with the idea of reflection. This focus was quite natural, and fully understandable in retrospect, since the dominant thinking about learning at that time was behaviouristic and cognitive from within the context of formal education, which emphasised memorisation. They suggested that reflection is a matter of recapturing experience, thinking about it and evaluating it. While they also recognised that experience is not just a cognitive phenomenon – they (1985: 20) write about 'behaviour, ideas and feelings' – their focus from a learning perspective was still cognitive.

Like Mezirow, they focused on reflection in its various forms and, in common with many others who wrote about experiential learning, they did not develop their thinking about experience. Boud and his colleagues, however, were much more concerned about the place of emotions in experience and learning from very early in their work, but they did not develop this aspect of their work systematically. Perhaps the focus on reflection rather than thought in its widest sense is *cul-de-sac* that learning theorists went and still are going down – since reflection is but one approach to thinking and our understanding of learning needs to be contextualised within an established academic framework about the nature of thought.

Boud, together with a variety of colleagues, has developed these initial ideas about the learning experience highlighting the fact that it can occur in different sites and in different ways, such as in problem-based and practice-based learning. His initial understanding has been influential in affecting the way that a great deal of practice, and subsequent research, has developed. Nevertheless, their contribution to learning theory per se is more limited because they have actually not developed their work about the nature of learning a great deal further than the early thinkers about learning.

At the same time, it is important to recognise that they, in common with a number of practitioners who used experiential teaching and learning methods, recognised the significance of the other dimensions of learning. Indeed, they were concerned that learners should be helped to attend to their feelings. Consequently, in role play and simulations, for instance, facilitators were taught that while it was important that they allowed learners to experience emotionally, they had to allow sufficient time to debrief students and allow them to unwind and reflect upon their emotional experiences thereafter.

Boud and his colleagues, like Kolb and many others of us who were concerned with experiential learning during this period, still tended to see experiential learning as separate from other forms of learning since they did not recognise learning as an existential phenomenon. One early theorist who did locate experiential learning within an existential framework was Edward Cell (1984).

Edward Cell and learning to learn from experience

Cell (1984) captured the title of the Faure Report (1972) *Learning to Be* in his opening chapter and from the outset of his work located learning within the struggle of being. But then Cell came to his studies on experiential learning from a different perspective to most other writers on the subject, since he was a professor of philosophy. Consequently, his approach to learning comes closest of any of the writers on experiential learning to that adopted here, and we will examine it quite extensively now.

Experiential learning, for Cell, is a process whereby we learn to become selves; he (1984: 4) maintains that:

Our existence as persons is something that we must create and maintain; sometimes there is an adventure and a joy but very often it is a struggle in the face of threats.

In order to become persons-in-the-world, we have to learn the culture of our life-world and we also have to learn to respond to the social pressures that are placed on us within this world. Cell talks much more about the powerlessness of the individual than he does about the social pressures exerted on people, and in this sense he conveys a sense in which inauthentic existence is the major expectation for the majority of people. We need to become significant persons – to have the power to make a difference and to exercise our autonomy. To this end Cell discusses two types of learning: functional and dysfunctional.

Functional learning, according to Cell, is 'the kind of learning that either contributes to our autonomy or enrichment, or is at least compatible with them while serving some other valuable aim' (1984: 17). Functional, in this sense, is used in relation to his understanding of the authentic human person – and in this he follows Carl Rogers' existentialist perspective. By contrast, dysfunctional learning occurs when we 'adopt the behaviour and beliefs expected of us by others' (1984: 19). Here, then, we see that his approach to the person is in accord with much of the discussion that occurred in the first part of the book.

However, Cell is also concerned about the situations within which this learning occurs and so he suggests four types of experiential learning: response learning, situation learning, transsituation learning and transcendent learning. Response learning is an S-R form of learning – the most rudimentary form when we respond to certain situations. It is behaviourist, operant conditioning, rote learning and so on. By contrast, situation learning begins with the way in which we change our interpretation of the situation and we then adapt previous learning to respond to the situation as we currently understand it. In a sense we can see how Mezirow adopted a similar position in his understanding of perspective transformation. However, this process of changing our interpretations of situations is more difficult for some people than for others, so that if we can learn how to do it then we are engaged in transsituation learning. Finally, we learn from time to time to create new concepts and interpretations and then we are engaged in creative learning.

In producing these four different types of experiential learning, Cell has followed a psychotherapeutic approach and has discussed ways in which individuals can be helped to adapt their approach to a situation to their own experience. However, he actually tells us nothing new about the process of learning but more about ways in which the situation can be managed and the person of the learner helped to grow and develop. He (1984: 60) suggests that:

We are what we do, and so it is in response learning that we become what we are. We are free when we are able to change in self-chosen ways, and it is in situation learning that we create alternatives to choose between.

Later on the same page Cell concludes that experiential learning occurs when direct interaction results in a change in behaviour, interpretation, autonomy or creativity. Now this final statement again confuses concept and function – but then he has a functional approach to learning, as we have already seen. Nevertheless, he has not exhausted the possibilities of the outcomes of the learning and he might actually be claiming that experiential learning occurs when a direct interaction between ourselves and our world results in change. Cell has begun to bridge the gap between experiential learning and existential learning and by so doing produces a theory of learning that fits comprehensively into the model discussed throughout this study.

Our final study of experiential learning in this chapter relates to the work of Weil and McGill and their own theoretical framework into which they seek to fit the various ways of looking at experiential learning.

Weil and McGill – four villages

The first international conference on experiential learning produced a quite influential book containing a number of papers that reflected the concern and enthusiasm for experiential learning in the 1980s. Perhaps the real significance of this resided in the fact that individual scholars were beginning to recognise that once we admit to subjective experience as a researchable fact, then our understanding of learning takes on different dimensions. Weil and McGill (1989) endeavoured to classify experiential learning into four major types, which they called 'villages'. 'Village' is an interesting word for a category because it reflects the idea that there is both similarity and diversity in each area. Their four villages are:

- *Village One*: accessing and accrediting learning from varieties of life experience in order to provide routes into higher education. Basically, they were talking about the 'validity' of outcomes of prior learning to embarking on formal education. That this village should come first reflects the concern at this time in broadening access to formal education through forms of accreditation.
- *Village Two*: ways of learning that provide a basis for bringing about change in curricula structures in formal education, and they included here everything from techniques to philosophies.
- *Village Three*: emphasises the experience as a basis for consciousness-raising in community action, so that the focus is on the relationship

between the individual experience and the social context within which it occurs.

- *Village Four*: is concerned with personal growth and development and so the focus is on the individual and interpersonal relationships.

Basically, these four villages utilise the different functions of learning to form criteria for the classification. But as we look at this diversity and at the variety of functions that are discussed, we need to ask whether it makes the term 'experiential' redundant. The term was very important at that time for the simple reason that for so long subjective experience was hardly regarded as a basis for scientific data and so it was necessary to reflect this emphasis. However, what this diversity captures is, in fact, the diversity of human learning which must always be based in human experience.

Conclusion

As we have seen, the growth and development of what has been called 'experiential' learning occurred in the 1980s; in a sense it was a sign of the times. However, the focus on the 'experience' was quite shallow inasmuch as the concept was rarely analysed in any depth and rarely led back to a philosophy of learning – but that was to be expected. 'Experiential' was a descriptor which moved our thinking beyond the stage of student-centred teaching and learning; it highlighted the focus of the practitioners and researchers on the way that they were looking at learning – and it was widely recognised that the learning experiences could be had in any place, so that work-based learning assumed considerable significance. In the same way, problem-based learning was, in reality, no more than focusing on the disjunctive situation which led to the experience. In other words, these forms of learning pointed us to the human person but, with few exceptions, (e.g. Cell 1984; Jarvis 1987), experientialists, whilst acknowledging Rogers' emphasis on looking at the relation between the process and the person, did not pursue this in any great depth. However, what occurred then was a very important step in our quest to understand the complex process of human learning. We are, perhaps, now in a position whereby we can ask whether we can ever achieve a comprehensive theory of learning and we turn to this in the final chapter of this opening volume.

Chapter 12

Towards a comprehensive theory of human learning?

One of the questions that this book has sought to answer has been whether we can actually have a comprehensive theory of learning and we are now in a position to answer it. We have examined fully my own work on learning and we have also looked at a very wide variety of other theorists, each of whom have touched upon some elements of learning, but none have offered a comprehensive theory. In this brief final chapter we will argue that while it is possible to discuss almost all of the constitutent elements in the learning process, we know insufficient about the influence of the individual variables to be able to have a theory that fully explains every aspect of the human process. Furthermore, if we were able to we would actually remove free will from the debate about the nature of humanity and, in the end, we would depersonalise learning and dehumanise the person. Consequently, we maintain that there is much more than we can learn about the factors that affect the learning process, so that while we can develop a more sophisticated theory than we have at present, we will never be able to produce a totally comprehensive one. We will illustrate this assertion in three brief sections: the person-in-the-world, learning and the person, and experience and its transformation. Finally, we will conclude with a brief discussion.

The person-in-the-world

It is important, when we consider that the learner is always in the world, to recognise that to try to study learning as something divorced from learner in the wider world is artificial and non-realistic. We might be able to trace paths through the process as we have done in Figures 1.5 and 1.6, but these are of neessity very general and tell us little about the specific situations within which learning occurs and how different situations affect the learning process.

It was hard for the early theorists of learning to isolate learning from the educational setting, so that many theories of learning were actually theories of learning and teaching; this is true from Confucianism to behaviourism and even to some of the experiential theories of learning. Yet we have become increasingly aware that there are other situations within which we learn, such as the workplace and the family and so on. Some of these situations are formal, others non-formal and so on. Yet the terms 'formal, non-formal and informal learning' have crept into the educational vocabulary when we have actually meant '*learning in* formal, non-formal and informal situations'. In the same way, we have talked of situated learning as if it is something different from other forms of learning, when all learning is situated and it is the different situations which might have a major influnece on the way that we learn and behave. Hence, we need to examine the extent to which we can devise sociological studies of learning, as well as psychological ones and sociological ones of education.

However, we are also confronted with another difficulty in studying learning since, as we have seen, the outcomes of learning are complex: some may be observable and even occasionally measurable, but for the most part it is impossible to discuss all the outcomes quite specifically since we may not know them all and, at best, we might be able to study more of them in carefully devised individual and small group research situations. We are also aware that individuals may not actually reveal the outcomes of their learning if they are in social situations where it would be unwise to discuss specific outcomes and unless these are observable then they will not be knowable to anyone except the learner.

Nevertheless, it might be possible to devise certain forms of sociologial research that would indicate some more of the effects of the variables of the social situation on the learning processes. We are aware, for instance, that power and influence, formality and informality, socio-economic class and status, gender, age and role and so on are all important variables in social action, but we have not yet attempted to understand fully how they affect the learning process. However, these all play a part when individuals act simultaneously in potential learning situations, but in the normal course of life it is hard to control for these variables when we study individual learning. In order to do this we would have to create artificial situations or study people in totally controlled environments, such as research laboratories – but then we have artificialised the learning situation and artificial conditions can tell us little or nothing about learning in the more normal situations. In addition, we need to examine the extent to which our processes of learning change with our holding different positions in social organisations and networks.

Consequently, we might wish to ask ourselves whether it is actually possible to devise valid sociological studies of learning. In other words, to what extent can we study the process of becoming the person-in-the-world?

Learning and the person

From the outset we have pointed out that the person is a complex phenomenon. In our definition of learning we have combined body and mind, but we pointed out that there is no conclusive argument that illustrates the precise relationship between body and mind. In addition, there are several factors in the body – genetic, biological and physical – all of which affect the way that the body operates in the world. We know insufficient about all of them and we have already suggested that it is possible to have a biological study of learning and even a study from a pharmacological perspective. We are aware of a little about the relationship between eating or physical exercise and learning ability, and we know sufficient to be able to point to certain affects of health on learning and learning on health.[1] But there is a great deal more to know about the way that we can control our learning, by controlling our bodies and so on. Certainly, there are, in forms of Eastern arts for instance, indications that a greater control of the body might lead to different learning abilities being developed.

In the same way, we do not know the precise relationship between the body and the mind. Yet we have shown how different theories of learning have assumed, without analytical discussion, the valdity of a theory of learning without having examined it in relation to our understanding of the mind–body relationship. For instance, if information processing demands a functional relationship and if we are unable to accept the functional theory of mind and brain, then we call into question information processing as a valid theory of learning. At best, it becomes an analogy. Hence, we do need to look carefully at the philosophical discussions that underlay learning theory and examine carefully the inter-relationship between psychological and philosophical thinking. We need a congruency between the two and we should not assume that once psychology emerged as a discipline that it displaced philosophical discussion in our quest to understand human learning.

In the same way, Freud's work has been with us a long time, yet we do not always know how the unconscious acts upon the conscious in learning situations. We are also aware of the dispute about the extent to which learning styles tell us anything about people's approach to learning or whether there is not such thing as learning styles per se since they actually reflect personality types, and that people with different personality types actually approach learning differently.

In addition, we have pointed out that the whole person involves the complete mind – knowledge, attitudes, emotions, beliefs, values and the senses, and we do not know sufficient about how our learning is affected by each of these all of the time, or how they affect our learning, or even how we might enhance each of these. Nor do we know of the inter-relationship between these and skills and between them and the various components of our body.

The human being is an extremely complex phenomenon of body and mind, and we need to develop an understanding of learning from the perspective of the physical sciences as well as from the social sciences. In addition, as we have a philosophy of the person, so we can develop a philosophy of learning, as I (Jarvis 1992) and Winch (1998) have indicated, and in this we were really only rediscovering some of the basic ideas about learning discussed by Confucian thinkers in the East and Locke and Rousseau, amongst others, in the West began. But these occurred before the development of psychology, which actually both enhanced our understanding of learning while, at the same time, it diverted our attention from other personal elements of learning. Now we are advocating a multi-disciplinary, and an interdisciplinary, approach to learning and recognise that there is still an underpinning philosophy which requires considerably more discussion in relation to our understanding of human learning.

Experience and its transformation

Oakeshott (1933) suggested that experience is one of the most difficult words in the philosophical vocabulary and we have noted how few scholars have tried to define it within the context of learning. Indeed, many theories omitted it from their considerations. But it is an essential element in human learning. As the person is always in the world, so our experiences are constructs of our perception and awareness of the world – our experiences of this external world are within us. We do not learn directly from the world, or directly from what we are taught; we learn from our experience of the world and our experience of what we are taught. We also need to understand much more fully the philosophical debates about the content of experience and the relationships between experience and reality. Educators, for instance, often claim that students are dull because they have not understood what we have taught them, but what we have taught them may be our reality (knowledge) but not in their experience (and therefore only information for them). We need to understand *their* experience since it is from this that they learn, and their experience is of the situation within which data are gathered.

But, as we have already pointed out, we are not always sure of all the variables in the social situation that act upon us as individuals, so that we cannot always be sure of the relationship between the external reality and what we have experienced of that reality from which we learn. What we know is that which is transformed is that which is already within the mind, and that the transformation process is itself a complex one combining the cognitive, emotive and behavioural, but how this interaction and transformation occurs still requires a great deal more research.

A comprehensive theory?

Learning is an extremely complex phenomenon and we have examined many different theories here. Each in their different ways have thrown light on one or more aspects of learning. Each has, therefore, helped us to understand the processes of learning better. None of them have actually explained the whole of the learning process, and this is the knub of the matter. What is clear is that there are elements of learning that must always be present: the person, as learner; the social situation within which the learning occurs; the experience that the learner has of that situation; the process of transforming it and storing it within the learner's mind/biography. Each of these four elements has innumerable, interacting variables, and different theories have highlighted different variables.

We are, therefore, confronted with at least three fundamental questions at this juncture:

- Is it possible to be able to control the learning process so that we get the desired outcomes of learning that some educators have assumed when they have argued for behavioural objectives in teaching and learning?
- Is learning a researchable phenomenon?
- Is it possible to have a comprehensive theory of learning?

Taking the first point: can we specify and control the outcomes of any learning situation? The assumption behind behavioural objectives is that we can do this, and so teachers are instructed to prepare lessons having behavioural objectives. But no teaching and learning situation takes all the variables that we have mentioned above into account in specifying the curriculum, nor in the actual process of teaching and learning. Indeed, such a curriculum approach, and the policy behind it, fails to recognise the complexity of the human being and, therefore, of human learning itself. It also fails to consider both the complexity of the person and the social situation within which the learning takes place. Finally, it also assumes that the teachers will be in a position to make the learners experience precisely what the curriculum specifies, and that the learners' experience is what the curriculum designer would have it be. This whole approach to behavioural objectives is over-simple because it fails to understand the complexity of human learning and to recognise that it is a human activity, so that it omits dominant elements and others that we may not always know and are certainly not always able to control.

But, in addition, we might ask whether we should actually try to do this. In this instance, we would not argue that the approach is over-simple but that it is morally questionable because it seeks to take from the learners their autonomy and authenticity and assumes that they can be manipulated in the process of teaching and learning. Indeed, such an approach fails to consider the humanity of the learners themselves. This conclusion does not, therefore automatically advocate a free and easy, or even a so-called progressive, approach to education. It is certainly not advocating that there should not be direction and development in children's learning. Indeed, the more informed that we are about learning, the more opportunities we ought to be able to provide for learners to learn in a wide variety of ways. Consequently, the more we know about learning, the more able we should be in designing teaching situations. However, this analysis does point to the fact that the person is at the heart of the process and that teaching and learning is always an I↔Thou relationship: it is always a moral relationship in which the humanity of the learners should be respected. Such respect means that learners should be given opportunity to reach beyond themselves – towards what Levinas' (1991) understands as 'infinity'. As Confucius advocated, everybody is educable and all can become sages – and we would add 'experts' as well.

Then we would, ask is learning a researchable phenomenon? Clearly, there are elements of it which are researchble but, as Jarvis and Parker (2005) have advocated, learning is an holistic phenomenon. Learning can be studied from a wide variety of different disciplinary standpoints – from the pure sciences to the social sciences and to the arts and humanities. But then, we have advocated that learning is about human living, even about life itself. We need a philosophy of learning and a pharmacology of learning; we need a sociology of learning and a psychology; we need a biology of learning and a neuroscienctific understanding of the learning process and so on. No one approach can tell us everything about learning, but we might only be able to study learning from one perspective at a time. Each will throw some light on the whole but none will capture its complexity, which is as complex as human living itself.

Finally, we can now ask, can we have a comprehensive theory of learning? In my previous work on learning I have always argued that we can never have such a theory, and at the end of this study I am more convinced than ever that this is the case. If we actually could understand every aspect of the learning process, then we would understand the person in society and we would be able to manipulate people like cogs in the complex machine of society, but we will never be able to do this in its totality – if we could, then we would understand life itself to the full. Each of our theories of learning adds a little bit more to our understanding of human life and learning, but we do not and cannot know everything about it. While we know a lot about social life, if we knew and understood everything, then society would be no more than a complex mechanism within which human beings apear to be flexible cogs – and this we are not. Hence, the objective of the next volume in this study is to ask some of these sociological questions and by so doing to return to something that I began much earlier (Jarvis 1985, 1986).

But, while we do not know everything there is to know about how the body, the brain and the mind interact, what we do know is that every person is a human existent born into human society and through individual learning the human essence emerges and develops, and that for as long as we live and stay engaged in society that learning continues. Ultimately, learning is intrinsic to human living and if we could fully understand human learning we would understand human life itself. Moreover, the fact that learning is intrinsic to human life also means that unless humanity destroys itself or is destroyed by some natural disaster, then humans will continue to learn for as long as humanity exists and, significantly, humanity and human society are continually developing. In other words, as Simpson (1995) has argued, humanity is an unfinished project.

Notes

1 A philosophical perspective on human learning

1 This book was awarded the C. O. Houle World Award for Adult Education Literature by the American Association of Adult and Continuing Education.
2 See, for instance, the paper by Alison Le Cornu in *Studies in the Education of Adults* (forthcoming – Oct. 2005), a copy of which I received about the time this work completed and before her paper was published.
3 Herein lies one of the fundamental paradoxes of this whole process. During the opening section of this book we will demonstrate quite conclusively that 'I' is a social construct and so, therefore, is 'Thou', so that the individual is a social construct and that our concentration on individualism is itself fundamentally misleading, if not in one sense, wrong.
4 In schools of perfumery, students learn different smells and over 1,400 different scents have already been isolated.
5 I have been told by a wine taster that there are over 120 different tastes of wine and so the number of tastes may be as great as the number of smells.

3 Learning in the social context

1 Some of the material in this chapter has been examined in detail in *Adult Education and Lifelong Learning: Theory and Practice* (3rd edition), Jarvis (2004).
2 We shall discuss this fully in the second volume.
3 This different approach to learning has led many in the West sometimes wrongly to accuse students from Confucial heritage countries of plagarism.
4 All the quotations within this quote come from Feigenbaum and McCorduck (1984).

4 Experience – from which we learn

1 In my own research (Jarvis 1980) into superstition I showed that underlying many superstitions was the endeavour to create these similar situations, i.e. one basis of magic is 'like produces like'. In contrast, religion, like learning, begins with the questioning process – a point to which we will return later in this chapter.
2 In the same way that disjuncture is a motivating factor, so reward and punishment are others and we will return to these in a later chapter.

5 The transformation of experience

1 My references to Piaget relate back to my own Masters degree dissertation (Jarvis 1972).
2 I have dealt quite fully with the distinction between being and having in *Paradoxes of Learning* (Jarvis 1992).
3 It could certainly be argued that Christian theology is a belief system constructed in response to questions of meaning many centuries ago, and that one approach the churches in the West might employ in seeking to retain their relevance would be to return to the questions of meaning rather than assuming that all the answers for one age are relevant to all other ages.
4 This is the nature of sectarianism.
5 Elsewhere, I (Jarvis 1997) have discussed the distinction between cultural and universal values; cultural ones being relative to the changes in society, whereas universal values being unchanging truths, although I argued that there is only one universal ethical principle – loving concern for the other.
6 See the discussion on memory below.

6 The person: changing and becoming more experienced

1 Some early thinkers, such as Augustine, used the idea of memory to include matters that have nothing to do with past conscious experience and which is not, therefore, learned (Taylor 1989: 134–5), but memory is always regarded here as something that occurs as a result of learning.
2 This might correspond to the de-ontological position in Ethics.
3 If I may be permitted to add a personal note, I found that after having been ill and then being forced to get physically fit my own desire to continue learning and to write was enhanced considerably, and this book is one of the outcomes of that.
4 There are a number of problems with the methodology of this study, as reported in their book (2004: 4), which do not tell us how their sample of 145 respondents were selected and also because they tried to match their findings to other research data. I do not think that the research methodology affects the individual benefits of learning, but the social benefits are more difficult to justify without their having recorded more detail about their research methodology.

7 Lifelong learning

1 It is in this paradox that Levinas introduces us to his understanding of ethics and religion. Ethics begins when the Other (the stranger) impinges on my spontaneity in the immediate situation – my freedom to do as I choose. Religion begins with the bond that binds the I and the Thou, which does not constitute a totality.
2 Maieutics: the Socratic method of eliciting knowledge through a process of questioning.
3 This statement deliberately makes no reference to anything beyond our earthly life from the cradle to the grave.
4 This conclusion reflects the position held by Confucius: 'Learning, from a Confucian perspective, cannot be separated from actual living and ought to be integrated into life. For Confucius, learning and living are not separate matters: Learning is life and life is learning' (Kyung 2004: 125).

8 Learning and action

1 In my own doctorate I discovered that members of professions, having professional orientations towards their work and working in bureaucratic organisations, were more likely to have low job satisfaction than were other members having more bureaucratic work ideologies (Jarvis 1977).

9 Cognitive theories

1 *The Analects* were written at about the time of Confucius, probably by some of his young followers (Liu 1955: 28–9).
2 From the *Doctrine of the Mean*, another of the major books of this period and one which Liu (1955: 32) suggests is closely associated with Confucius.
3 *The Great Learning* is one of the earliest books from the time of Confucius – some of it is late, but other parts appear to be quite contemporaneous with Confucius (Liu 1955: 30–1).

10 Emotions and learning

1 I have relied heavily on the material that Goleman reports which relate to the learning processes, but those wanting to understand the way that the emotions affect the whole of human functioning might read both of his books and follow up many of his references.
2 See the work of Joseph LeDoux; only one reference (1993) given in the list of references at the end of this book, as an example.

11 Experiential learning

1 Boud studied at the University of Surrey at the same time as Heron was developing his own work on facilitating teaching and co-counselling there.

12 Towards a comprehensive theory of human learning?

1 Just after I had written the first draft of this chapter there was report in the media that children drinking a small amount fish oil each day were much more controlled and able to learn better than they did before they included this in their diet, and also there was a great deal of debate about the nature of the menu for school meals and the effects that different meals might have on learning.

References

Adam, B. (1990) *Time and Social Theory*. Cambridge: Polity.

Adorno, T. (1973) *The Jargon of Authenticity*. Evanston: Northwestern University Press.

Alheit, P., Bron-Wojciechowska, A., Brugger, E. and Dominicé, P. (eds) (1995) *The Biographical Approach in European Adult Education*. Vien: Verband Wiener Volksbildung.

Allman, P. (1984) 'Self-help learning and its relevance for learning and development in later life' in Midwinter, E. (ed.) *Mutual Aid Universities*. London: Croom Helm.

Apter, M. (1989) 'Negativism and the sense of identity' in Breakwell, G. (ed.) *Threatened Identities*. London: Wiley.

Argyris, C., Putnam, R. and Smith, D. (1985) *Action Science*. San Francisco, CA: Jossey-Bass.

Argyris, C. and Schön, D. (1974) *Theory in Practice: Increasing Professional Effectiveness*. San Francisco, CA: Jossey-Bass.

Aslanian, C. and Brickell, H. (1980) 'Americans in transition: life changes and reasons for adults learning' in *Future Directions in a Learning Society*. New York: College Board.

Bandura, A. (1977) *Social Learning Theory* (2nd edition). Englewood Cliffs, NJ: Prentice-Hall.

Bandura, A. (1989) 'Human agency in social cognition theory', *American Psychologist*, 44: 1175–84.

Bartlett, F. (1932) *Remembering: A Study in Experimental and Social Psychology*. Cambridge: Cambridge University Press.

Bateson, G. (1972) *Steps to an Ecology of Mind*. San Francisco, CA: Chandler.

Bauman, Z. (1995) *Life in Fragments*. Cambridge: Polity.

Bauman, Z. (1999) *In Search of Politics*. Cambridge: Polity

Bauman, Z. (2000) *Liquid Modernity*. Cambridge: Polity.

Bauman, Z. (2002) *Society under Siege*. Cambridge: Polity.

Bauman, Z. (2003) *Liquid Love*. Cambridge: Polity.

Bauman, Z. (2004) *Identity*. Cambridge: Polity.

Beck, U. (1992) *Risk Society*. London: Sage.

Belenky, M., Clinchy, B., Goldberger, N. and Tarule, J. (1986) *Women's Ways of Knowing*. New York: Basic Books.

Benner, P. (1984) *From Novice to Expert*. Menlo Park, CA: Addison-Wesley.

Berger, P. L. and Luckmann, T. (1966) *The Social Construction of Reality*. London: Allen Lane/Penguin.

Bergson, H. (1998 [1911]) *Creative Evolution*. New York: Dover.

Bergson, H. (1999 [1965]) *Duration and Simultaneity*. Manchester: Clinamen.

Bergson, H. (2001 [1913]) *Time and Freewill*. Mineola, IO: Dover.

Bergson, H. (2004 [1912]) *Matter and Memory*. New York: Dover.

Birren, J. (1963) 'Psychophisiological relations' in Birren, J., Butler, R., Greenhouse, S., Sokoloff, L. and Yarrow, M. (eds) *Human Aging: A Biological and Behavioural Study*. Washington, DC: US Government Printing Office.

Blasi, I. (1988) 'Identity and the development of the self' in Lapsey, D. and Power, F. (eds) *Self, Ego and Identity: Integrative Approaches*. New York: Springer-Verlag.

Borger, R. and Seaborne, A. (1966) *The Psychology of Learning*. Harmondsworth: Penguin.

Botkin, J., Elmandjra, M. and Malitza, M. (1979) *No Limits to Learning*. Oxford: Pergamon.

Boud, D., Keogh, R. and Walker, D. (eds) (1985) *Reflection: Turning Experience into Learning*. London: Croom Helm.

Bourdieu, P. (1973) 'Cultural reproduction and social reproduction' in Brown, M. (ed.) *Reproduction in Education, Society and Culture*. London: Sage.

Brookfield, S. (1987) *Developing Critical Thinkers*. San Francisco, CA: Jossey-Bass.

Bruner, J. (1990) *Acts of Meaning*. Cambridge, MA: Harvard University Press.

Buber, M. (1959) *I and Thou*. Edinburgh: Clarke.

Candy, P. (1991) *Self-direction for Lifelong Learning*. San Francisco, CA: Jossey-Bass.

Cattell, J. R. (1963) 'Theory of fluid and crystallised intelligence: a critical experiment', *Journal of Educational Psychology*, 54(1).

Cell, E. (1984) *Learning to Learn from Experience*. Albany, NY: State University of New York Press.

Chalmers, D. (1996) *The Conscious Mind*. Oxford: Oxford University Press.

Cheng, X. (2000) 'Asian students' reticence revisited', *System*, 28: 435–46.

Chiang, M. (1924) *A Study of Chinese Principles of Education*. Shanghai: The Commercial Press.

Chu, H. (1990) *Learning to be a Sage: Selections from the Conversations of Master Chu, Arranged Topically*. Berkeley, CA: University of California Press.

Claxton, G. (1999) *Wise Up: The Challenge of Lifelong Learning*. London: Bloomsbury.

Cole, M. and Scribner, S. (1978) 'Introduction' in Cole, M. *et al.* (eds) *L. S. Vygotsky – Mind in Society*. Cambridge, MA: Harvard University Press.

Coleman, J. (1990) *Foundations of Social Theory*. Cambridge, MA: Belknap Press of the Harvard University Press.

Collins Dictionary of the English Language (1979). Glasgow: Collins.

Cooper, D. (1983) *Authenticity and Learning*. London: Routledge and Kegan Paul.

Cooper, D. (1990) *Existentialism*. Oxford: Blackwell.

Côté, J. and Levene, C. (2002) *Identity Formation, Agency and Culture: A Social Psychological Synthesis*. Mahwah, NJ: Lawrence Erlbaum.

Crabbe, J. (ed.) (1999) *From Soul to Self*. London: Routledge.

Crane, T. (ed.) (1992) *The Contents of Experience*. Cambridge: Cambridge University Press.

Crane, T. (2001) *Elements of Mind*. Oxford: Oxford University Press.

Cranton, P. (1994) *Understanding and Promoting Transformative Learning*. San Francisco, CA: Jossey-Bass.

Csikszentmihalyi, M. (1990) *Flow: The Psychology of Optimal Experience*. New York: Harper and Row.

Cusack, S. and Thompson, W. (1998) 'Mental fitness: developing a vital aging society', *International Journal of Lifelong Education*, 17(5): 307–17.

Dahlgren, L.-O. (1984) 'Outcomes of learning' in Marton, F., Hounsell, D. and Entwistle, N. (eds) *The Experience of Learning*. Edinburgh: Scottish Academic Press.

Delors, J. (1996) *Learning: The Treasure Within*. Paris: Unesco.

Dewey, J. (1916) *Democracy and Education*. New York: Free Press.

Dewey, J. (1933) *How We Think*. Boston, MD: D.C. Heath.

Dewey, J. (1938) *Experience and Education*. New York: Collier.

Dominice, P. (2000) *Learning from our Lives*. San Francisco, CA: Jossey-Bass.

Dreyfus, H. and Dreyfus, S. (1977) 'Uses and abuses of multi-attribute and multi-aspect model of decision making'. Unpublished paper. Dept of Industrial Engineering and Operations Research, University of California, Berkelely.

Engeström, Y. (1987) *Learning by Expanding*. Helsinki: Orienta-Konsultit.

Engeström, Y. (1990) *Learning, Working and Imagining*. Helsinki: Orienta-Konsultit.

Entwistle, N. (1981) *Styles of Learning and Teaching*. Chichester: Wiley.

Erikson, E. (1963) *Childhood and Society*. New York: Norton.

European Commission (1995) *Teaching and Learning: Towards the Learning Society*. Brussels: European Commission.

European Commission (2001) *Making a European Area of Lifelong Learning a Reality*. Brussels: European Commission COM (2001) 678 final.

Falk, P. (1994) *The Consuming Body*. London: Sage.

Faure, E. (1972) *Learning to Be*. Paris: Unesco.

Feigenbaum, E. and McCorduck, P. (1984) *The Fifth Generation*. New York: Signet.

Festinger, L. (1957) *A Theory of Cognitive Dissonance*. Evanston, IL: Row, Peterson.

Field, J. (2000) *Lifelong Learning and the New Educational Order*. Stoke-on-Trent: Trentham.

Fisher, R. (1982) *Social Psychology*. New York: St Martin's Press.

Fowler, J. (1981) *Stages in Faith Development*. San Fransisco, CA: Harper and Row.

Fromm, E. (1942) *The Fear of Freedom*. London: Routledge and Kegan Paul (reprinted as an ARK paperback in 1984).

Fromm, E. (1949) *Man for Himself*. London: Routledge.

Gadamer, H.-G. (1978) *Philosophical Hermeneutics*. Berkeley, CA: University of California Press.

Gadamer, H.-G. (1986) *The Relevance of the Beautiful and Other Essays*. Cambridge: University of Cambridge Press.

Gagné, R. (1977) *The Conditions of Learning* (3rd edition). New York: Holt, Rinehart and Winston.

Gagné, R., Briggs, L. and Wager, W. (1992) *Principles of Instructional Design* (4th edition). Fort Worth, TX: Harcourt, Brace and Jovanich.

Gardner, H. (1983) *Frames of Mind* (2nd edition). New York: Basic Books.

Geertz, C. (1964) 'Ideology as a cultural system' in Apter, D. (ed.) *Ideology and Discontent*. New York: Free Press.

Gehlen, A. (1988) *Man: His Nature and Place in the World*. New York: Columbia University Press.

Gergen, K. (1994) *Realities and Relationships: Soundings in Social Construction.* Cambridge, MA: Harvard University Press.

Giddens, A. (1991) *Modernity and Self-identity.* Cambridge: Polity.

Gilhooly, K. (1996) *Thinking: Directive, Undirected and Creative* (3rd edition). Amsterdam: Academic Press.

Goffman, E. (1971 [1959]) *The Presentation of Self in Everyday Life.* Harmondsworth: Penguin.

Goffman, E. (1961) *Asylums.* Harmondsworth: Penguin.

Goffman, E. (1968) *Stigma.* Harmondsworth: Penguin.

Goleman, D. (1996) *Emotional Intelligence.* London: Bloomsbury.

Goleman, D. (1998) *Working with Emotional Intelligence.* London: Bloomsbury.

Gouldner, A. (1957–8) 'Cosmopolitan and locals: towards an analysis of latent social roles', *Administration Science Quarterly,* 2.

Greenfield, S. (1999) 'Soul, brain and mind' in Crabbe, J. (ed.) *From Soul to Self.* London: Routledge.

Habermas, J. (1981) *The Theory of Communicative Action,* Vol. 1. Cambridge: Polity.

Habermas, J. (1987) *The Theory of Communicative Action,* Vol. 2. Cambridge: Polity.

Habermas, J. (1990) *Moral Consciousness and Communicative Action.* Cambridge: Polity.

Hammond, C. (2004) 'The impacts of learning on well-being, mental health and effective coping' in Schuller, T., Brassett-Grundy, A., Green, A., Hammond, C. and Preston, J. (eds) *The Benefits of Learning.* London: RoutledgeFalmer.

Handy, C. (1990) *The Age of Unreason.* London: Anchor.

Harré, R. (1998) *The Singular Self.* London: Sage.

Heidegger, M. (1968) *What is Called Thinking?* New York: Harper and Row.

Heller, A. (1984) *Everyday Life.* London: Routledge and Kegan Paul.

Hodgkiss, P. (2001) *The Making of the Modern Mind.* London: Athlone.

Houle, C. (1984) *Patterns of Learning.* San Francisco, CA: Jossey-Bass.

Hsun, T. (1928) *The Works of Hsun Tse,* translated by H. Dubs. London: Arthur Probsthain.

Hull, C. (1943) *Principles of Behaviour.* New York: Appleton-Century Crofts.

Hull, C. (1952) *A Behaviour System.* New Haven, CT: Yale University Press.

Illeris, K. (2002) *The Three Dimensions of Learning.* Roskilde, Denmark: Roskilde University Press.

Ivy, G., MacLead, C., Petit, T. and Markus, J. (1992) 'A physiological framework for perceptual and cognitive changes in ageing' in Craik, F. and Salthouse, T. (eds) *The Handbook of Ageing and Cognition.* Mahwah, NJ: Lawrence Erlbaum.

James, D. and Coyle, C. (1998) 'Physical exercise, IQ scores and working memory in older men', *Education and Ageing,* 13(1): 37–48.

Jarvis, P. (1972) *Religious Socialisation in the Junior School.* Unpublished M.Soc.Sc., University of Birmingham.

Jarvis, P. (1977) 'A profession in process: the relationship between occupational ideology, occupational position and role strain, satisfaction and commitment of Protestant and Reformed ministers of religion'. Unpublished Ph.D. thesis, University of Aston.

Jarvis, P. (1980) 'Towards a sociological understanding of superstition', *Social Compass,* 27: 285–95.

Jarvis, P. (1985) *The Sociology of Adult and Continuing Education.* London: Croom Helm.

Jarvis, P. (1986) *Sociological Perspectives on Lifelong Education and Lifelong Learning*. Athens: University of Georgia, Dept of Adult Education.

Jarvis, P. (1987) *Adult Learning in the Social Context*. London: Croom Helm.

Jarvis, P. (1992) *Paradoxes of Learning*. San Francisco, CA: Jossey-Bass.

Jarvis, P. (1997) *Ethics and the Education of Adults in Late Modern Society*. NIACE: Leicester.

Jarvis, P. (1999) *The Practitioner Researcher*. San Francisco, CA: Jossey-Bass.

Jarvis, P (2001) *Learning in Later Life*. London: Kogan Page.

Jarvis, P. (2004) *Adult Education and Lifelong Learning: Theory and Practice* (3rd edition). London: RoutledgeFalmer.

Jarvis, P. (2005) 'Transforming Asian education through open and distance learning – through thinking' in *Proceedings of Transforming Asian Education through Open and Distance Learning*. Hong Kong: Hong Kong Open University.

Jarvis, P. and Parker, S. (eds) (2005) *Human Learning: A Holistic Perspective*. London: RoutledgeFalmer

Jenkins, R. (2004) *Social Identity*. London: Routledge

Kagan, I. (1971) 'Developmental studies in reflection and analysis' in Cashdow, A. and Whitehead, I. (eds) *Personality, Growth and Learning*. London: Longman.

Kant, E. (1993) *Critique of Pure Reason*. London: Dent.

Keddie, N. (1980) 'Adult educaton: an ideology of individualism' in Thompson, J. (ed.) *Adult Education for a Change*. London: Hutchinson.

Kelly, G. (1955) *The Psychology of Personal Constructs*. New York: Norton.

Kennedy, P. (2002) 'Learning cultures and learning styles: (myth)understanding about adult (Hong Kong) Chinese learners', *International Journal of Lifelong Education*, 21(5): 430–45.

Kirkegaard, S. (1959) *Either/Or*, Vol. 2. Princeton, NJ: Princeton University Press.

Knowles, M. (1980) *The Modern Practice of Adult Education* (revised edition). Chicago, IL: Association Press.

Knowles, M. (1989) *The Making of an Adult Educator*. San Francisco, CA: Jossey-Bass.

Koestler, A. (1964) *The Act of Creation*. London: Hutchinson.

Kohlberg, L. (1986) *The Philosophy of Moral Development*. San Francisco, CA: Harper and Row.

Kolb, D. (1984) *Experiential Learning*. Englewood Cliffs, NJ: Prentice-Hall.

Köhler, W. (1925) *The Mentality of Apes*. London: Routledge and Kegan Paul.

Kyung Hi, K. (2004) 'An attempt to elucidate notions of lifelong learning: *analects*-based analysis of Confucius' ideas about learning', *Asia Pacific Education Review*, 5(2): 117–126.

Lacey, A. (1989) *Bergson*. London: Routledge

Lave, J. and Wenger, E. (1991) *Situated Learning*. Cambridge: Cambridge University Press.

LeDoux, J. (1993) 'Emotional memory systems in the brain', *Behavioural and Brain Research*, 58.

Lee, W. O. (1996) 'The cultural context for Chinese learners: conceptions of learning in the Confucian tradition' in Watkins, D. and Biggs, J. (eds) *The Chinese Learner*. Hong Kong: CERC and Victoria: ACER.

Lengrand, P. (1975) *An Introduction to Lifelong Education*. London: Croom Helm.

Levinas, E. (1991) *Totality and Infinity*. Dordrecht, Germany: Kluwer.

Levinson, D., Darrow, C., Klein, D., Levinson, M. and McKee, B. (1978) *The Seasons of a Man's Life*. New York: Knorf.

Levinson, D. and Levinson, J. (1996) *The Seasons of a Woman's Life*. New York: Ballentine.

Levitas, R. (1990) *The Concept of Utopia*. New York: Phillip Allan.

Lifton, R. J. (1961) *Thought Reform and the Psychology of Totalism*. Harmondsworth: Penguin.

Lindley, R. (1986) *Autonomy*. London: Macmillan.

Liu, Wu-Chi (1955) *A Short History of Confucian Philosophy*. Harmondsworth: Penguin.

Locke, J. (1993 [1690]) *An Essay Concerning Human Understanding*. London: Dent.

Loevinger, J. (1976) *Ego Development*. San Francisco, CA: Jossey-Bass.

Longworth, N. and Davies, K. (1996) *Lifelong Learning*. London: Kogan Page.

Lowe, E. (1992) 'Experience and its objects' in Crane, T. (ed.) *The Contents of Experience*. Cambridge: Cambridge University Press.

Luckmann, T. (1967) *Invisible Religion*. London: Macmillan.

Luckmann, T. (1983) *Life-World and Social Realities*. London: Heinemann.

McAdams, D. (2001) *The Person*. Fort Worth, TX: Harcourt College Publishers.

McGill, I. and Beaty, L. (2001) *Action Learning* (2nd edition). London: Kogan Page.

McGill, I. and Brockbank, A. (2004) *The Action Learning Handbook*. London: RoutledgeFalmer.

MacMurray, J. (1979 [1961]) *Persons in Relation*. Atlantic Highlands, NJ: Humanities Press.

Macquarrie, J. (1973) *Existentialism*. Harmondsworth: Penguin.

Marcel, G. (1976) *Being and Having*. Gloucester, MA: Peter Smith.

Marsick, V. and O'Neil, J. (1999) 'The many faces of action learning', *Management Learning*, 30(2): 159–76.

Marton, F. and Booth, S. (1997) *Learning and Awareness*. Mahwah, NJ: Lawrence Erlbaum.

Marton, F., Dall'Alba, G., Tse, L. K. (1996) 'Memorizing and understanding: the keys of the Paradox?' in Watkins, D. and Biggs, J. (eds) *The Chinese Learner*. Reprinted in 1999. Hong Kong: Comparative Education Research Centre, University of Hong Kong and the Australia Council for Educational Research.

Marton, F. and Säljö, R. (1984) 'Approaches to learning' in Marton, F., Hounsell, D. and Entwistle, N. (eds) *The Experience of Learning*. Edinburgh: Scottish Academic Press.

Maslin, K. T. (2001) *An Introduction to the Philosophy of Mind*. Cambridge: Polity.

Maslow, A. (1968) *Toward a Psychology of Being*. New York: Van Nostrand.

Merriam, S. and Caffarella, R. (1991) *Learning in Adulthood*. San Francisco, CA: Jossey-Bass.

Merton, R (1968) *Social Theory and Social Structure* (enlarged edition). New York: Free Press.

Mezirow, J. (1977) 'Perspective transformation', *Studies in Adult Education*, 9(2): 153–64.

Mezirow, J. (1981) 'A critical theory of adult learning and education', *Adult Education*, 32(1): 12–113.

Mezirow, J. (1990) 'How critical reflection triggers learning' in Mezirow, J. *et al.*, *Fostering Critical Reflection in Adulthood*. San Francisco, CA: Jossey-Bass.

Mezirow, J. (1991) *Transformative Dimensions of Adult Learning*. San Francisco, CA: Jossey Bass.

Mezirow, J. (2000) 'Learning to think like an adult' in Mezirow, J. *et al.*, *Learning as Transformation*. San Francisco, CA: Jossey-Bass.

Mezirow, J., Darkenwald, G. and Knox, A. (no date) *Last Gamble on Education*. Washington, DC: Adult Education Association of the United States of America.

Miller, N. and Dollard, J. (1941) *Social Learning and Imitation*. New Haven, CT: Yale University Press.

Moser, P., Mulder, D. and Trout, J. (1998) *The Theory of Knowledge*. New York: Oxford University Press.

Newman, F. and Holzman, L. (1997) *The End of Knowing*. London: Routledge.

Nietzsche, F. W. (1969) *Thus Spoke Zarathustra*. Harmondsworth: Penguin.

Noonan, H. (2003) *Personal Identity* (2nd edition). London: Routledge.

Nyiri, J. (1988) 'Tradition and practical knowledge' in Nyiri, J. and Smith, B. (eds) *Practical Knowledge: Outlines of a Theory of Traditions and Skills*. London: Croom Helm.

O'Neill, C. (2003) 'Learning to be Me'. Unpublished Ph.D. thesis, University of Surrey.

O'Sullivan, E. (1999) *Transformative Learning*. London: Zed Books.

Oakeshott, M. (1933) *Experience and its Modes*. Cambridge: Cambridge University Press.

Organisation of Economic Cooperation and Development (1996) *Lifelong Learning for All*. Paris: OECD.

Ormrod, J. (1995) *Human Learning* (2nd edition). Columbus, OH: Merrill.

Parker, P. (2005) 'The biology of learning' in Jarvis, P. and Parker, S. (eds) *Human Learning: A Holistic Perspective*. London: RoutledgeFalmer, pp. 16–31.

Pavlov, I. (1927) *Conditioned Reflexes*. London: Oxford University Press.

Pedlar, M. (1997) 'Interpreting action learning' in Burgoyne, J. and Reynolds, M. (eds). London: Sage.

Peters, R. (1973) 'Freedom and the development of the free man' in Doyle, J. (ed.) *Educational Judgements*. London: Routledge and Kegan Paul.

Peterson, R. *et al.* (1979) *Lifelong Learning in America*. San Francisco, CA: Jossey-Bass.

Piaget, J. (1929) *The Child's Conception of the World*. London: Routledge and Kegan Paul.

Polanyi, M. (1962) *Personal Knowledge*. Chicago, IL: University of Chicago Press.

Polanyi, M. (1968) *The Tacit Dimension*. London: Routledge and Kegan Paul.

Popper, K. (1979) *Objective Knowledge* (revised edition). Oxford: Oxford University Press.

Preston, J. and Hammond, C. (2002) *The Wider Benefits of Further Education: Practitioner Views*. London: University of London, Centre for Research on the Wider Benefits of Learning.

Putnam, R. (2000) *Bowling Alone*. New York: Simon and Schuster.

Revans, R. (1980) *Action Learning: New Techniques for Action Learning*. London: Blond and Briggs.

Revans, R. (1982) *The Origins and Growth of Action Learning*. Bromley: Chartwell-Bratt.

Riegel, K. (1973) 'Dialectical operations: the final period of cognitive development', *Human Development*, 16(3): 315–24.

Rogers, C. (1951) *Client-Centered Therapy*. Boston, MA: Houghton-Mifflin.

Rogers, C. (1969) *Freedom to Learn*. Columbus, OH: Merrill.

Rogers, C. (1983) *Freedom to Learn for the 80's* (2nd edition). New York: Merrill.

Rogers, C. and Freiberg, H. J. (1994) *Freedom to Learn* (3rd edition). New York: Merrill.

Rose, A. (ed.) (1962) *Human Behavior and Social Processes*. London: Routledge and Kegan Paul.

Rousseau, J.-J. (1911 [1762]) *Emile*. London: Dent.

Ryle, G. (1963) *The Concept of Mind*. Harmondsworth: Penguin. (First published by Hutchinson, London, 1949.)

Ryle, G. (1979) *On Thinking*. Oxford: Blackwell.

Scheler, M. (1980) *Problems of a Sociology of Knowledge*. London: Routledge and Kegan Paul.

Schilling, C. (1993) *The Body and Social Theory*. London: Sage.

Schön, D. (1971) *Beyond the Stable State*. Harmondsworth: Penguin.

Schön, D. (1983) *The Reflective Practitioner*. New York: Basic Books.

Schön, D. (1987) *Educating the Reflective Practitioner*. San Francisco, CA: Jossey-Bass.

Schroyer, T. (1973) 'Forward' in Adorno, T. (ed.) *The Jargon of Authenticity*. Evanston, IL: Northwestern University Press.

Schuller, T. (2004) 'Three capitals' in Schuller, T., Preston, J., Hammond, C., Brassett-Grundy, A. and Bynner, J., *The Benefits of Learning*. London: RoutledgeFalmer.

Schuller, T., Baron, S. and Field, J. (2000) 'Social capital: a review and critique' in Baron, S., Field, J. and Schuller, T. (eds) *Social Capital*. Oxford: Oxford University Press, pp. 1–38.

Schuller, T., Preston, J, Hammond, C., Brassett-Grundy, A. and Bynner, J. (2004) *The Benefits of Learning*. London: RoutledgeFalmer.

Schutz, A. (1967) *The Phenomenology of the Social World*. London: Heinemann.

Schutz, A. and Luckmann, T. (1974) The *Structures of the Life-world*. London: Heinemann.

Searle, J. (1992) *The Rediscovery of the Mind*. Cambridge, MA: MIT Press.

Selman, R. (1980) *The Growth of Interpersonal Understanding*, cited in Habermas, J. (1990) *Moral Consciousness and Communicative Action*. Cambridge: Polity.

Sheehy, G. (1995) *New Passages: Mapping Your Life Across Time*. Toronto: Random House of Canada.

Simpson, L. (1995) *Technology, Time and the Conversations of Modernity*. London: Routledge.

Singer, J. (1975) *Daydreaming and Fantasy*. London: Allen and Unwin.

Singer, J. (1978) 'Studies of Daydreaming' in Pope, K. and Singer, J. (eds) *The Stream of Consciousness*. New York: Wiley.

Skinner, B. (1938) *The Behavior of Organisms*. Englewood Cliffs, NJ: Prentice-Hall.

Skinner, B. (1953) *Science and Human Behavior*. New York: Macmillan.

Skinner, B. (1971) *Beyond Freedom and Dignity*. Harmondsworth: Penguin.

Stein, J. (2005) 'Brain and learning' in Jarvis, P. and Parker, S. (eds) *Human Learning: A Holistic Perspective*. London: RoutledgeFalmer, pp. 32–49.

Stern, W. (1938) *General Psychology from a Personalistic Standpoint*. New York: Macmillan.

Sternberg, R. (1997) *Thinking Styles*. Cambridge: Cambridge University Press.

Stikkers, K. (1980) 'Introduction' in Scheler, M. (ed.) *Problems of a Sociology of Knowledge*. London: Routledge and Kegan Paul

Strauss, A. (ed.) (1964) *George Herbert Mead on Social Psychology*. Chicago, IL: University of Chicago Press.

Stroobants, V., Jans, M. and Wildemeersch, D. (2001) 'Making sense of learning for work: towards a framework of transitional learning', *International Journal of Lifelong Education*, 20(1–2): 114–26.

Taylor, C. (1989) *Sources of the Self*. Cambridge: Cambridge University Press.

Thorndike, E. (1913) *Educational Psychology: The Psychology of Learning*, Vol. 2. New York: Teachers College Press.

Thorndike, E. (1928) *Adult Learning*. London: Macmillan.

Tillich, P. (1962) *The Courage to Be*. London: Fontana.

Toennies, F. (1957) *Community and Society*. MI: Michigan State University Press. (Published in the UK as *Community and Association*, London: Routledge and Kegan Paul.)

Tough, A. (1979) *The Adult's Learning Projects* (2nd edition). Toronto: OISE.

Turner, B. (1996) *The Body and Society* (2nd edition). London: Sage.

Turner, R. (1962) 'Role taking: process versus conformity' in Rose, A. (ed.) *Human Behavior and Social Processes*. London: Routledge and Kegan Paul.

Turner, V. (1969) *The Ritual Process*. Harmondsworth: Penguin.

Valberg, J. (1992) 'The puzzle of experience objects' in Crane, T. (ed.) *The Contents of Experience*. Cambridge: Cambridge University Press.

Van Gennap, A. (1960 [1908]) *The Rites of Passage*. London: Routledge and Kegan Paul.

Vygotsky, L. S. (1978) *Mind in Society* (edited by M. Cole, V. John-Steiner, S. Scribner and E. Souberman). Cambridge, MA: Harvard University Press.

Vygotsky, L. (1988) *Thought and Language*. Cambridge, MA: MIT Press.

Wagner, H. (1970) *Alfred Schutz – On Phenomenology and Social Relations*. Chicago, IL: University of Chicago Press.

Wallis, G. (1926) *The Art of Thought*. London: Jonathan Cape.

Watkins, D. and Biggs, J. (eds) (1996) *The Chinese Learner: Cultural, Psychological and Contextual Influences*. Hong Kong: CERC and Victoria: ACER.

Watson, J. (1925) *Behaviorism*. New York: Norton.

Weil, S. and McGill, I. (eds) (1989) *Making Sense of Experiential Learning*. Buckingham: Open University Press and Society for Research in Higher Education.

Wertheimer, M. (1912) 'Experimentelle Stüdien über das Sehen von Bewegung', *Zeitschrift für Psychologie*, 61: 161–265.

Wilkin, H. (1971) 'Psychological differentiations' in Cashdown, A. and Whitehead, I. (eds) *Personality, Growth and Learning*. London: Longman.

Williamson, B (1998) *Life-worlds and Learning*. Leicester: NIACE.

Wilson, J. (1972) 'Indoctrination and rationality' in Snook, I. (ed.) *Concepts of Indoctrination*. London: Routledge and Kegan Paul.

Winch, C. (1998) *The Philosophy of Human Learning*. London: Routledge.

Yeaxlee, B. (1929) *Lifelong Education*. London: Cassell.

Index